Treasury of Newfoundland Stories

Volume III

Classic Spy Tales & Epic Sea Adventures

BREAKWATER
P.O. Box 2188, St. John's, NL, Canada, A1C 6E6
WWW.BREAKWATERBOOKS.COM

A CIP catalogue record for this book is available from Library and Archives Canada.
Copyright ©2018 Jack Fitzgerald
ISBN 978-1-771031-073

COVER DESIGN: Maurice Fitzgerald

We acknowledge the support of the Canada Council for the Arts, which last year
invested $153 million to bring the arts to Canadians throughout the country.
We acknowledge the financial support of the Government of Canada and the
Government of Newfoundland and Labrador through the Department of Tourism,
Culture, Industry and Innovation for our publishing activities.

PRINTED AND BOUND IN CANADA.

Canada Council   Conseil des Arts   Canadä   Newfoundland
for the Arts   du Canada   Labrador

Breakwater Books is committed to choosing papers and materials for our books that
help to protect our environment. To this end, this book is printed on a recycled paper
that is certified by the Forest Stewardship Council®.

RECYCLED
Paper made from
recycled material
FSC   FSC® C103567

Treasury of Newfoundland Stories

Volume III

Classic Spy Tales & Epic Sea Adventures

I dedicate *Classic Spy Tales and Epic Sea Adventures*
to the memory of Ambrose Cahill.

Ambrose passed away on April 19, 2017, at the age of ninety-four. He was a close friend for half a century, and I benefited from his Irish-Newfoundland wit and extensive knowledge of the Southern Shore and its colourful heritage. In the days when a tour "up the shore" referred to all the communities from Bay Bulls to St. Mary's, Ambrose coined the term "The Irish Loop," which took a decade or two to spread to the point where Cahill's "Irish Loop" has been incorporated into the Newfoundland Place Names category and has long replaced "Up the Shore" in tourist promotions. Among my forty books published to date are many references to the name Ambrose Cahill and the many wonderful anecdotes, both funny and tragic, that have been preserved. Needless to say, Ambrose will be missed.

CONTENTS

~~~

CONTENTS

~~~

INTRODUCTION

Classic Spy Tales and Epic Sea Adventures represents the third volume in the *Treasury of Newfoundland Stories* by Jack Fitzgerald. This volume is Jack's forty-first published book and provides readers with a stunning collection of true Newfoundland stories which are every bit as gripping and compelling as the title suggests.

The objective of the author in compiling the *Newfoundland Treasury* series is to build an extensive collection of true Newfoundland stories, folklore, and offbeat narratives for Newfoundlanders and friends of Newfoundlanders, at home and abroad, to collect. The series is a must for Newfoundland history enthusiasts and home libraries.

Classic Spy Tales chronicles many spy stories supporting the deep involvement of German intelligence efforts and attacks in and around Newfoundland and Labrador during the two world wars.

While Newfoundlanders were often left in the dark about the dangers swirling around them, plenty of attention was being paid by military strategists in Berlin, London, and Washington. The result was the enormous effect spy information sent to Berlin had on the allied war efforts and defence policies in WWI and WWII.

It focuses on many unique cloak-and-dagger spying activities and German naval intrusions against Newfoundland and Labrador throughout both wars. The long lost Spring Rice Document from WWI, recovered by Fitzgerald, plays an important role in this section.

Classic Spy Tales presents several major challenges to the existing wartime history of both world wars. In addition to researching Newfoundland, Canadian, American, and British sources, Fitzgerald sought out German records related to warfare and spying in and around Newfoundland as well.

The *Epic Sea Adventures* section offers an extraordinary collection of Newfoundland's most exciting and classic sea stories with topics as varying as sea disasters, unique sea tales, and remarkable and bizarre encounters involving Newfoundland seamen and strange creatures.

Before the infamous sinking of the *Titanic*, the steamship *Arctic* sank in Newfoundland waters and captured newspaper headlines around the world. The fate of the *Arctic* was used later, when journalists sought out a disaster comparable to the *Titanic* tragedy. Here we read a lively and dramatic story which shamed many Newfoundlanders and has been mostly ignored in Newfoundland history.

There is also the spectacular story of the ship loaded with dynamite burning in St. John's Harbour and the valiant battle by firefighters to save the city from destruction.

Readers will be amazed at the history of giant squid in Newfoundland waters, the stories of unmatched heroism at sea, and the true exploits of the *Edgecombe*, which set out from St. John's in 1841. This story involves adventure and treachery that ranks as perhaps the world's most famous epic sea tale and became the inspiration for Robert Louis Stevenson's *Treasure Island*.

Many of Fitzgerald's earlier books, still sought after by readers, have gone out of print, but the best of those stories have been revised and included in this series. These are just a few examples from the many lively and dramatic Newfoundland *Classic Spy Tales and Epic Sea Adventures* found in Volume III.

PART ONE

~~~

CLASSIC SPY TALES

CHAPTER ONE

The Man Called Intrepid

~~~

In 1951, Premier Joseph R. Smallwood established a crown corporation to oversee economic development in New-foundland and Labrador. A crown corporation was defined as one that was at least ninety percent owned by the provincial government, making it exempt from federal taxes. This led to the development of the Newfoundland and Labrador Company (NALCO), which began with capital provided by the Newfoundland government and an impressive group of New York investors headed by Sir William Stephenson, who was appointed as the first chairman of NALCO.

Although some of the developers who arrived in New-foundland in the fifties were scoundrels, Stephenson was known to be an honest and astute businessman who had acquired a great deal of wealth despite humble beginnings. But there was more to William Stephenson than met the eye. In fact, during WWII he had lived a double life. However, the details of his secret life, and the impact he had on the outcome of the world's greatest armed conflict, were concealed in a vault and not to be opened until forty years after the end of WWII.

At the core of Stephenson's history is a story as farfetched as many of the world's most popular spy tales, which makes Stephenson's exploits even more remarkable for being true. The seeming absurdness of this man's accomplishments—absurd because his physical appearance obscures feats of ingenuity, cunning, raw nerve, and physical prowess—had a profound effect on the outcome of WWII.

Prior to the end of WWII, the only photograph of Stephenson remained among British intelligence records sealed in archival vaults, and during the war, Winston Churchill secretly ordered that Stephenson's pictures be purged from all newspapers. Years ago, while researching the activities of Dr. Alfred Valdmanis in Newfoundland, I stumbled upon a photograph of Valdmanis and Stephenson taken in the Colonial Building in 1951. Apart from Stephenson's brief involvement with NALCO, the photograph seemed unimportant at the time. However, when I came across an intelligence picture of Britain's top spy, made public in 1974, I realized this master spy was the same man that Joey Smallwood had appointed to the chair of NALCO in 1951.

Not only did Stephenson act as Churchill's most trusted intelligence agent, but he also worked diligently, under the instruction of his government, to gain the trust of none other than Adolf Hitler. Only when the seal was removed from the Britain Security Coordination's wartime secrets did the world learn the name of the British citizen turned spy who infiltrated Hitler's inner circle. Unlike Hitler, however,

Churchill made sure his double agent was known only by a code name: Intrepid.

After Stephenson informed Churchill of Germany's increased militarization, the two men reasoned that if they couldn't change the government's disastrous policy of appeasement in 1935 they would secretly develop a plan to make sure Britain, at least, had an intelligence organization to meet the German challenge when it occurred.

Under his code name, Stephenson was the same double agent who trained the squad of assassins responsible for the death of Hitler's heir-apparent, General Reinhard Heydrich, who was in charge of developing the program to annihilate the Jewish race. In fact, Intrepid operated a training camp near Toronto for the assassins who successfully assassinated Heydrich and many others. Among those training there was Ian Fleming, who became Intrepid's second in command. After the war, Fleming turned to writing his famous James Bond 007 novels.

Stephenson did not write a book, but he agreed to be interviewed for the one written by William Stevenson (no relation), whose book, *A Man Called Intrepid*, became a bestseller and later a Hollywood smash hit. So the man who risked his life for the Allies in wartime by embedding himself within the Führer's inner circle and who inspired the story of the most famous fictional spy in history, James Bond, was actually hired by Joey Smallwood to oversee resource development in the province of Newfoundland.

Stephenson was a wealthy businessman, but not materialistic, an expert on the world's political systems, but he shunned publicity. Although well connected to the elite of Europe and America, he was a humble man. Above all, he was an inventor and a genius, factors which spiked his rapid growth of wealth following the end of the First World War. His business activities enabled him to travel freely on several continents—a truly great asset for any double agent. All in all, he was just the type of man Hitler's intelligence service was recruiting, making him the perfect operative for Churchill. And for a short time, he worked for Joey Smallwood and the province of Newfoundland.

Alfred Valdmanis (standing) and Sir William Stephenson, the man formerly known as Intrepid, at the Colonial Building in St. John's in 1951. (Archives and Special Collections, Queen Elizabeth II Library, Memorial University, Joseph R. Smallwood Collection: 16.01.001)

CHAPTER TWO

The Truth About the Atlantic Charter

CHURCHILL DIARY SAYS ATLANTIC CHARTER NEVER EXISTED

When Sir Winston Churchill published his memoirs in 1953, he boldly asserted that the Atlantic Charter—a document supposedly stating the Allies' war objectives—did not exist. Churchill provided proof in the form of the actual document he and Franklin Delano Roosevelt verbally agreed to release to the press as a cover story for the meeting. In 1941 the name Atlantic Charter was not used, nor was it intended to be used, and Churchill noted he first heard the title in 1945 and was upset the document had not been destroyed. The document used in 1941 had not been signed by either of the world leaders, though they did make verbal agreements, but Churchill did discover a document with the signatures of both leaders written in the same hand. FDR died in 1945 shortly before Churchill could confront him.

President Franklin D. Roosevelt and Prime Minister Winston Churchill aboard the HMS *Prince of Wales* in Placentia Harbour, August 10, 1941. (US Naval History and Heritage Command, Catalog #: NH 67211)

Today, almost eighty years later, the cover story used at the time for the purpose of the joint meeting is promoted as the Atlantic Charter, while the true reason for their risky meeting at Placentia is ignored. Churchill said sarcastically, "Everyone claims to have read the document but no one knows what is in it!"

The actual history in no way diminishes Newfoundland's important role in WWII. Without such a meeting, and without the results it produced, the outcome of the war would have been quite different. It gives this province a more important reason to celebrate an eightieth anniversary.[1]

---

[1] Winston Churchill, *Triumph and Tragedy: The Second World War Volume VI* (Boston: Houghton Mifflin, 1953) 392-393. For an image of the original forged document, see Winston Churchill, *The Grand Alliance: The Second World War Volume III* (Boston: Houghton Mifflin, 1950), 476.

THE TRUTH ABOUT CHURCHILL AND FDR MEETING AT PLACENTIA

In August 1941, the US was still a neutral country and England was the underdog against Germany. Russia, under attack, had already adopted a scorched earth policy, but with limited supplies and weapons, was not expected to hold out in a long war. Hitler was telling his colleagues that England had lost the war and would soon surrender. It was a time of worldwide danger and uncertainty. With German U-boats dominating the Atlantic in 1941, it would have taken a matter of great urgency for the prime minister of England to cross the Atlantic. Was drawing up principles to guide the world after the war of such urgency?

It was under these conditions that the historic meeting between President Franklin D. Roosevelt and Prime Minister Winston Churchill was held at Ship Cove in Placentia Bay, Newfoundland. Although it has long been claimed that the Placentia Bay meeting marked the first time the two met, they did meet on a previous occasion many years before. That meeting took place on July 29, 1918, at Gray's Inn, London, when both were guests at a dinner for the War Cabinet. Roosevelt was annoyed when Churchill said he had no memory of the event.[2]

The meeting in Placentia Bay is best remembered for the eight principles put forward in a joint statement, which by 1945 was known as the Atlantic Charter and later inspired the founding of the United Nations after the war. However,

[2] William Manchester, *The Last Lion: Winston Spenser Churchill Alone, 1932-1940* (New York: Little, Brown and Co, 1988).

the Placentia meeting was actually concerned with issues far more important at the time than any plans of improving the already existing League of Nations or creating a new force aimed at keeping world peace after the war. First, the war had to be won.

While the world was digesting the news that Prime Minister Churchill and President Roosevelt had secretly met in Placentia Bay, senior diplomats and military officials, acting on the top-secret aspects of the meeting, were moving to activate decisions made there to help change the course of the war. Churchill and Roosevelt sent a joint message to Joseph Stalin, president of Russia, from the Placentia Bay meeting. The contents of this message are disclosed later in this chapter.

WHY THE MEETING?

Roosevelt decided to meet with Churchill after carefully considering the report by the president's personal representative, Harry Hopkins, of a meeting he held with the prime minister in London in mid-July 1941. Hopkins was accompanied on that visit by several top American military strategists. Months earlier, Lord Phillip Kerr, Marquis of Lothian, the British Ambassador to Washington, had informed the Americans that England was running out of money to fight the war.[3] The Americans were trying to determine if the German invasion of Russia, launched on June 22, would have any effect on the Lend-Lease supplies Britain needed from the United States. During the meeting,

---

[3] Churchill had met FDR years before but had no memory of the meeting.

one US General expressed the opinion that England could not withstand an invasion. He argued that England stood to lose everything by trying to spread its forces too thin. Churchill and his military strategists explained the reasoning behind their actions, which appeared to convince the Americans that the prime minister was on the right course. Roosevelt agreed with Churchill's defence that the enemy needed to be confronted wherever he was found. The meeting with Hopkins concluded with a recommendation that the two leaders meet.

The prime minister anxiously awaited the president's response, which came near the end of July by way of another visit to the prime minister's Downing Street residence around mid-July 1941 by Harry Hopkins. The prime minister was delighted when Hopkins informed him that Roosevelt was very interested in meeting with him, "in some lonely bay or other." Churchill had never met the president in person although they had been in regular and constant contact with each other over the previous two years. He immediately agreed to the meeting.[4]

The prime minister felt he and Roosevelt had urgent issues to discuss. Churchill was perhaps the one leader who never wavered in his steadfast conviction that Hitler would be defeated. Churchill accurately forecasted that the war would turn in his favour in 1942. Yet, unlike Roosevelt, Churchill had given some thought to an international organization to assure peace in the world after the war ended.

As expected, the prime minister's cabinet approved of the

---

[4] Winston Churchill, *The Grand Alliance: The Second World War Volume III* (Boston: Houghton Mifflin, 1950).

meeting even though Clement Atlee, deputy prime minister, had some concerns about Churchill's safety travelling on the Atlantic with so much German U-boat activity.

The meeting was set for August 9, and Ship Cove, Placentia Bay, Newfoundland, was chosen as the place of rendezvous. The British military arranged for their largest and latest battleship, the HMS *Prince of Wales*, to take Churchill and his party to Newfoundland under escort. Roosevelt travelled to Placentia on the USS *Augusta*.

To protect the secrecy of the meeting, Churchill instructed Atlee to deal with enquiries about the prime minister's absence with the reply, "I cannot undertake to deal with rumour."

DANGEROUS CROSSING

Atlee had just reason to be concerned over the dangers on an Atlantic crossing. In June and July, the German U-boat fleet had increased its numbers and had sunk eighty-three ships on the Atlantic.[5] Just weeks before the Ship Cove, Placentia Bay, meeting, the United States Navy began its anti-submarine patrols of the Atlantic from the USN Base at Argentia nearby. This may have been a factor in the choice of Placentia Bay for the meeting.

Churchill often risked his own safety during the war. He once crossed the Atlantic on the *Queen Mary* to meet with Roosevelt while the ship carried five thousand German prisoners of war. The trip remained top secret until after the

---

[5] Robert H. Ferrell and John S. Bowman, eds, *The Twentieth Century: An Almanac* (New York: World Almanac Publications, 1984).

war, but Churchill said, at the time, he did not fear the Germans because they were being guarded by armed British soldiers. After the attempted assassination against him in Baltimore, he brushed it aside with humour.

During the crossing, the *Prince of Wales* ran into two dangerous situations. The first involved the weather. Just two days at sea a heavy wind storm struck, and the ship's captain was forced to make a choice between slowing down or moving full speed ahead, alone, without the escort vessels. The admiral of the fleet, Sir Dudley Pound, gave the order, "Full steam ahead!" When the winds settled, the escort vessels caught up with them.

The next problem was the presence of several U-boats in the area. Admiral Pound chose to set a zig–zag course which succeeded in evading the enemy. However, during the process, it was necessary to order absolute wireless silence. This gave Churchill a chance to relax. He read a novel called *Captain Horatio Hornblower* by C. S. Forester. He noted in his memoirs, "I found it vastly entertaining." It did cause some anxiety later among military officers in the Mid-East Headquarters who thought *Hornblower* was a code name for a mission they were not told about.

In the evenings, Churchill watched films with the officers and crew. His favourite was *Lady Hamilton*, which he found inspirational and viewed five times.[6]

Churchill expressed to his colleagues the advantages of the forthcoming meeting in Newfoundland. In his memoirs he wrote:

---

[6] Ibid.

Moreover, a conference between us would proclaim the ever closer association of Britain and the United States, would cause our enemies concern, make Japan ponder, and cheer our friends. There was also much business to be settled about American intervention in the Atlantic, aid to Russia, our own supplies, and above all the increasing menace of Japan.[7]

The Ship Cove meeting had a much greater impact on turning the fortunes of war in favour of the Allies than previously thought.

LEADERS ARRIVE IN PLACENTIA BAY

On Saturday, August 9, 1941, as the two warships drew abreast of each other in Placentia Bay, with their escort vessels keeping a close watch, Churchill and Roosevelt saluted each other. The Royal Marine Band played "The Star Spangled Banner," and the American band played "God Save the Queen." After the period of formalities concluded, Churchill boarded the *Augusta* and greeted the president. The two leaders held discussions relating to their agenda while the military strategists began their meetings.

Churchill sparked loud laughter among guests at the dinner held on the first night of the Ship Cove meeting with his comment about the Russians. He had brought a pot of caviar with him from London, which had been a gift he received from Stalin. While offering it to be shared by his guests, he quipped, "It is so good to have such a treat, even if it means

---

[7] Ibid 247.

fighting on the side of the Russians to get it."

It was during the preliminary discussion between the two leaders that Roosevelt suggested it would be helpful if they formulated a joint declaration to determine certain broad principles to guide the policy discussions to follow. That night, Churchill drew up a list of six principles and the next morning presented them to the president. The president made several changes to the wording in the list and then added two more principles. At that point, to Churchill's disappointment, there was no mention, even in a general way, of the need to organize any sort of peace organization after the war.

Over the next three days, several conferences were held dealing with urgent war-related issues, including strategies to deal with the looming threat to peace from Japan. Some of these meetings were exclusively attended by the military strategists while Churchill and Roosevelt met separately.

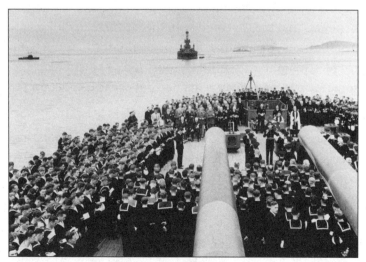

Church service on the deck of the HMS *Prince of Wales* in Placentia Bay. (US Naval History and Heritage Command, Catalog #: NH 67208)

KEY ISSUES DISCUSSED

The Placentia Bay meeting developed strategies that were instrumental in changing the course of the war. These included extending the Lend-Lease Program to help Russia, increasing aid to England, delaying Japan's entry into the war through diplomatic stalling, and relieving Britain of some of its military commitments.[8]

In August 1941, both Britain and the United States held grave concerns over the possibility of Japan entering the war by attacking British or Dutch possessions in the East Indies or Malaya. During the Placentia Bay meeting, the two world leaders agreed on joint actions to be taken should their fears become reality. Two weeks before Roosevelt and Churchill met, they froze all Japanese assets in the United Kingdom and the United States. On August 17, as a result of the Ship Cove meeting, the League of Nations warned the Japanese against taking aggressive steps in the Pacific. Both leaders felt the Japanese were intending to go to war, and Churchill's hope was that the US could keep the Japanese in diplomatic negotiations for another four or five months so England could strengthen its military position. The strategy had some success, and Japan remained out of the conflict for the next four months.[9]

Another of the issues discussed by the two leaders had special significance for Russia and no doubt played a role in winning the war. This matter dealt with Russia's needs in order to repel the German invasion taking place. The

[8] The US agreed to take over Britain's commitment to the Portuguese government to protect them in the event they were forced to establish a government in exile.

[9] John Keegan, *The Second World War* (New York: Penguin, 1989).

idea originated at the Placentia Bay summit for a conference to take place in Moscow from September 28 to October 1, 1941. The Moscow Conference was attended by W.V. Harriman, representing the United States, and Lord Beaverbrook, representing the British. Russia was represented by Vyacheslav Molotov.

The outcome of that conference was the signing of a joint declaration by Britain and the United States to provide aid to the Soviet Union in its fight against the Axis. This led to the decision on October 30 by the United States to offer the Soviets one billion dollars' worth of supplies under the Lend-Lease Program. Escorted convoys were arranged to deliver the supplies Russia needed.[10] About six weeks after the Moscow meeting, the United States amended the Neutrality Act of 1939 to enable American merchant ships to be armed and to call at ports of belligerents.[11]

RUSSIA'S IMPORTANCE TO THE WEST

Aiding Russia against Germany was of primary importance to Churchill and Roosevelt in 1941. It kept the Germans tied down on the eastern front, giving England time to increase its military arsenal in preparation for a European invasion and the US time to strengthen its own military and to take up military strategic positions in the Atlantic while keeping the war away from America.

Churchill had placed Lord Beaverbrook in full charge of the

---

[10] Robert H. Ferrell and John S. Bowman, eds, *The Twentieth Century: An Almanac* (New York: World Almanac Publications, 1984).

[11] Winston Churchill, *The Grand Alliance: The Second World War Volume III* (Boston: Houghton Mifflin, 1950).

question of American supplies to Russia, and Roosevelt relied much on his personal representative, Harry Hopkins, to keep him up to date on the issue. He sent Hopkins to Moscow prior to the Placentia Bay meeting to meet with Stalin and obtain detailed information on the Soviet position. Hopkins returned in time to join Churchill in departing on August 4 for the Newfoundland meeting. In a note to Roosevelt on the same day, Churchill remarked, "Twenty-seven years ago today, the Huns [Germans] began their last war. We must make a good job of it this time." During the cross-Atlantic trip, Hopkins filled Churchill in on Stalin's views.

Before leaving for the meeting, Churchill arranged for Lord Beaverbrook, who was on another mission at the time, to fly over to Newfoundland on August 11 to participate in the discussions with the president. He instructed his senior officials to ensure Beaverbrook brought all urgent papers with him. His directions were to secure the documents in a weighted bag so if the plane crashed the information would not be found. Another trusted advisor, Arthur Purvis, was scheduled to take a flight the same day, at Churchill's request, to attend the meeting in Ship Cove.

Churchill wanted Lord Beaverbrook's and Arthur Purvis's expertise available in discussions on the division of supplies between Great Britain and the Soviet Union. He also relied on these two for a Canadian perspective during the meetings. Both left Prestwick in separate planes on the same day. Beaverbrook arrived safely at St. John's and met withChurchill on the 12th. Minutes after take-off, the plane carrying Purvis crashed into a nearby hill. All on board were killed.

STALIN RECEIVES MESSAGE FROM SECRETIVE PLACENTIA MEETING

On August 12, 1941, the two world leaders sent a joint state-ment from Ship Cove to Stalin related to discussions they had just completed involving aid to Russia. That statement was not shared with the public and did not include any references to any charter. It read:

12 Aug. '41

We are at the moment co-operating to provide you with the very maximum of supplies that you most urgently need. Already many shiploads have left our shores, and more will leave in the immediate future.

We must now turn our minds to the consideration of a more long-term policy, since there is still a long and hard path to be traversed before there can be won that complete victory without which our efforts and sacrifices would be wasted.

The war goes on upon many fronts and before it is over there may be yet further fighting fronts that will be developed. Our resources, though immense, are limited, and it must become a question as to where and when those resources can best be used to further to the greatest extent our common effort. This applies equally to manufactured war supplies and to raw materials.

The needs and demands of your and our armed services can only be determined in the light of the full knowledge of the many factors which must be taken into consideration in the decisions that we make. In order that all of us may be in a position to arrive at speedy decisions as to the apportionment of our joint resources, we suggest that we prepare for a meeting to be held at Moscow, to which we would send high representatives who could discuss these matters directly with you. If this conference appeals to you, we want you to know that, pending the decisions of that conference, we shall continue to send supplies and materials as rapidly as possible.

We realise fully how vitally important to the defeat of Hitlerism is the brave and steadfast resistance of the Soviet Union, and we feel therefore that we must not in any circumstances fail to act quickly and immediately in this matter of planning the programme for the future allocation of our joint resources.[12]

Churchill was pleased when Roosevelt agreed that the American navy would take over patrol of the American-Iceland segment of the Atlantic, thus relieving the hard-pressed British of some of their convoy duties. This strengthened the British in dealing with the U-boat threat on the Atlantic.[13]

THE JOINT ANNOUNCEMENT

The two leaders agreed to issue a joint statement on August 14, which would be confined to mentioning the most publicaly acceptable positive parts of the agreement dealing with the issue of aid to the democracies and, in particular, the principles regarding a better future for civilization.

---

[12] Ibid., 444.

[13] Staff of the *New York Times*, Churchill in Memoriam (New York: Bantam, 1965).

An important point made by Churchill referred to item eight, which as it stood would disappoint the English people because it lacked any mention of establishing, even in general terms, an international organization for keeping peace after the war.

Roosevelt's motivation in putting forward the eight points was to influence American opinion. The idea of an outright commitment for American involvement in the League of Nations would not have gone over well with the American people. They were not then members of the League. Churchill confided to Atlee:

> Having regard to our views about the League of Nations or other international organisations, I would suggest the following amendment after the word "essential": *"pending the establishment of a wider and more permanent system of general security."*
>
> He will not like this very much, but he attaches so much importance to the Joint Declaration, which he believes will affect the whole movement of United States opinion, and that I think he will agree.
>
> It would be most imprudent on our part to raise unnecessary difficulties. We must regard this as an interim and partial statement of war aims designed to assure all countries of our righteous purpose, and not the complete structure which we should build after victory.[14]

14   Ibid., 443.

JOINT DECLARATION BY PRESIDENT AND PRIME MINISTER, AUGUST 12, 1941

The two leaders agreed that:

Their countries seek no aggrandizement, territorial or other.

They desire to see no territorial changes that do not accord with the freely expressed wishes of the peoples concerned.

They respect the right of all peoples to choose the form of Government under which they will live; and they wish to see sovereign rights and self-government restored to those who have been forcibly deprived of them.

They will endeavor, with due respect for their existing obligations, to further the enjoyment by all States, great or small, victor or vanquished, of access, on equal terms, to the trade and to the raw materials of the world which are needed for their economic prosperity.

They desire to bring about the fullest collaboration between all nations in the economic field, with the object of securing for all improved labour standards, economic advancement, and social security.

After the final destruction of the Nazi tyranny they hope to establish a peace which will afford to all nations the means of dwelling in safety within their own boundaries, and which will afford assurance that all the men in all the lands may live out their lives in freedom from feat and want.

Such a peace should enable all men to traverse the high seas and oceans without hindrance.

They believe that all the nations of the world, for realistic as well as spiritual reasons, must come to the abandonment of the use of force. Since no future peace can be maintained if land, sea, or air armaments continue to be employed by nations which threaten, or may threaten, aggression outside of their frontiers, they believe, pending the establishment of a wider and permanent system of general security,[15] that the disarmament of such nations is essential. They will likewise aid and encourage all other practicable measures which will lighten for peace-loving peoples the crushing burden of armaments.[16]

Churchill was elated over the final draft of the declaration; in particular, item eight in which Roosevelt included the prime minister's addition regarding a permanent system of general security. Churchill commented in his memoirs:

The fact alone of the United States, still technically neutral, joining with a belligerent Power in making such a declaration was astonishing. The inclusion in it of a reference to "the final destruction of the Nazi tyranny", based on a phrase appearing in my original draft, amounted to a challenge which in ordinary times would have implied warlike action.

Finally, not the least striking feature was the realism of the last paragraph, where there was a plain and bold intimation that after the war the United States would join with us in policing the world until the establishment of a better order.[17]

[15] These were Churchill's words which FDR verbally accepted in order to have the whole statement accepted. Without them, there was no commitment to the idea.

[16] Ibid., 443.

[17] Ibid., 444.

CALAMITY IN ST. JOHN'S FINAL NIGHT OF MEETING

On the final night of the meetings, there were some anxious moments in St. John's about ninety miles from the scene. An unidentified aircraft had suddenly approached the city, which had been blacked out due to wartime regulations. Anti-aircraft guns protecting the city were alerted and ready to fire when the identity of the plane was determined.[18] When officials learned the plane was carrying a special guest of Churchill, the searchlights went out and an all clear was sounded. It was Lord Beaverbrook, a member of Britain's wartime cabinet and trusted friend of the British prime minister. Beaverbrook was the unidentified expected guest whom Churchill referred to at the meetings only as the "newspaperman."

Beaverbrook was en route to the meeting in Placentia Bay but had no way of getting there from St. John's. The Newfoundland Railway stepped in and made special arrangements for a train to take Beaverbrook to Argentia. Almost everybody on Churchill's ship was asleep when he arrived at 5 a.m. He joined the meetings with the two world leaders and then returned by train to St. John's. From there, he took an evening flight to Washington to continue discussions with American officials on behalf of Churchill and Roosevelt and likely to assist in laying the groundwork for the Moscow meeting.

Contrary to public belief, the charter (Joint Statement) was never signed. The likely reason for this was that the eight

---

[18] Two anti-aircraft guns were stationed in a field east of the Hill-o-Chips in the east end of St. John's.

principles were meant to be a joint statement that guided the agenda at the meeting. It was later that these principles were given a stronger emphasis along with the label the "Atlantic Charter."

Three days before the meeting at Placentia Bay took place, a radio station in Cincinnati, Ohio, reported that Washington sources stated the president was to meet Churchill somewhere in the Atlantic. It was not until six days after Churchill returned to England that he told his people of the meeting with the American president held "somewhere in the Atlantic."

Churchill began his address to the British Nation with the words:

> In a spacious landlocked bay which reminded me of the west coast of Scotland, powerful American warships, protected by a strong flotilla, and far-reaching aircraft, awaited our arrival and as it were, stretched out a hand to help us.[19]

On August 14, the unsigned joint statement was released to the world. The cover-up document served its purpose, which was to divert public attention from the life-and-death issues which the Placentia Bay meeting had dealt with.

On December 8, 1941, the United States, following the December 7 attack on Pearl Harbour, declared war on Japan. The Senate voted 82-0 in favour of war, and the House of

[19] Winston Churchill, *The Grand Alliance: The Second World War Volume III* (Boston: Houghton Mifflin, 1950).

Representatives voted 388-1 in favour. Representative Jeanette Rankin, the first elected woman representative, voted against it. Rankin, a pacifist, also opposed the US entry into WWI.[20] The US declared war on Germany and Italy on December 11, 1941.

---

[20] Robert H. Ferrell and John S. Bowman, eds, *The Twentieth Century: An Almanac* (New York: World Almanac Publications, 1984).

CHAPTER THREE

The Fate of the *Prince of Wales*

~~~

Just four months after the Placentia Bay meeting, all Britain was shocked after learning the *Prince of Wales* and the *Repulse* were sunk in a two-hour battle with Japanese shore-based aircraft. British military historian John Keegan writes:

> The loss was a disaster for which no one in Britain was prepared. Not only did it upset all preconceptions about Britain's ability to command distant waters through naval power; it struck cruelly at the nation's maritime pride. "In all the war," wrote Winston Churchill, "I never received a more direct shock."[1]

Following the Placentia Bay meeting, the *Prince of Wales*, the most important battleship in the British fleet, had moved on to its next mission. That assignment was to join

---

[1] John Keegan, *The Second World War* (New York: Penguin, 1989).

with the *Repulse* at Colombo then move on to Singapore to strengthen British forces in the east.[2]

The simultaneous news of the surprise attack on Pearl Harbour and the beginning of the Japanese invasion of the Malay Peninsula at Singora, 450 miles north of Singapore, shocked British military leaders. The Admiralty was concerned over the vulnerability of its two major battleships in Singapore and immediately sent a message for them to "go to sea and vanish among the innumerable islands." The message arrived too late, and both battleships had already departed from Singapore on December 8, with intentions to cover the British Army's lines along the Malay Peninsula. They were accompanied by four destroyers.

A DEVASTATING BLOW TO THE BRITISH

Jack Ford, whose story is told in the book *The Jack Ford Story*, was one of the soldiers on guard duty the night of December 9 when the *Prince of Wales* and the *Repulse* sailed by the RAF's Seletar Airbase at Singapore on their way down the coast to defend the Malaya Peninsula. Ford recalled:

> I watched them pass and head towards the Japanese fleet. A fellow soldier, an Englishman, said to me, "We'd be in a nice state now if we lose the *Prince of Wales* and the *Repulse*." It wasn't long after that a voice on the radio was telling us that the *Prince of Wales* and the *Repulse* had been sunk by the Japanese. I said, "We are doomed, we are doomed. We got no

[2] G.W.L Nicholson, *More Fighting Newfoundlanders* (St. John's: Govt. of Newfoundland and Labrador, 1969).

fleet now. The *Prince of Wales* and the *Repulse* are gone, the *Exeter* was sunk in the Java Sea, three or four other destroyers are gone and an American fleet was destroyed at Pearl Harbour. We got no chance in God's world."[3]

Recalling that event, Ford acknowledged the superiority of the Japanese pilots and aircraft:

We lost four or five aircraft that went to defend the *Repulse* and *Prince of Wales*. The Japanese easily challenged us in the sky. Their pilots had been training for a long while and they were flying in superb aircraft that could accelerate to three hundred miles per hour. The top speed for our planes was a little more than one hundred miles an hour. We couldn't stay in the sky at all, they shot us out of it. I remember my friend, Jack Ryall, a Scotsman, who flew one of the planes which I worked on. When he was ordered to go into that battle, he said to me, "Thanks for looking after us, but I am afraid this is going to be a suicide mission." I never saw him again. He was shot down over Kuantan defending the *Prince of Wales* and *Repulse*. These kinds of things happen in war. We had lost most of our aircraft and soon after the Japs approached Singapore from Malaya. Other RAF squadrons came to Singapore to join us in fighting the invaders.[4]

---

[3] Jack Fitzgerald, *The Jack Ford Story: The Newfoundlander in Nagasaki* (St. John's: Creative, 2008).

[4] Ibid.

A few weeks after the sinking of the two British warships, the Japanese sent down divers to retrieve the British-made radar equipment. It was a major undertaking, and when completed, the equipment was sent to Japan where its scientists used it to develop radar for its own military.[5]

WALLACE CAKE

Wallace Cake was one of the survivors of the *Prince of Wales*. Later when Cake read an account of the epic battle in which the Japanese claimed to have dropped wreaths where the ship went down, he commented, "All the wreaths that I saw dropped, exploded." Cake was among those rescued by British destroyers and taken to Singapore.[6]

About eight weeks later, Cake was assigned to serve on the 2,000-ton patrol ship *Vyner Brooks*. Soon after, that ship was attacked by Japanese bombers and sunk eight miles from the Malayan shore. Cake recalled, "I forgot my life jacket when we abandoned ship so I had to swim the eight miles to shore without it. The ship was carrying many nurses and children who made it safely to shore."

Before dawn next morning, horrors took place that caused Cake to have nightmares the rest of his life. Not one of the nurses was still alive by dawn the next morning. Japanese soldiers had taken them into the jungle where they were raped and beaten throughout the night.

---

[5] Gordon Thomas and Max Morgan Witts, *Enola Gay* (New York: Pocket Books, 1977).

[6] This story on Cake is based on articles he wrote for the *Canadian Legion Veteran's Magazine*, December 1958 and March 1959, and *Comrade in Arms* by Herb Wells.

Cake was among the survivors who evaded the Japanese and spent the next two days on the edge of the jungle near the Malayan shore. They did hear the screaming of the nurses throughout the night. "It was horrible for us. There was not a thing we could do about it," recalled Cake. He always had trouble telling their story because of the atrocities associated with it. He later recalled:

> Of about sixty persons in our party on the beach, only twelve of us reached the nearest town alive. The others were killed by a Japanese patrol. We were taken by the Japanese to the small town of Montuck and after two months there we were sent to Palembang, Sumatra. There were about two thousand British in the camp when we got there.[7]

At Palembang, there were 2,000 British POWs and about 150 men assigned to each straw hut. Jack Ford was also a prisoner there before being moved to Singapore and then Nagasaki. Strips of bamboo were used for bedding, and there were no blankets provided. Prisoners were forced to work from 8 a.m. to 9 p.m. seven days a week and were paid five cents a day. The five cents were paid with one- and five-cent notes. Cake looked forward to his work when he was moved to the docks to unload food cargoes. He said:

> It was better to be beaten up once in a while for stealing a little food than to slowly starve to death. There was one case where a fellow dropped a case and was beaten by the guard. The poor fellow lost his temper and hit the

---

[7] *The Canadian Legion Veteran Magazine*, 1958.

guard hard enough to knock him down. Three
or four of the guards tied his hands and beat
him to death.[8]

In the few months leading up to the atomic bombing of
Japan, which ended the war, conditions were almost
intolerable for prisoners. Rations were reduced to 240
grams of rice daily and twenty to thirty men were dying of
starvation every day. Those who died were buried in a
corner of the prison and when that reached its capacity, they
were buried in the jungle outside the camp. By the summer
of 1945, Wallace Cake had dropped from 140 to 82 pounds.
Cake wrote:

> The British Medical Officer in the camp said
> that we could not last any longer than another
> two months. Fortunately for us, the war ended.
> We had no idea of what was happening until
> August 22 when we were told what we had been
> waiting for almost four years to hear—the war
> is over. The news proved to be too much
> for some of the men and some of them went
> absolutely hysterical. The RAF flew over and
> dropped supplies of food and clothing.[9]

The Japanese remained in control of the camp until the
British arrived. A Captain Takahashi, who had bullied and
tormented the prisoners, suddenly became very supportive
of them. Cake recalled, "He must have lost twenty pounds
through the exercise during that month, and by now has
probably lost his neck."

[8] Ibid.
[9] Ibid.

Cake said there were a few Japanese soldiers who acted decently towards the prisoners. They had to be careful in any help they offered because, if caught, they too would be punished.

CHAPTER FOUR

Berlin Knew
Newfoundland's Weakness

~~~

The complacency that existed in St. John's during WWII was shaken on March 3, 1942, when U-boat 587 fired torpedoes at St. John's in the first German attack on North American soil. How did Newfoundland military secrets reach Berlin?

Newsweek Magazine, on July 13, 1942, reported that information reaching Berlin from St. John's, Newfoundland, led to the sinking of several ships in the North Atlantic.[1]

However, by that time German U-boats had already carried out their first attack on North American soil at St. John's, which was followed six months later with the sinking of ships at Lance Cove and Wabana, both on Bell Island. In the case of the November 1942 attack on Wabana, U-boat Command in Germany was previously aware of a weakness

---

[1] Gerhard Bassler, *Vikings to U-boats: The German Experience in Newfoundland* (Montreal: McGill-Queen's, 2006).

in Bell Island defences and relayed this information to U-boats in Conception Bay.

German intelligence was also aware of the defences protecting St. John's harbour as well as the regularly scheduled air surveillance of the city. Was there a spy at work in Newfoundland? Or did German intelligence have other means of gathering information?

With WWII in its third year, a War Exposition was held in Chicago which highlighted the first attack on the American continent at St. John's less than three months previous. The display was made up of fragments of two torpedoes, which the exhibition noted were fired upon St. John's by an enemy submarine.

Several sealing vessels were entering St. John's harbour when the torpedo attack was launched, and the sealers heard the explosions. Research shows that, on March 3, there were actually three torpedoes fired at St. John's by U-boat 587 under the command of Captain Ulrich Borcherdt. The U-587 was patrolling near St. John's after participating in an attack on convoy *ons-67* off the Newfoundland coast. Three days after the attack on St. John's, U-587 sank the 900-ton Greenland escort *Hans Egeda* off St. Pierre-Miquelon.[2]

Although some claim Bell Island was the site of the first submarine attack on North America, those attacks actually took place in September and November of 1942, more than six months after the attack on St. John's.

---

[2] Michael Hadley, *U-boats Against Canada* (Montreal: McGill-Queens,1989). Laurence Peterson, *The First U-boat Flotilla* (Annapolis: Naval Institute Press, 2002). Jak P. Mallman Showell, *U-boat Command and the Battle of the Atlantic* (St. Catherines: Vanwell, 2000), 150.

Newfoundlanders in the early days of WWII viewed the conflict as a foreign war and felt confident they were secure from enemy attack. However, the German strategy to bring the war to the North American coast, code named Drumbeat, got underway in early January 1942 when the first of a series of waves of German U-boats entered Newfoundland and Canadian coastal waters. U-587 was part of the fourth wave sent here in March.[3] Newfoundland expended its efforts by concentrating on preparing a volunteer home defence and helping the war effort by sending money and volunteers to Britain's aid.

The importance of the colony's strategic position was not fully appreciated in Newfoundland, but was immediately recognized in other capitals of the world. Washington, Ottawa, London, and even Berlin assessed its importance, and from the start, included Newfoundland and its coastal waters in its individual military strategies. Washington and Ottawa viewed Newfoundland as the battle line between North America and Europe in the event England fell and hostilities spread to this continent. England, which was dependant on its imports from North America for its survival, recognized the importance of Newfoundland's coastal waters at first, and as the war progressed, developed an appreciation for the strategic importance of the port of St. John's.

Berlin, early in the war, began implementing military policies aimed at preventing the supply of Britain's needs from North America by blocking its ports and sinking its merchant vessels. Operation St. John's was a specific military mission of the German's aimed at St. John's and part of the larger Operation

[3] Ibid.

Drumbeat, which included the St. Lawrence, Halifax, and American ports.

THE FUEHRER'S STRATEGY

The most important strategy in disrupting Hitler's grand plan was developed by Churchill's double agent, William Stephenson, and implemented by the prime minister's underground spy organization, the BSO. In preparation for D-Day, a couple of dozen carefully chosen agents were parachuted behind enemy lines with top-secret documents intended to fall into German hands. These phony documents succeeded in convincing Hitler that the British were planning on crossing the English Channel at its narrowest point. While Hitler moved his main force to surprise the Allied forces, Churchill's and Roosevelt's troops landed elsewhere. This changed the war.

One of the BSO agents parachuted behind enemy lines days before D-Day was John Finn, who was later employed by CJON Radio and Television.[4]

But long before the D-Day preparations, at a conference with his naval commanders in Berlin on December 12, 1941, Adolph Hitler decided to launch a major U-boat offensive against ports in America.[5] While the main target of this operation was the United States, Newfoundland and Canadian coastal waters became targets as well. Upon Hitler's

[4] This information was included in Intrepid's top-secret documents, which remained sealed for forty years after the war. I interviewed Finn for an earlier book, and he mentioned parachuting into France before D-Day, but revealed nothing else.

[5] Operation Drumbeat followed the declaration of war on Germany by the United States a week before.

instructions, his U-boats were ordered to penetrate the northern end of the coastal route between Newfoundland and New York near the homeward-bound ports of convoys.[6]

British mapping of U-boat activity between December 7, 1941, and July 31, 1942, shows U-boat activity along Newfoundland's coast from the Grand Banks to St. John's, then north to Conception Bay and Notre Dame Bay. U-boat activity increased and expanded in the following six months with high concentrations in the Strait of Bell Isle area, which earned the name Torpedo Junction.[7]

The convoys operating out of Canadian and American ports travelled within 600 miles of Newfoundland's coast from Port aux Basques to St. John's and north to Notre Dame Bay. In the first month of Operation Drumbeat, thirty-one ships of nearly 200,000 tons had been sunk on the Atlantic Coast in Newfoundland, Canadian, and American waters. By the end of February losses in the Atlantic increased to seventy-one ships, nearly all of them in the American zone.[8]

On July 1, 1941, the US Navy started anti-submarine patrols from bases in Newfoundland.[9]

AVALON PENINSULA KEY DEFENCE IN NORTH AMERICA

The Avalon Peninsula was perhaps one of the best fortified and defended areas in North America during World War II.

---

[6] Winston Churchill, *The Hinge of Fate: The Second World War Volume IV* (Boston: Houghton Mifflin, 1950) 109.

[7] Ibid., 110.

[8] Ibid., 124.

[9] Robert H. Ferrell and John S. Bowman, eds, *The Twentieth Century: An Almanac* (New York: World Almanac Publications, 1984).

There were the strong RCN presence in St. John's harbour, American and Canadian bases located in the city, and the Royal Canadian Air Force (RCAF) at Torbay. Argentia was not only the most expensive of the American overseas bases, but it was also home to the largest single US task force in the Atlantic.

Argentia housed facilities for both the US Navy and the US Army. On its north side was the naval base and naval air station, and on its south side was the US Army base Fort McArthur. The massive task force at Argentia included six escort carriers, fifteen destroyer escorts, a second artillery group, an aircraft artillery company, an anti-aircraft artillery company, an anti-motor torpedo boat battalion, and an infantry company. By 1943, a total of 12,403 soldiers were stationed there.

The naval base and air station served both American and Allied anti-submarine air patrols and task force escorts. US Army personnel patrolled the east side of Placentia Bay. Not only was Argentia protected with searchlights, but the Americans installed searchlights at Dunville and Fox Island.

The establishing of a base at Argentia was a boon for the Placentia area, and it employed between ten and fourteen thousand people during its construction. In 1955 the USN took over Fort McArthur when the Atlantic Barrier Force and an Airborne Early Warning Wing were formed to operate from there. In later years, the base was used for American and Canadian oceanographic studies.[10]

During August 1941, at Argentia, the Anglo-American

---

[10] Joseph R. Smallwood, *Encyclopaedia of Newfoundland and Labrador: Volume 1* (St. John's: Newfoundland Book Publishers, 1981).

agreement was signed that gave the United States Navy (USN) control over almost all Royal Canadian Navy (RCN) operations beyond the twelve-mile territorial limit. Two separate RCN commands coordinated the agreement: The Flag Officer, Newfoundland at St. John's, and the Commanding Officer, Atlantic Coast, in Halifax. They were responsible for the naval operations in their respective areas plus the provision of escort groups for the Atlantic convoys under USN control.[11]

The Argentia base was built at a cost of fifty-two million dollars, which was a huge sum of money in the 1940s. It was a base for anti-submarine patrols over the North Atlantic, and it played a major role in winning the Battle of the Atlantic.

WINSTON CHURCHILL FELT ARGENTIA MOST IMPORTANT

The United States war chiefs agreed that should the war spread to America and to the Pacific, the Atlantic and European theatre should be regarded as decisive. Hitler must be defeated first, and on this conception American aid in the Battle of the Atlantic was planned. Preparations were started to meet the needs of joint ocean convoys. This is where Argentia came in. In March 1941, American officers visited Great Britain to select bases for their naval escorts and air forces. Work on these began immediately. Meanwhile the development of American bases in British territory in the West Atlantic, which had begun in 1940, was proceeding rapidly.

---

[11] Marc Milner, *The U-boat Hunters* (Toronto: University of Toronto Press, 1994).

Churchill noted the importance of the Argentia Base in his memoirs:

> The most important for the North Atlantic convoys was Argentia, in Newfoundland. With this and with harbours in the United Kingdom American forces could play their fullest permissible part in the battle, or so it seemed when these measures were planned.
>
> Between Canada and Great Britain are the islands of Newfoundland, Greenland and Iceland. All these lie near the flank of the shortest, or great-circle, track between Halifax and Scotland. Forces based on these "stepping-stones" could control the whole route by sectors. Greenland was entirely devoid of resources, but the other two islands could be quickly turned to good account.[12]

Lt. Col. Timothy J. Regan, on July 2, 1945, addressing American Forces at Pepperrell, made the following commentary:

> When the base was first constructed, it looked as though the enemy would overrun Britain. They already had weather stations in Iceland and Greenland. Their submarines were running practically unchecked in the North Atlantic. The actual and immediate danger to Canada and the US was very real indeed. A base from which we could protect our eastern cities and factories was the number one priority in our defence plans. The answer to that was Newfoundland. This has become a clenched fist challenging the Germans to come farther. The Germans were driven from Iceland and their stations destroyed on Greenland after the Newfoundland Base was secure. While you were here and seeming to

---

[12] Winston Churchill, *The Grand Alliance: The Second World War Volume III* (Boston: Houghton Mifflin, 1950), 138.

be inactive, your very presence was helping to keep the European War confined to Europe.[13]

Exhaustive studies of German documents and volumes of interviews with WWII members of the German military by Canadian scholars affirm that German U-boats carried out intelligence-gathering missions in Newfoundland.[14] Several examples supporting this are found in U-boat experiences around Newfoundland's coast. Also revealed is that while the Germans landed two spies on Canadian soil during WWII, none were set ashore in Newfoundland. However, one German spy en route to the United States was captured near Cape Race and taken to Argentia.

A German U-boat scouted the area around Bell Island at night, seeking out possible targets and weaknesses. Bell Island was an important target for Germany because it supplied thirty percent of Canada's iron ore to process into steel. Any pertinent information gathered was radioed or passed on by U-boats returning to Germany from Newfoundland waters to the commander of U-boats in Berlin[15] who, after studying the information, advised several U-boat captains in the Conception Bay area that Wabana would be a good target for a night attack. The Germans discovered a weakness in the Bell Island defences, which contributed to the success of the U-boat attack at Wabana.

[13]   Quoted in Jack Fitzgerald, *A Day at the Races* (St. John's: Creative, 2003).

[14]   The information on U-boat activities was collected from the following: Michael Hadley, *U-boats Against Canada* (Montreal: McGill-Queens,1989); James B. Lambe, *The Corvette Navy: True Stories from Canada's Atlantic War* (Halifax: Nimbus, 2010); Edwin P. Hoyt, *U-boats Offshore: When Hitler Struck America* (New York: Stein and Day, 1978); and. Marc Milner, *The U-boat Hunters* (Toronto: University of Toronto Press, 1994).

[15]   At different stages of the war, U-boat Command Headquarters was located at Lorient, France; Hamburg and, in 1942, Berlin, Germany.

THE "SHARK KEY" CODE

U-boats collecting and sending radio messages to Germany often put themselves at risk as well as presenting target opportunities for the allies. The "Shark" key used by the U-boat fleet was not broken by British intelligence until December 1942. Author John Keegan explained: Up to that time, the British used High Frequency Direction Finding (HF/DF or Huff Duff) to detect and locate shadowing U-boats from the transmissions they sent back to U-boat headquarters, and so for convoys to be rerouted or protecting aircraft summoned. Meanwhile, because of the Admiralty's ill-advised persistence in the use of a book code instead of a machine cipher, the B-Dienst (German Intelligence) was able to read convoy traffic and direct wolf packs on to chosen routes with sometimes disastrous effect.[16]

One of the secrets hidden in British archives was that William Stephenson, known by the code name Intrepid, had already decoded Germany's infamous Enigma, but to reveal the secret would have alerted the Germans and could have spelled disaster for the Allies' future plans.

U-BOATS SPIED ON ST. JOHN'S, HARBOUR

St. John's also came under the watchful eye of an intelligence gathering U-boat. Captain Ruggeberg of U-513, which carried out the successful attack on Bell Island on September 5, 1942, scouted St. John's Harbour area for more than two weeks under the protection of a heavy fog. During the operation, he came so close to a Canadian destroyer outside

[16] John Keegan, *The Second World War* (New York: Penguin, 1989).

St. John's Harbour that they nearly collided. Captain Ruggeberg failed to find any easy targets but he succeeded in gathering intelligence.

The information he sent to Hamburg was helpful in the developing of Operation St. John's in which the Germans succeeded in laying mines outside the Harbour. Ruggeberg informed Hamburg that St. John's was protected by a single escort ship guarding its entrance and a daily and constant air surveillance. Of special interest was how Newfoundland's capital city regulated its lighting. The U-boat captain, referring to Atlantic ports, noted that all lights burned under peacetime conditions except for the restrictive use of lighting at St. John's, Cape St. Francis, Bull Head and Ferryland. Michael Hadley, in his book *U-boats Against Canada* stated, "Newfoundland alone exercised regular control over its navigation lights."

When the U-513 was leaving the area of St. John's on September 29, it encountered and sunk the 7,174-ton SS *Ocean Vanguard* just three and a half miles out.

SOMETIMES SECRETS LEAKED OUT

A lid was kept on the German U-boat attacks in coastal waters off Newfoundland and Canada in the early days of the war, but with the strong military presence in Newfoundland, and with both St. John's and Bell Island coming under attack, the public knew the war had spread from across the Atlantic. On March 5, 1942, Lt. William Strange of Plans and Operations in Naval Service Head-quarters in Ottawa revealed to the press:

It is obvious to everyone who reads the news that submarines now are operating not far from the North American coasts. This is no occasion for surprise, and certainly none for anything approaching dismay. Such attacks may make the headlines, but they should not–in the public mind–be permitted to occupy unreasonable prominence. The "trench warfare of the seas," was essential to sustain Britain against Axis aggression, its success should not be measured by the frequency of U-boat attacks from whatever quarter, but from the volume of tonnage actually delivered to England.[17]

U-BOATS LURKING ON SOUTH COAST

Intelligence gathered by the Germans was the basis for U-541, under the command of Kurt Peterson, moving to position his U-boat between the south coast of Newfoundland and St. Pierre on September 3, 1944. In this case, B-Dienst intercepted and decoded a secret message from the Allies that the troop ship *Lady Rodney* would be passing through that area after leaving Sydney, Nova Scotia, for St. John's. While in this area, Peterson sighted the 2,140-ton SS *Livingstone*, and torpedoed it. The vessel, which was carrying supplies from Boston for Fort Pepperrell Base, went to the bottom of the Atlantic. Of the twenty-eight people on board, fourteen people survived the sinking and were rescued by the HMCS *Barrie* and taken to St. John's.

---

[17] Quoted in Michael Hadley, *U-boats Against Canada* (Montreal: McGill-Queens, 1989).

Despite the lore relating to German spies and saboteurs operating in Newfoundland, Germany actually showed little interest in developing secret-agent networks in either Newfoundland or Canada. U-boat historian Jak Mallmann Showell suggests that the lack of interest was due, in general, to the proven lack of dependability of agents.

Showell chronicles a list of several incidents in which U-boats either landed or attacked on Canadian and Newfoundland soil. In respect to Newfoundland, he adds to our knowledge of several major German involvements, including the landing of the weather station at Labrador by U-537 in October 1943; the sinking of two vessels at Wabana by U-518 in November 1942; and the sinking of two vessels at Lance Cove in September 1942.

In respect to Canadian soil, the author lists two attempts by U-boats to rescue prisoners of war. Noted are the U-262 attempt to pick up escaped POWs on May 2, 1943, and the U-536 attempt to pick up escaped POWs on September 27-28, 1943. Both missions ended in failure. In the past, most Newfoundland writers fail to mention the first attack on North American soil on March 3, 1942, when St. John's Harbour was fired upon by U-boat 587 under Captain Ulrich Borcherdt. The U-587 was part of the fourth wave of German U-boats sent out to North American coastal waters in early 1942 as part of Operation Drumbeat.[18]

THE SPY AT ARGENTIA

During August 1944, the USN captured a German spy, who

18   Ibid.

was en route to the United States, and took him to Argentia. The spy was on board U-1229, which left Norway on July 26, 1944, on a special mission to land a spy at Winter Harbour, Maine. At the time of his capture, he had three thousand dollars in his possession.

The USS *Bogue*, an aircraft carrier, sighted U-1229 southeast of Cape Race on August 12, 1944. The U-boat dove, but was unable to escape the air attack launched by the *Bogue*. It surfaced long enough for Captain Zink and his crew to abandon ship just before it sank. The forty survivors of U-1229 were taken on board the *Bogue* and interrogated. During this process, the Americans learned of the U-boat's mission and identified the spy. Upon arrival at Argentia, they turned him over to military authorities.[19]

Since the war, there have been many unsubstantiated stories of German spies being executed at Argentia. Eileen Houlihan, a school teacher at Freshwater during the war years, recalled an intriguing story that suggests executions by firing squad may have taken place at Argentia. Her source was the unpublished memoirs of Brother F. Foran, a native of Argentia who served as principal of Holy Cross School in St. John's in the late 1940s and early 1950s. His family operated the lighthouse at Point Latine, near Argentia. Mrs. Houlihan recorded that Brother Foran recounted how an American soldier came to their door one day and told his mother not to be concerned if she heard gunfire in the area. Looking over the shoulder of the officer, Mrs. Foran could see three men standing behind him. Two were soldiers carrying rifles, and a third man stood between them. The

[19] Herb Wells, *Comrades In Arms: A History of Newfoundlanders in Action*, Second World War (St. John's: self-published, 1986), 102.

officer at the door advised Mrs. Foran not to be concerned about the sound of gunfire in the area that day. Soon after, she heard gunfire. According to Brother Foran, rumours spread throughout the community that an American soldier who had deserted his post on shoreline patrol was executed for desertion, which in wartime was a severe offence.[20]

Mrs. Houlihan writes:

> Judging from the number of graves on Boot Hill there must have been many attempts at sabotage and espionage. Traitors were executed by firing squad and buried at Boot Hill on the opposite side from the people who were killed by accident. These graves were unmarked and were exhumed after the war.[21]

While wartime records revealed two German spies having been landed in Canada and a few in the United States, the only reference to spies in Newfoundland was of the one aboard U-518 when it attacked Bell Island and the spy arrested and held at Argentia. The former was on a mission to Canada and had no connection with gathering intelligence in Newfoundland. The latter was on a mission to the United States when captured.

It is interesting to note that, despite the fears of many in

---

[20] During the 1990s I communicated with U.S. Naval Intelligence in West Virginia, the Pentagon and the Congressional Library in Washington asking for a general confirmation that any prisoners had been executed on American bases in Newfoundland. None of the sources answered the question, but I did succeed in obtaining the American Counter-Intelligence Report on the K of C Fire of 1942. The question of such executions, whether of deserters or German spies, is a subject yet to be dealt with by writers and historians. American authorities were not cooperative when I sought a definitive answer.

[21] Eileen Houlihan, *Uprooted! The Argentia Story* (St. John's: Creative, 1992).

Newfoundland, the arson of the Knights of Columbus Hostel in St. John's on December 12, 1942, was not the work of German saboteurs; no mention of it has ever been found among German records or mentioned during interrogations and post-war interviews with German military officials.

In the early 1980s, Bren Walsh, a noted Newfoundland journalist and author, met with an American judge advocate at the Pentagon and left that meeting with the truth about who started the Knights of Columbus fire in 1942, which claimed ninety-nine lives. In December 1984, Bren turned up at Dick's Bookstore on Water Street to attend the release of my book *Newfoundland Disasters*. He called me aside and revealed he had written a book on the fire and planned to have it published. He divulged that the fire was not the work of a German arsonist but an American in St. John's. The Dunfield Enquiry had correctly found that it was the work of a pyromaniac. The man had been arrested and tried for the crime and was sentenced to a military prison. I invited Bren to attend a weekly radio show I did with VOCM announcer Pat Murphy. Bren declined but promised that as soon as his book was released he would accept my invitation. Next day I discussed Walsh's finding and his offer to appear on our radio show with Pat. I included a report on the amazing revelation, including the pyromaniac's name in that broadcast.

Unfortunately Walsh passed away before his book was completed. I learned he had entrusted a family member with his papers. Several years later, when these had not been released, I investigated the story further and contacted officials at the Pentagon to find out about the prisoner. They were ready to cooperate with me but needed more specific information. A spokesman explained that military prisoner records were held for twenty years. I was unable to provide more specific information. A member of Walsh's family confirmed they were aware of Walsh's discovery but had lost track of the documentation. In my research, I did obtain a copy of the US Military Enquiry into the fire from the Congressional Library. I pursued the matter with the Pentagon officials and the American Central Intelligence offices in West Virginia. The outcome of that effort is provided in detail in the revised edition of my book *Newfoundland Disasters.*

In respect to the records of German spy networks, it can no longer be argued that such records are still being kept secret. Especially when there are ample records regarding the landing of German spies in Canada, the United States, Ireland, and other countries. As Showell argues, even when U-boat logs have been destroyed, military researchers can and have reconstructed missing history from U-boat Command records.

FAILED TO ESTABLISH A SPY RING

Hadley's research into wartime German documents reveals that Germany was not operating any spy network in Newfoundland or Canada. They did succeed in landing two agents on Canadian soil with one turning himself into Canadian authorities and the other, through his own bumbling, being captured within twenty-four hours after making a successful landing on the Quebec shore. Surprisingly, the German Command gave little consideration to sending secret agents to Canada until the spring of 1942, two and a half years into the war.[22] Top level German naval staff emphatically believed, in December 1942, that secret agents were not reliable. It was this belief that prompted U-boat Command to refuse to send a U-boat to Iceland to rescue an agent there. However, in rare cases, they were willing to take great risks to rescue POWs as they attempted in Quebec.

The spy landed in Quebec was forty-one-year-old Lt. Werner von Janowski, who was no stranger to Canada. He immigrated to Ontario in the 1930s, lived near London, and was employed as a farm worker. He played the cello and told friends he came from a prominent German family. Another hobby he showed much interest in, but meant nothing to friends and neighbours at the time, was photography. He frequently travelled around the province taking pictures of public buildings and waterfront areas. Just before the war, he returned to Germany where the economy was growing while Canada was still in a depression. There are references in German-authored books to his having joined the French Foreign Legion during the pre-war period, which caused German authorities to consider him subversive and refuse him acceptance into their military. Whether this claim was true or not, von Janowsi eventually became a member of a special sabotage unit where he earned the confidence of his superiors who chose him for the Canadian mission.

This German spy had a close connection with Newfoundland. He was the only passenger on U-518 under Captain Wilhelm Wissmann when it made a successful surface attack on Wabana, Bell Island, on November 2, 1942. That story is told in another part of this book. The U-518 was on

[22] Jak P. Mallmann Showell, *U-boats at War: Landings on Hostile Shores* (Annapolis: Naval Institute Press, 2000).

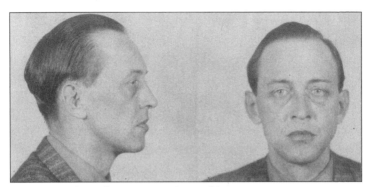

RCMP mugshot of Werner von Janowski (National Archives of Canada: mugshots of Janowski, C-107138)

a double mission, which was to land von Janowsi somewhere on Quebec's shore and to scout Newfoundland waters for any possible shipping targets. A week after the Wabana attack, the spy was landed on Quebec soil.

On November 9 at about 3:30 a.m., U-518 surfaced as close to Sawyer's Point, Quebec, as possible then launched a rubber dinghy to land von Janowski. Separating Sawyer's Point from the village of New Carlisle was Point de New Carlisle, which with its hill of wooden trees hid the landing site from the village.

The landing was successful, but surprised Captain Wissmann when he realized the landing beach was next to a road and CNR rails. When a car turned a curve in the road, its lights shone directly onto the submarine and those on deck had to lie low. Surprisingly, they avoided detection.

The landed spy was to make contact with Adrian Arcand, leader of the Canadian Fascist Party. However, Arcand and ten of his associates had been arrested and jailed two years before. It confirmed for the RCMP that there was no

German spy network operating in Canada; otherwise, German intelligence would have known this.

Though there may not have been an actual spy ring based in Canada, William Stephenson, the man called Intrepid, and his top-secret BSO had in fact compiled a list of Canadians and immigrants listed in German records as supporters of the Third Reich. Intrepid also assembled a similar list of Americans which included senators and labour leaders, among others.

Now in Canada, the agent von Janowski was burdened with three suitcases. One, which he buried on the beach, contained a German naval uniform, his alibi if caught. In such a case, he would claim he was a U-boat commander defecting. Otherwise, he would be treated as a spy and executed.

He carried the remaining two suitcases with him as he walked alone from Sawyer's Point into the village of New Carlisle. One case carried his transmitter for communication with Hamburg, and the other case was his spy kit which included a twenty-five calibre gun, brass knuckles, five-thousand dollars in outdated Canadian bills, 1,000 dollars in twenty-dollar American gold pieces, and some emergency rations of chocolate and dextrose tablets. He had Canadian registration and a taxi licence, and went by the name William Branton. In the same suitcase were several English books, to be used for code purposes, one of which was *Mary Poppins* by P.L. Travers.[23]

Suspicion that he was a German spy began when he arrived to register at the hotel in New Carlisle and told the hotel

---

[23] Michael Hadley, *U-boats Against Canada* (Montreal: McGill-Queens,1989).

clerk that he had arrived there on a bus. This alarmed the clerk because there was no bus that day. The spy continued to attract attention by spending outdated Canadian money and dropping Belgian matches. Since people in the area already feared the Germans may land spies in Quebec, the clerk reported his suspicions to the police, which led to von Janowski's arrest.

Having completed his assignment, Captain Wissmann advised Hamburg that his mission had been successful and that the agent was landed on Canadian soil. He then slipped away and returned to seeking targets in Newfoundland coastal waters. Wissman was not aware that, twenty-four hours after being landed on Canadian soil, von Janowski was arrested and the process of turning him into a double agent had begun.

As a double agent for the RCMP, he kept in touch with his controllers in Hamburg, but after eight months of trying, he was unable to get any valuable information from them. Canadian authorities were at a loss to explain why the Germans did not respond to radio messages sent to Hamburg over an eighteen-month period. Some blamed it on the American press, in particular *Newsweek*, which on November 23, 1942, reported that a German agent had been landed in Quebec a few weeks earlier. However, there is another explanation:

> His minders got what they bargained for at first because it was quickly discovered that his radio transmitter was not powerful enough to reach Germany. Fortunately, while living in Canada before the war, von Janowski had been trained as a radio repair mechanic and thus it was plausible for him to be able to fit a booster to increase

the output of his equipment. This helped a little, but the abundance of background noise in the atmosphere still made reception difficult.[24]

The RCMP handed von Janowski over to work with the British for the remainder of the war.

The Germans were more anxious to get Lt. M. A. Langbein[25] on Canadian soil than they were with von Janowski. This is obvious from the fact that the U-213 mission carrying Langbein was sent directly to land the spy, unlike the U-518 mission carrying von Janowski, which searched Newfoundland waters for a target before going to the St. Lawrence to drop him off.

On May 13, 1942, U-213, under the command of Captain Amelung von Varendorff, landed the German agent on Canadian soil, but not without difficulty. The captain had planned on landing at Melvin's Beach near Saint. John, New Brunswick, but the coastline was rugged in that area, and it took three hours to find a suitable site about thirty miles southwest of Saint John. Langbein arrived on shore dressed in full uniform so that, if caught, he could claim status as a prisoner of war and avoid the death penalty for convicted civilian spies.[26]

Langbein is said to have had a photographic memory and had lived in Canada from 1928 to 1932 where he worked in Alberta and Manitoba. His mission was to gather

[24] Jak P. Mallmann Showell, *U-boats at War: Landings on Hostile Shores* (Annapolis: Naval Institute Press, 2000).

[25] It is believed the initials M.A. meant mechanical artillery rather than the spy's initials. This was done to explain why he was not knowledgeable about submarines.

[26] Michael Hadley, *U-boats Against Canada* (Montreal: McGill-Queens,1989).

information on locations of Canadian industries and report on activities in the port of Halifax. Langbein was given specific orders not to engage in sabotage, even though he had been trained by the German Army in espionage and had completed a mission in Romania. This spy was given Canadian identification papers under the name Alfred Hoskins of 182 Young Street, Toronto, and a sum of money that included seven thousand dollars in large American bills and twelve dollars in old Canadian money.

With its mission completed, U-213 joined a group of subs operating off the coast of New York seeking shipping targets. After a few days without success, it returned to Germany. On July 23, 1942, U-213 was sunk by the sloops HMS *Erne* and *Sandwich*, 160 miles off Santa Maria. All fifty men on board died.[27]

What Langbein's German handlers did not know about their agent was that he had become disillusioned with Nazism and once inside Canada went on to spend his money. Most of the money given him by the Germans was spent in brothels. On November 1, 1944, he gave himself up to Canadian naval authorities.

Langbein was interned in a Canadian POW camp and repatriated to Germany after the war.

U-BOAT WITH JAPANESE SCIENTISTS IN NEWFOUNDLAND WATERS

U-boat 234 received the message from Berlin that the war was over and that it should surrender to an Allied country.

---

[27] Kenneth Wynn, *U-boat Operations of the Second World War: Volume I* (London: Chatham, 1997).

This U-boat was heading towards Newfoundland to surrender, but for some unknown reason, changed its course and was intercepted by the USS *Sutton*, which escorted the sub to the Portsmouth Naval Yard. U-234 was carrying a shipment of uranium and heavy water to be used in developing an atomic bomb. Two Japanese scientists, who were accompanying the shipment to Japan, committed suicide rather than surrender.[28]

GERMAN SOURCES

Officers of the German B-Dienst (Observer's Service) gathered intelligence from many sources, including allied newspapers and magazines from captured planes, boats, and prisoners. They used wireless intercepts and decrypts of code transmissions to collect information on convoy movements. The U-boat fleet collected intelligence which was useful to B-Dienst. During May 1941, England obtained important intelligence and equipment that gave it a major advantage over German Intelligence. A German weather ship was captured off Iceland on May 7.

Among military papers found aboard it were secret documents relating to the Germans' master coding machine known as Enigma. English luck got even better two days later when they captured a U-boat and retrieved a cipher machine and code books.[29] These were used by the cryptographers of the Government Code and Cipher School at Bletchley, England, which monitored the signals sent between U-boats

---

[28] Jack Fitzgerald, *The Jack Ford Story: The Newfoundlander in Nagasaki* (St. John's: Creative, 2008).

[29] Robert H. Ferrell and John S. Bowman, eds, *The Twentieth Century: An Almanac* (New York: World Almanac Publications, 1984).

and from U-boat headquarters in Germany.[30] The Germans never discovered their loss during the war. The find proved invaluable to the Allies.

THE IRELAND CODE

The German Navy was well prepared to assist any of its crews taken as prisoners of war. Each U-boat captain was given a code called the Ireland Code because of its focus on the letters I and R. The alphabet from A to I represented a dot in Morse Code, from J to R represented a dash, and from S to Z represented a gap. The captain, writing home, was able to inform German intelligence of any information he had that would be helpful, including escape plans and locations where escaped prisoners could be rescued by U-boats. The system was used several times and although U-boats were sent in accordance with the code instructions, in both cases, the prisoners were recaptured before arriving at their rendezvous points.[31]

PRIME MINISTER CHURCHILL CONCERNED

Prime Minister Winston Churchill held deep concerns over the threat of U-boats in the Atlantic. In his memoirs, he wrote, "The U-boat attack was our worst evil. It would have been wise for the Germans to stake all upon it. I remember hearing my father say, 'In politics when you have got hold of a good thing, stick to it.'"[32] Fortunately, as history recorded, the Germans did not.

---

[30] John Keegan, *The Second World War* (New York: Penguin, 1989).

[31] Michael Hadley, *U-boats Against Canada* (Montreal: McGill-Queens, 1989).

[32] Winston Churchill, *The Grand Alliance: The Second World War Volume III* (Boston: Houghton Mifflin, 1950).

The Allies had expected the Germans to pay more attention to North American ports after the United States entered the war. Less than one month before the torpedo attack on St. John's, on February 10, Britain gave the United States twenty-four of its best equipped anti-submarine trawlers and ten corvettes with trained crews for the American Navy. Prime Minister Churchill stated in his memoirs, "These were welcomed by our Ally, and the first arrived in New York early in March. It was little enough, but the utmost we could spare."[33]

During the war, the home defence had fifteen hundred coast and sky watchers scattered in every community throughout Newfoundland. Their duty was to report any unusual occurrence from land or sea to the military. Coast-watchers in St. John's saw the explosions against the cliffs on both sides of the entrance to the harbour.

The coast-watchers who witnessed the event recovered as many of the pieces of metal as possible and turned over the collection to the military in the city for examination. Experts examining the pieces determined that the metals were parts of German torpedoes. However, the Nazi attack was not reported in Newfoundland papers until almost two months after Canadian newspapers broke the story. There is speculation that authorities at first did not want to release news of the attack because they feared it would panic the local population.

In his narrative on the *History of Signal Hill National Historic Park and Area to 1945*, James Candow recorded that the first torpedo exploded at 2:54 p.m. on March 3, 1942, in front of

[33] Winston Churchill, *The Hinge of Fate: The Second World War Volume IV* (Boston: Houghton Mifflin, 1950), 117.

Fort Amherst, and the second went off just two minutes later on the opposite side of the Narrows. A general alarm was sounded at Fort Amherst, and the guard was doubled at Fort Chain Rock,[34] but there were no more further developments. There was speculation the Germans were targeting an ammunition supply ship moored in St. John's harbour.

One of the few people who knew the secret was David C. Smith, a frogman (diver) with the Newfoundland Dockyard. Smith lived on Hamilton Avenue opposite the Bennett Avenue intersection in St. John's. He was working underwater when the torpedoes hit. He said the water around him suddenly took on tremendous force and shot him towards the surface and almost out of the water. The water in St. John's harbour was fifty feet deep in 1942. When speaking with the press after the war, Smith recalled:

> Fortunately, they were poor marksmen and each time they missed the mouth of the landlocked harbour, the torpedoes would explode harmlessly on the cliffs off Fort Amherst. But for that, I'd not be here to tell of it and St. John's harbour would probably have been in shambles. The harbour bottom was covered with between six to eight feet of silt and getting a solid footing was a problem and that added to the hazard of underwater sea operations. Working as a diver was always an adventure and thrill each time you went down. You never knew what to expect.

Other exhibits at the Exposition included items from conquered countries in Europe and from England. England's

---

[34] Fort Chain Rock was on the northern side of The Narrows overlooking Chain Rock in St. John's Harbour.

display included some of the boats used in the evacuation from Dunkirk.

In preparing for home defence, the Newfoundland Government was concerned over the possibility of German Naval attacks on St. John's Harbour. Historian Allan Fraser noted in his writings:

> Since St. John's Harbour is an exposed anchorage, prompt measures must be taken to protect the entrance through the narrows, by means of a net. On the advice of the Commander-In-Chief of the America-West Indies Naval Squadron, a three inch jack stay carrying a one inch wire net 240 feet long, eighteen feet deep and with a mesh ten feet by six feet was manufactured immediately and placed in position during November 1939. The centre of the jack stay of the net is eight feet below surface. The net itself can be raised and lowered by means of winches. It took three to five minutes to lower it and five to ten minutes to raise it.

The entrance to St. John's Harbour was so shallow that it would have been very difficult, if not impossible, for a submarine to enter the harbour submerged. The object of the net was to foul the propellers of a submarine as it surfaced. The net was damaged on November 22, 1939, by the SS *Castlemore* when it entered the harbour. This delayed the system from going into operation until May 1940.

The U-boats that attacked Newfoundland were developed by German Admiral Karl Donitz, who had served in WWI as a submarine captain. These and the attack strategy for using them were adopted by the German Navy in World War II. Donitz had worked and experimented with his idea during the period after WWI while Germany was denied having submarines by the Treaty of Versailles.

To counter this disadvantage, he experimented with small, fast submarines whose effectiveness was as surface torpedo boats. He created an effective strategy for these vessels in which several would form a "Pack" to track down and attack a convoy boat. These units could identify approaching convoys, and with the help of "Radio Command" on shore, they would concentrate on one convoy and overwhelm it with mass sinkings.

Once Germany gained control of the French Atlantic ports, these "Wolf Packs" gained the naval advantage over England from mid-1940 to 1943. This had dire consequences on Britain, which was so heavily dependent on its imports. German access to Atlantic ports, combined with the Wolf Pack threat on the Atlantic, was of primary concern to Allied countries.

LIGHTHOUSE KEEPER GERRY MYRICK HELPED AMERICANS FIND U-BOAT

On March 1, 1942, two days before the German torpedo attack on St. John's, a U-boat was sighted by the lighthouse keeper at Cape Race. Within hours, the 88th Squadron of the United States Army Air Force (USAAF) at Argentia were in the area off the Cape Race coast in pursuit of U-boat 656, which was under the command of a Captain Kroning.

It was a day like any other day for Gerry Myrick at the Cape Race Lighthouse when something unusual caught his attention in the waters off the coast. He watched a submarine periscope penetrate the water and surface. Myrick was not alarmed at first because he thought it was an American sub from Argentia. His mood quickly changed when he saw uniformed German sailors coming on deck. Quickly, he sent a radio message to the US Naval Station at Argentia.

The U-boat moved on and soon after American planes flew over the area. Myrick lost sight of them as they continued out to sea. It appeared nothing had happened so Myrick continued on with his duties.

A month later, Myrick heard the sound of motor-engines coming down the unpaved, pot-holed road to the lighthouse. He was startled when several American Naval jeeps stopped and several high-ranking officers got out and approached him. Once they were satisfied that Myrick was the man who had reported the sighting of the German sub, they told him that American planes had caught up with the U-boat twenty-five miles south southeast of Cape Race and sunk it.

After thanking him, they presented the lighthouse keeper with a medal and a certificate signed by the Secretary of the USN expressing his appreciation for Myrick's vigilance. The incident was never revealed to the public until after the war.[35]

CODE NAME "OPERATION ST. JOHN'S"

In 1943, the German Navy developed a strategy aimed at

---

[35] A varied account of this incident was told in my book *Newfoundland Adventures*. Recent research on German U-boat activity in Newfoundland waters verified the sinking of U-656 and enabled me to confirm and name the U-boat seen by Myrick: Showell, *U-boats at War*, and Hadley, *U-boats Against Canada*.

tipping the war in their favour. By placing mines around major ports along the western coast of North and Central America, they felt that they could tie down tens of thousands of troops and equipment that would otherwise participate in the expected Allied invasion in Europe. Simply put, it meant-keep them fighting over here so that they can't fight over there. The first phase of this strategy targeted St. John's and Halifax. German Intelligence was aware of the intense convoy activities and naval presence in the ports of St. John's and Halifax.

On May 11, 1943, the German Navy approved its top-secret order, which they called Operation St. John's.[36] This mission was the first stage in its much larger plan. The operation began with U-119 and U-120 placing mines off St. John's and Halifax during June 1943. It was U-119 that laid the first minefield of WWII in Canadian waters on June 1, 1943. The RCN became aware of these and sent out minesweepers. Since Canada had assigned most of its minesweepers to convoy escort duty, the few left were not adequate for the latest threat to North American shipping. More minesweepers were commissioned to be built.

On September 28, U-220, a sixteen hundred ton mine layer under Captain Barber, left a French port en route to Newfoundland coastal waters. Its objective was to lay magnetic mines along the convoy lanes off the coast of St. John's. Naval leaders in Berlin had been supplied with intelligence information by U-513 on convoy and naval activities out of St. John's. After sinking ore carriers at Bell

---

[36] Operation St. John's was aimed at closing down St. John's Harbour and interrupting convoy deliveries to England. It was part of Operation Drumbeat, which aimed at closing down North American ports for the same reason.

Island in 1942, the U-513 collected intelligence on military movements in the St. John's Harbour area.[37] The St. John's mines were laid at intervals of 400m and at depths ranging from 50 to 350m.

RCN minesweepers discovered the operation when, on October 11, they destroyed a floating mine off St. John's. When eight more were located the next day, the military quickly closed the port of St. John's and rescheduled and rerouted convoys.

The only victims of Operation St. John's were the 3,478-ton American cargo vessel *Delisle* and the 3,721-ton British vessel the SS *Penolver*. Both ships were part of Convoy WB65 from Wabana to Sydney, Nova Scotia. Everyone on board the *Penolver* was rescued, but twenty-seven of the forty-one man crew of the *Delisle* were lost. These tragedies of war occurred just fifteen miles south of Cape Spear.

American aircraft caught up with U-220 in the mid-Atlantic and sent her to the bottom of the ocean.[38]

GERMAN FLAG RAISED AT CAPE SPEAR

On February 1, 1944, not far from the entrance to St. John's Harbour, a German U-boat was facing a crisis—one so serious, that Captain Werner Weber had arbitrarily decided that his only recourse was to abandon and scuttle his ship. With a German flag in his hand, the thirty-five year old Captain of U-boat 845 walked to the bridge to announce his decision.

---

[37] Michael Hadley, *U-boats Against Canada* (Montreal: McGill-Queens, 1989).

[38] Marc Milner, *The U-boat Hunters* (Toronto: University of Toronto Press, 1994).

This scene unfolded in daytime near shore just a half mile northeast of the Cape Spear Battery after U-845 had grounded on a rock, identified by the RCN as "Old Harry," which had a depth of twenty-eight feet.

What followed next was a remarkable set of circumstances involving Canadian Naval Intelligence that led to a major embarrassment for the Canadian Army and the closing of the port of St. John's for three days.

This incredible story came to the attention of Naval Intelligence four months after the incident and only after U-boat 845 was sunk by the Navy following a prolonged battle. Details of the incident at Cape Spear were gathered during the interrogation of the forty-five survivors of the fifty-four man crew of the U-boat.

At that stage of the war, U-boat commanders were allowed more discretion in selecting their missions. The Germans realized they had lost the Battle of the Atlantic and were attempting to pin down as much of the Allied military power as possible on this side of the Atlantic to weaken their efforts in Europe. On January 25, 1944, Captain Werner moved into waters off the coast of St. John's with the intention of attacking ships inside the harbour. This 740-ton U-845 had experienced a series of mechanical failures prior to this date and morale was low among the crew.

Werner adjusted his strategy after learning of the boom defences at the harbour entrance, combined with his knowledge that the German Navy had mined the area outside the narrows. Instead, he planned to wait for his prey near the harbour at periscope depth and then to follow and attack it. Although the German edition of *Sailing Directions* described the underwater dangers in the area, Werner acted as though he was not aware of them. These directions noted that the eastern approach to St. John's Harbour was uneven, and that the Post War Signal Station at Cape Spear rose to an elevation of 264 feet.

On February 1, an opportunity to score a sinking came when the corvette HMS *Hadleigh Castle* entered the area en route from Argentia to St. John's. Remaining submerged, Weber followed his target and ingloriously grounded on "Old Harry" less than one thousand yards from the Cape Spear Battery. The impact was hard. Michael Hadley, in his book *U-boats Against Canada*, described the damage:

> The rudders jammed amidships, she could only get clear after considerable time and anxiety by going full speed astern. With one rudder useless, two ruptured diving tanks, the caps of two forward torpedo tubes jammed, and the jumping wires snapped, Weber considered the damage sufficiently serious to abandon ship and scuttle.

When Weber made his intentions known, Engineering Officer Otto Strunk was convinced he was acting prematurely. Strunk succeeded in convincing the Captain to give him a chance to repair the steering gear. In order to do this, the sub had to surface and move off coast. In broad daylight the U-845 surfaced within view of the Cape Spear Battery and moved farther out to sea, leaving behind a trail of oil slick. German records of the event simply noted that "Weber 'touched bottom' and 'withdrew to seaward to repair the damage.'"[39]

---

[39] Michael Hadley, *U-boats Against Canada* (Montreal: McGill-Queens, 1989).

Before leaving Newfoundland waters on February 9, 1944, U-845, about ten miles east of Cape Spear, fired and hit the SS which had just left St. John's. The U-845 felt it had sunk the ship and it left for the Flemish Cap. The attack prompted the immediate closing of St. John's harbour which lasted for three days as the RCN conducted mine sweeping operations.

The U-845 was sunk off Ireland in March 1944.[40]

Canadian Naval Intelligence, embarrassed by the incident, initiated an investigation into how this could have happened in broad daylight so near the Cape Spear Battery. What they learned was disturbing. The radar operator at Cape Spear followed precisely the established procedures to operate only during the hours of darkness or on days when visibility fell below five thousand yards. At dawn on February 9, the operator picked up a target within two and a half miles, then turned off his radar. Intelligence found no record of the air force or navy having been informed of the radar find.

The RCAF Meteorological Division found that visibility was unlimited during the time U-845 lay on the surface off Old Harry. Almost six months later the Army claimed that it had a recollection of snow flurries with limited visibility on February 9. Michael Hadley's reaction to the incident was, "The peacetime mentality in Canadian waters, of which U-boat commanders frequently spoke must have prevailed at Cape Spear. U-845 experienced all the tactical advantages the Canadian coast could offer."

---

[40] Marc Milner, *The U-boat Hunters* (Toronto: University of Toronto Press, 1994).

GERMAN ATTACK ON NEWFOUNDLAND SHIP

In July 1940, a Moira Gordon boarded the *Geraldine Mary* to travel to London, England, to marry her fiancé Derek Bowring, an officer with the 166th Newfoundland Regiment. The ship was owned by the Anglo-Newfoundland Development Co. Ltd. and was being used to transport newsprint from Newfoundland.

The *Geraldine Mary* left Botwood on July 19 to join a convoy out of Halifax on its way to the United Kingdom. The convoy, code-named HX60, was unknowingly sailing straight into the path of three German U-boats, which had orders to attack all North-American convoys.

U-52, under the command of Otto Salman, on August 4, upped periscope and slammed a salvo of torpedoes into the Newfoundland cargo ship.[41] The blasts broke the ship in two, sending her to the bottom of the ocean. Only one person died in the attack, all others were rescued by other vessels in the convoy. The victim was H. C. Thompson of Mortier Bay. Miss Gordon married Derek Bowring. She passed away in 1990, and Derek Bowring died at his home in Topsail near St. John's during December 2010 at the age of ninety-three.

FRIENDLY FIRE

The HMS *Honeysuckle* was nearly sunk in St. John's Harbour on June 7, 1941, by fire from the guns stationed on Signal Hill. The Honeysuckle had flashed the wrong signal

---

[41] Herb Wells, *Comrades in Arms: A History of Newfoundlanders in Action, Second World War* (St. John's: self-published, 1986).

while entering the harbour. As a result, gunfire was directed across her bow. The problems were straightened out and the ship was allowed to continue into the harbour.

SHOWED CONTEMPT FOR GERMAN ATTACKERS

Many ships were torpedoed on the Atlantic during WWII, but the reaction of one particular captain and crew set their experience apart from any other. In this case, the vessel was owned by the Grand Bank Fisheries and came under German attack during September 1941.

After torpedoing the boat, the Germans remained in the area until the Newfoundlanders had safely abandoned the ship in a lifeboat. The captain of the submarine asked the Newfoundland Captain, a man named Thompson, if he wished to be towed to the Azores where they would be safe. Thompson shook his fist at the Germans and told them to "Go to hell!" He and his crew trusted their survival to fate, "…rather than be saved by a group of Nazis."

As the sub pulled away, the angered captain fired a volley of shells at the Newfoundlanders but none hit. Thompson and crew rowed for three days and nights with little water and no food. They reached the Azores and were given clothing and food. From there, they were shipped home to Grand Bank.

CATAPULT ARMED MERCHANTMEN

An allied convoy of ships on its way to war-stricken England came under heavy attack on August 3, 1942, by a German submarine wolf pack off the southeast coast of Newfoundland. The attack caused the convoy to split up and one ship, the *Ocean Empire*, headed towards Newfoundland pursued by a submarine.

The *Ocean Empire* was what the military called a CAM (Catapult Aircraft Merchant) and was equipped with a rocket-propelled catapult designed to launch a single Hawker Hurricane. The Hurricanes were dubbed Suicide Planes by ordinary seamen, and for good reason: once launched, they couldn't land back on the ship so had to be ditched in the Atlantic. They were developed to provide air protection for convoys in the area called "The Pit" which was a huge area in the mid-Atlantic outside the air-covered areas east of Newfoundland, south of Iceland and west from the British Isles.

CAMs were actually merchant ships large enough to be converted to handle one or more catapult systems. Spitfire and Hurricane fighters were mounted on these long catapult structures, which were located on the ship's bow. They earned the name "Suicide Planes" because once they were airborne they could not return to the ship. The pilot had to ditch the plane and parachute into the ocean hoping to be rescued. Flying these planes took nerves of steel and a great deal of courage. Ordinarily, escort commanders refrained from using them until weather conditions were suitable enough to enhance rescue operations to recover the pilot. That was not always possible.

The U-boat's pursuit of the *Ocean Empire* lasted into the following day. Heavy fog moved in and settled off Cape Race.

Meanwhile, the *Ocean Empire* was on a collision course with the rugged Newfoundland shoreline.

Half the *Ocean Empire* was left high and dry at Long Point near Cape Race. The Captain tried to refloat the vessel by dumping into the ocean part of the ship's coal cargo, which was carried in the forward holes. He expected this would make the stern heavy and cause her to refloat. The attempt failed. As the fog lifted two ships appeared on the scene; one to try and refloat her and the other to destroy her if the first effort failed.[42]

By 11 a.m. the *Foundation Franklin* towed the damaged *Ocean Empire* off the land and north along the coast towards St. John's, where she was to undergo repairs. However, the *Ocean Empire* never made it. She was being kept afloat by air trapped beneath the forward hatches. Just off Calvert, the hatches gave out and the ship went to the bottom.

Naval historian Herb Wells revealed in his book *Comrades in Arms* that the *Ocean Spray* had engaged the enemy and its Spitfire plane was lost in the battle.

Naval pictures of the *Ocean Empire* taken before she sunk showed the aircraft was not on the ship. The Navy concluded that the plane had been launched to fight off its U-boat attackers.

---

[42] James B. Lambe, *The Corvette Navy: True Stories from Canada's Atlantic War* (Halifax: Nimbus, 2010).

WHY U-69 WAS IN CABOT STRAIT

In early October 1942, some twenty U-boats split up into two Wolf Packs, with one group to patrol at the edge of the Air Gap—this was the Allies' name for the area too far away from Newfoundland to be reached by aircraft. The German's referred to the same area as the Black Pit. It was there that they scored their greatest number of hits.

Three of these U-boats, including U-69, wandered from the pack and ended up in the Cabot Strait. Meanwhile, German intelligence had learned that the *Caribou* had left North Sydney in Convoy SPAB escorted by a minesweeper. They also learned that another convoy identified as SC104 was made up of forty-seven merchant ships escorted by the RN destroyers *Viscount* and *Fame* and four corvettes. This convoy was attacked by the Germans and eight ships were sent to the bottom of the Atlantic in just three days. On October 9, Graf sighted the *Carolus* and torpedoed it. Eleven people died as a result of that sinking.

Intelligence was of paramount importance in the Battle of the Atlantic, and the British Forces gained superiority over the German B-Dienst. Newfoundland played a key role in turning the tide of battle because of its military air and naval bases, from which attacks on U-boats were frequently launched. Another military asset was St. John's Harbour, which was a key port for the Allied Naval forces throughout the long confrontation. Information gathered from intelligence services enabled the Allies to reroute convoys, add to the number of escort vessels, and send long range aircraft to fight off the U-boats. Keegan pointed out the importance of additional aircraft.

CHAPTER FIVE

German Logbooks and the Bell Island Attack

~~~

On Saturday, September 5, 1942, a German U-boat attacked and sunk two iron-ore carriers anchored between Little Bell Island and Lance Cove, waiting to join an overseas convoy. Conception Bay waters were calm and the skies overcast when Commander Rolf Ruggeberg manoeuvred U-boat 513 beneath the water's surface to a position directly in line with the ore carrier *Lord Strathcona*. He ordered his crew to torpedo the ore carrier, but when they pulled the switch nothing happened. The crew had forgotten to set the battery from charge to fire. The torpedoes left their tubes and quickly sank.

The U-boat then surfaced and was spotted by the Newfoundland cutter *Evelyn B* which was moving near the southwest corner of Kelly's Island and heading out to sea. At a range of fifteen hundred yards the *Evelyn B* opened fire and the shell passed near the U-boat's periscope. The sub dived and retaliated, firing two torpedoes which struck and sank the ore carrier SS *Saganaga* nearby.

The *Evelyn B* and the Free French ship *PLM 27*[1] made an effort to get away. Because the U-boat was in shallow waters, she could not move with her accustomed ease. When the *Lord Strathcona* swung around suddenly, it struck the U-boat's tower, forcing her into the mud of the shallow harbour. Once more the U-boat sent off two torpedoes and this time they hit the *Lord Strathcona*, sending her to the bottom. The Germans were unable to reload the torpedoes fast enough, and as they escaped out of Conception Bay, they missed a final opportunity to sink the *Evelyn B*.

In his book *U-boats at War*, Jak Mallmann Showell describes the attack on the *Saganaga* and *Lord Strathcona* based on German records. He states:

> This action started about midday with the first of two massive explosions aboard the *Saganaga*. A couple of men, together with a good collection of deck furniture, were hurled high into the air shortly before the scene was surrounded by an astonishing cloud of smoke and flames. Less than a minute later, there was nothing left, other than bubbling water where the ship had been. The first officer of the *Lord Strathcona*, Ross Creaser, appearing on deck at about the same time as the second torpedo struck the *Saganaga*, saw his colleagues getting one of their boats ready to pick up survivors. Quickly he ordered a message to be sent to the nearby fort, saying that there was a submarine in the bay. Then

[1] Free France was the part of France not occupied by the Germans. The occupied part was Vichy France.

watching the *Saganaga* disappear, he jumped into the next boat setting out to search for anyone remaining in the turbulent water. He had just left his ship when that too flew into the air to sink in less than two minutes.

Four hours later, two anti-submarine boats turned up at Wabana to begin a hunt of Conception Bay for U-513. Thirty people died on the *Saganaga*; however, the *Lord Strathcona*'s crew had abandoned ship when they saw how the battle was shaping up.

The captain of the *Evelyn B* was given a special award for bravery for sticking with his ship and fighting off the U-boat attack.

In response to the attack on the *Saganaga*, the Newfoundland Militia was placed on alert. "W" Force, the Canadian led unit comprised of Canadian and Newfoundland forces, rushed a forty millimetre Bofors anti-aircraft gun to Topsail and sent a corvette travelling at full speed to the southern end of Conception Bay. The German U-513 escaped the gunfire and made its retreat.

The military assessment completed after the attack determined that the Militia's Defence Battery on Bell Island was too poorly positioned to be effective against an attack from the west on shipping anchorage. Unfortunately, it was the only suitable area for a battery.

Mallmann Showell notes that despite the widespread defensive measures the Bell Island attacks sparked, "U-boats penetrated deep into Canadian waters to reap impressive harvests in the treacherous coastal shallows."

On November 2, 1942, at 3:30 a.m., U-boat 518 captained by Friedrich Wissmann torpedoed the SS *Rose Castle* and the Free French ship *PLM 27*, killing forty men and destroying the wharf on Bell Island. The incredible aspect of the November attack was that it was a four-hour surface attack. This took place just two months after the Lance Cove assault by a U-boat. The *PLM 27* was the same vessel that joined the *Evelyn B* in fighting off the Germans during the Lance Cove attack.

In the days prior to this incident, Wissmann became aware of a special message from the Commanding Officer of U-boats in Berlin suggesting special conditions existed in the Wabana area that would make an attack easy. The message was sent to U-520 and U-521, but since both were engaged at the time, Captain Wilhelm Wissmann of the U-518 advised Berlin that he would go check out the area. Wissmann was already on a mission to drop off a German spy on Canadian soil. That story is told elsewhere in this book. The assignment left him with discretion to take advantage of opportunities to destroy Allied shipping that might arise.

Berlin based its suggestion on recent intelligence gathered by U-boats from the area of Bell Island, showing that the army searchlights covering Wabana were operating contrary to their own regulations. Captain Wissmann later recorded that the operation of these protective lights "spelled their doom," and actually helped him complete his successful mission. According to Michael Hadley:

> The regular defensive sweep of army searchlights illuminated U-518's target at sufficiently reliable intervals

to facilitate a definitive surface attack with little risk of detection and retaliation. The army defenders had disregarded their Standing Orders which explicitly called for irregular intervals.[2]

The crews of both ships were sleeping and caught by surprise when attacked. The *Rose Castle* was owned by Dominion Steel and commanded by William J. McDonald. The *PLM 27* was captained by J.B. Chance and was owned by the Ministry of War Transport in London and manned by the Free French.

The *Rose Castle* was anchored between the Scotia Pier and Lance Cove. There were very few rescue boats available, and

The Scotia Pier, on Bell Island, was damaged during U-518's attack on the *Rose Castle* (Photograph Gerald Milne Moses, Library and Archives Canada, PA-188854)

2   Michael Hadley, *U-boats Against Canada* (Montreal: McGill-Queens, 1989).

after the attack, the survivors made it to shore on their own. The U-518 launched its attack by firing at a coal boat. The torpedo missed the boat and hit the wharf, causing an explosion which shook the whole island and roused the population from their sleep. The SS *Flyingdale* was damaged when the torpedo struck the wharf.

The lights illuminated the target sufficiently for U-518 to successfully complete its mission and escape. Three targets were aimed at, but only the 7,803-ton *Rose Castle* and the 5,633-ton *PLM* were sunk.[3] The U-boat left the area travelling at full surface speed around the south end of Bell Island and then turned outward toward Western Bay.

A Digby bomber caught up with the U-518 about forty miles east of Cape Race, and the U-boat narrowly avoided being hit by one of four bombs dropped. The U-518 was able to escape when a sudden thick fog moved in over the area.

The two U-boat attacks on Bell Island caused the Canadians to vacate the Wabana anchorage completely, replacing it with the construction of anti-torpedo nets off the Wabana wharves. The attacks had a disruptive effect on Allied shipping schedules and coastal defence patrols.

Special Constable Norm Noseworthy was on the telephone in his office when the power from the explosion knocked him over and broke every window in the office. Pieces of the wharf landed two hundred feet away. The Militia on the island returned fire but missed its target, killed a cow, and tore up cabbage and potato patches at St. Philips.

---

[3] Jak P. Mallmann Showell, *U-boats at War: Landings on Hostile Shores* (Annapolis: Naval Institute Press, 2000).

Of the forty-three crew members of the *Rose Castle*, twenty-eight were killed during the U-boat attack. Twelve of the *PLM 27*'s fifty crew members also died. The twelve French victims were waked side by side at the police station at Wabana. Their bodies were returned to their homes in France for burial after the war.

The bell of the *Rose Castle* washed ashore and was later recovered and placed on display at the Canadian Legion Club on Bell Island. A part of the torpedo which destroyed the wharf was recovered by a Canadian corvette and taken to St. John's for examination.

THE GOOD DOG SHEP

An interesting anecdote regarding the sinking of the ore ships at Bell Island involved the dog owned by a French crewman on the *PLM*.

For months after, the dog searched the island for her master, and people who saw her high on the cliffs thought she was a wolf. Residents got used to her and named her Shep. The story of Shep's devotion and bravery became known when survivors of the attack told her story. Shep was on board the ore carrier when the torpedo hit. Seconds after the explosion, Shep plunged into the water and began searching for her master. When she couldn't find him, she grabbed another sailor by the clothing and swam with him to the shore several hundred yards away.

Shep ended up in a good home on Bell Island, and he was able to respond to commands in both English and French.

At first, a man named O'Neill took her in and cared for her. It took some time before the dog understood commands given in English, but she did. Pat Fitzpatrick became Shep's second owner and he would sometimes shout, "A ship! A ship!" and the dog would race to the cliff, perhaps hoping to see her master.

CHAPTER SIX

German Logbooks and the Sinking of the *Caribou*

~~~

On October 14, 1942, just forty miles southwest of Port aux Basques, the SS *Caribou*, a Newfoundland Railway ferry vessel, was blasted out of the water by the German U-boat, U-69, under the command of Captain Ubric Graff. The *Caribou*, ostensibly a passenger ferry, was carrying 237 people; forty-six were crew members, seventy-three were civilians, and 118 were military personnel. Of the total on board, 136 lives—men, women, and children—were lost.

However, it took almost thirty years for the public to discover it was a German torpedo that sent the *Caribou* to the bottom. As late as 1962, there had still been no proof that the *Caribou* had been sunk by a German U-boat.

A Canadian Broadcasting Corporation special feature on the *Caribou* disaster was aired in 1962. Tom Fleming, a surviving officer of the ill-fated vessel, was asked whether the submarine that sank the *Caribou* was ever identified. His reply was that it never had. He added that he did not believe any record had been found which would link a German U-boat to the sunken *Caribou*. Since that time, military historians have produced detailed accounts of U-boat activities during WWII.

U-69 was known to her crew as the "Laughing Cow." Graf wrote in his log in October 1942 the following:

> At the beginning of October, the U-69 entered Cabot Strait and proceeded into the Gulf of St. Lawrence on October 9th. It destroyed the small British Steamer *Carolus* of 2, 573 tons. Since there was no other prey in sight, the U-boat made for the open sea and on the 11th of October passed through the Cabot Strait. Three days later on the 14th of October the U-69 sank the British steamer *Caribou* of 2,222 British registered tons.[1]

Once confirmation was made that the *Caribou* was indeed sunk by the Germans, another controversy arose. Gerald S. Bastow, a former aide-de-camp to the Governor-General of Canada and an Air Force Wing Commander, who was on the ship that fateful night, observed, "People have asked the question, 'Was the *Caribou* a legitimate target?' As far as the *Caribou*'s officers were concerned, it was not a question of will they sink us, but when will it happen?" Bastow asserted that naval authorities had insisted on night crossings despite the fact that the ship's captain and the Newfoundland Railway officials were opposed to it.[2]

---

[1] Jack Fitzgerald, *Newfoundland Disasters* (St. John's: Creative, 2003).
[2] Ibid.

While some historians have described the attack on the *Caribou* as cowardly, others argued there was military justification for the sinking. Many felt the Germans believed the *Caribou* was being used to ferry troops, and, in fact, there were troops on the ship that night. Other evidence put forward to militarily justify the sinking was the fact that the *Caribou* was flying the Red Ensign and was listed in *Janes Fighting Ships* as a troop transport.

Herb Wells points out why the U-boat captain would believe it was a legitimate military target. He explained:

> The forty-six man crew in wartime would be treated as merchant seamen and therefore military personnel. The *Caribou* was being escorted by the *Grandmere*, a sophisticated escort vessel which would have made any U-boat Commander suspicious. The SC104 Convoy (departed in same month) was given one escort ship for every eight ships in the convoy. In comparison, the *Caribou* had its own escort vessel.[3]

From the life-saving precautions taken by the ship's owners, it appears they too realized the presence of danger on the North Sydney-Port aux Basque ferry run. The *Caribou* had six lifeboats each capable of holding one hundred people. There were fourteen emergency rafts, three hundred life belts, and a considerable amount of life saving apparatus. A wireless radio had been installed in one of the lifeboats. The vessel was fitted with life rafts in case lifeboats were damaged or broken during an attack. This improvement saved many lives when the attack did come.

---

[3] Herb Wells, *Comrades in Arms: A History of Newfoundlanders in Action, Second World War* (St. John's: self-published, 1986).

U-69 was on the surface directly ahead of the *Caribou* when it fired the torpedo that hit and sunk it. Just four minutes after the hit, the boilers of the *Caribou* exploded. Captain Graff watched the vessel sinking and only submerged when he saw the HMS *Grandmere* about a thousand metres away move to ram him. None of the six depth charges dropped by the escort vessel hit U-69.

Almost a week later, on October 20, U-69 attacked a ship in the Wabana-Sydney Convoy sixteen miles southwest of Ferryland Head. The torpedo failed to explode due to a faulty detonator. That vessel was the *Rose Castle*, the same vessel torpedoed at Wabana on November 2 by U-518.[4]

THE BLACK PIT PATROL

In early October 1942, some twenty U-boats split up into two Wolf Packs with one group to patrol at the edge of the Air Gap—the Allies' name for the area too far away from Newfoundland to be reached by aircraft. The German's referred to the same area as the Black Pit. It was there that they scored their greatest number of hits.

Three of these U-boats, including U-69, wandered from the pack and ended up in the Cabot Strait. Meanwhile, German intelligence had learned that the *Caribou* had left North Sydney in Convoy SPAB, escorted by a minesweeper. They also learned that another convoy, identified as SC104, was comprised of forty-seven merchant ships escorted by the RN destroyers *Viscount* and *Fame* and four corvettes.

---

4 Michael Hadley, *U-boats Against Canada* (Montreal: McGill-Queens,1989).

This convoy was attacked by the Germans, and eight ships were sent to the bottom of the Atlantic in just three days. On October 9, Graf sighted the *Carolus* and torpedoed it. Eleven people died as a result of that sinking.

CHAPTER SEVEN

Amazing Revelations After the War

One example of the value of having access to a port off the coast of North America and closer to the United Kingdom involved the successful effort of England to transport a large part of its treasury to Canada during the early days of the war when a German invasion of England was a real possibility.

This was one of the amazing stories after the war. It was the story of the treasury-carrying convoy which got into trouble in Newfoundland waters. One of the ships carrying the precious cargo was the HMS *Batory*. That ship itself was no different than countless others entering the port during the war. It was the ship's cargo that was important. So important that had its existence been known, it likely would not have made it across the Atlantic. It was something the German Navy would have prized.

This story began in early 1940 when Prime Minister Winston

Churchill considered the likelihood of a German invasion of England all but certain. After discussing the possibilities with his war cabinet, a decision was made to send a major part of the British treasury to Canada for safe keeping. If England did fall, the British had a secret plan to carry on the war from Canada.

Within ten days of that meeting, a fortune of several billion dollars in gold and securities was ready for transportation across the Atlantic. The first shipment went out successfully on the British cruiser *Emerald*. On July 8, the remainder of the valuable cargo left British ports in five ships, altogether carrying almost two billion dollars in gold. Four destroyers accompanied the fleet until they were twenty miles from England, out of reach of the German Air Force. Although targets for U-boats, they were all capable of travelling at a high speed.

One of the gold carrying ships, the *Batory*, developed engine trouble as the little fleet was passing through Newfoundland waters. The admiral in charge decided that, rather than slow down the fleet and risk becoming targets for U-boats, he would send the *Batory* to the St. John's Dockyard for repairs. The *Bonaventure* was assigned to escort her.

On the two ships combined, there was a total of a quarter of a billion dollars. Near St. John's, they ran into a heavy fog which caused the vice-admiral on the *Bonaventure* grave concern. He ordered the vessels to reduce speed, and they made it to St. John's safely.

The *Batory* was repaired in St. John's, and the two ships went on to re-join the treasure fleet at Halifax. From there a heavily guarded train took the fortune to Montreal, where it was placed in the basement of the twenty-four story Sun-Life Assurance Building. Not even the highest Newfoundland government officials had any knowledge of the event until after the war.

NEWFOUNDLANDERS GIVEN CANADIAN STATUS IN 1941[1]

Through an act of the Canadian Parliament, Newfoundlanders were classed as Canadians during the war to facilitate travelling to and from the United States.

Under section 18 of the Canadian Foreign Exchange Conduct Regulations, a Newfoundlander was classed as, and was to receive the same treatment as, a resident of Canada. In 1941, in order to exercise stricter control over the travelling of residents of Newfoundland to the United States and Canada, it was agreed by the Canadian and Newfoundland authorities that residents should be in possession of the Canadian Foreign Exchange Control Boards Travel Permit—Form H. Under the agreement, Newfoundlanders travelling in that way were considered to be in the same category of residents of Canada travelling to the USA and were subject to Canadian rules and regulations governing such travel permits.[2]

A CANADIAN EMBARRASSMENT

The Canadian military's most embarrassing incident during WWII was no doubt an event that took place in St. John's during 1942. The town was a busy port with visiting

[1] Jack Fitzgerald, *Battlefront Newfoundland* (St. John's: Creative, 2010).
[2] Fraser M286 PANL p242

warships from many nations and was thought to be a likely spot for German espionage. The Canadian Forces at St. John's were participants in a special Canadian security week. The week was aimed at testing Canada's military security both in Newfoundland and across Canada. A secret known only to the top command of the Canadian Forces involved the staging of an incident to test not only the military but the public alertness in the city of St. John's. An unidentified man was dressed in a Nazi uniform. His mission was to see how far he could get in the city without being detected. The outcome shocked the military.

The Nazi impersonator walked freely around St. John's and socialized without being detected. He stopped people on the streets to ask for directions; visited stores and walked along Water Street and New Gower Street, the city's busiest thoroughfares. He found the people very friendly and trusting.

However, a more startling reaction took place when he visited Winterholme on Rennie's Mill Road, which housed the offices of the Canadian Military Command in St. John's. The Nazi impersonator stopped and chatted with the sentries on duty, who not only allowed him into the building, but left him on his own inside. The impersonator went directly into the office of the commanding officer. In reporting the episode to Ottawa, the military commander explained that most people and many soldiers had never seen a Nazi uniform.

Just a few months prior to this, the British military held a similar security week in London. They sent two uniformed Nazi impersonators into the streets. The two went undetected for three hours before being challenged and apprehended by British soldiers.[3]

MORE DANGER IN NEWFOUNDLAND WATERS

The German U-boats were not the only threat to ships sailing in Newfoundland waters during World War II. Naval mines began turning up in coves and bays around the island, and after the war, several dozen explosive mines were identified just outside the St. John's Narrows. It was believed that these had been put there by the Germans who had made unsuccessful attempts to mine the waters outside Halifax, Nova Scotia. Not all mines found in Newfoundland were placed by the Germans. Some were mines laid by the English which had broken away from their moorings in European waters and drifted across the Atlantic.

A special force of experts in mine disposal named The Rendering Mines Safe Crew (RMSC) was formed to deal with the problem during the war. This unit was made up of a commanding officer and five men. They handled many harrowing incidents which threatened fishermen, communities, and even children playing on beaches.[4]

In 1941, few people in Newfoundland had any knowledge of mines and mine laying submarines. So when Llewellyn Curtis, a fisherman from La Scie Harbour, was fishing near the Horse Islands, he saw a strange object bobbing in the water. He recognized an opportunity to take its mooring wires to moor his motorboat.

---

[3] Jack Fitzgerald, *Untold Stories of Newfoundland* (St. John's: Creative, 2004).

[4] The work of the RMSC remained secret until after the war.

He wasted little time in attaching it to his boat and towing it back to La Scie. There he solicited the help of several neighbours in hoisting it onto the wharf and then rolled it a long distance to his store. He boasted about the strange object he had found at the fishing grounds to no less a person than the local Newfoundland Ranger. The Ranger recorded the incident his notebook:

> He opened it up to show the insides. I looked at the object from a distance and immediately concluded it was a mine. It somewhat resembled a bell buoy and was the size of a bark pot. On the outside there were eight pointed steel projections about six inches in length and a half inch in diameter. Curtis removed these. At both ends there were steel plates bolted to the body of the mine. Curtis removed one of the bolts in the centre of this plate and with it a small trap door came off. Through this small opening I saw wires and batteries all apparently in good condition.

The RMSC was called in by the Ranger and the object was identified as a mine. Fortunately it had not exploded when tampered with. The commanding officer's report stated, "It was a miracle that the people living in the little cove where the mine was landed were not blown to pieces."[5]

It became necessary for the RMSC to hold meetings in fishing communities to explain the dangers of these mines.

A special problem had developed outside St. John's Harbour where a number of mines were identified after the war

---

[5] Many other such experiences of the RMSC are told in Jack Fitzgerald, *Untold Stories of Newfoundland* (St. John's: Creative, 2004).

and remained as a threat to ships using the harbour. When authorities became aware of the problem in 1945, a team of British and Canadian minesweeping experts were assigned to remove the mines.

One of the two commanding officers of the effort was Lieutenant-Commander James Badcock of Carbonear; the second was Lieutenant-Commander Jack Davis of Saint John, New Brunswick.

Later, while serving with the famous Dover-patrol Sweepers during 1940-41, Badcock was injured while disarming a mine and had the heels of both feet shattered. The injury left him with a limp for the rest of his life.

British papers described the Newfoundland sweeping operation as, "A very difficult job which was executed with skill and determination by the little ships of the Black Ensign Fleet."

This team of experts worked from dawn to dusk for several weeks until they finally accomplished their mission. The commanders held conferences each night with the men to record progress and to iron out difficulties.

The operation used nine British minesweepers to keep main shipping channels from the harbour clear for shipping while the Canadian vessel *Kipawa* placed dans, or buoy markers, to identify the mines for the sweepers.

Some of the mines were actually brought to shore and dismantled by team members Lieutenant George Rundell and Lieutenant Ceaman Wells. The two leaders worked up to their waists in water to steer deadly explosives around the rocks and shoals until they arrived safely on shore. *The Evening Telegram* reported, "Lt. Commander Badcock had the satisfaction of seeing every mine accounted for."

Rundell was awarded the George Medal for mine disposal work when the Nazis made abortive attempts to block off Halifax Harbour in 1942 and 1943.

CHILDREN PLAYED WITH BOMB

In another case, children in a fishing cove on Newfoundland's north coast tossed rocks at a hornet mine stranded on the shore, hoping to see it explode. According to the RMSC report:

> Two young men had discovered the 'buoy' as they called it and dragged it right up on the beach. Then the children started to have fun. The aim of some of them was unerring, but luckily the mine remained intact. One of the villagers even suggested dragging the thing to the top of a fairly high crag and then letting it roll down to see what would happen.

The RMSC destroyed the mine then called a meeting of adults and children to explain the dangers these mines presented. Not all fishermen were inexperienced in handling these mines. The RMSC applauded the merchant Jack Roberts and his helper, Sam.

> Observing two fishermen with an object in tow, he put to sea accompanied by his helper. Approaching the fishermen's boat he realized that what the fishermen thought was a molasses puncheon was in reality a mine. He advised them accordingly and they immediately cut

it loose. Roberts and the helper then secured the mine, towed it to a place of safety and moored it. But as they reached the shore a storm arose. The mine's anchor broke loose and the women of the village were in a state of nervousness as they watched the mine bob about on the turbulent waves.

Roberts and his helper set out again in heavy weather and, without regard for their own safety, put a tow line on the mine. Then they towed it to an isolated spot in the bay and with great difficulty moored it again. This time it stayed put. Roberts went ashore and contacted naval authorities. The Islands are inaccessible in heavy weather but the RMS ship felt its way through the treacherous waters and rendered the mine safe. Everyone in the village was relieved.

ORIGINS OF THE NAVAL MINES

RMSC records report that the mines discovered by citizens around Newfoundland were of British origin:

> In accordance with International Law, British mines are rendered harmless once they break away from their moorings. But no mine is too safe. Sometimes the switch freezes and won't break when the mine drifts away. Had there been German mines, I shudder to think what would have happened, and certainly in two cases the villagers did not know of what origin they were.

Declassified German records since the war have revealed that the German mines placed around St. John's Harbour and Halifax Harbour were engineered to flood themselves automatically after three months thus rendering them harmless. This was done so as not to threaten U-boats participating in Operation Drumbeat or other missions in this area.[6]

The cases of mines neutralized by the RMSC were given to fishermen who used them as barking kettles, which proved to be ideal for making herring nets.

THE GALLANT JACK LEGROW OF BAULINE

When a flotilla of the Royal Navy launched an attack on the German-Axis held Madagascar, Leading Seaman Jack Legrow was not part of the landing crew. However, his courage and quick thinking brought him into the middle of the battle where he successfully assisted fellow seaman who had been pinned down on a beach by an unrelenting enemy assault.

Legrow, a resident of Bauline, a small community just north of St. John's, was a crewman on one of the 11th ("Empire Pride") Landing Craft Flotilla which, on September 10, 1942, moved into formation for an attack at Green Beach at Majunga, on the west side of the 900-mile-long island of Madagascar.

> The flotilla launched its attack from a position about a quarter mile from Green Beach. At about 250 yards from the beach, the flotilla was subjected to a vigorous attack from enemy machine-gun fire. All the boats brought up bows onto the sea wall. The army officer in Legrow's boat, along with two gunners, scram-

[6] Jak P. Mallmann Showell, *U-boats at War: Landings on Hostile Shores* (Annapolis: Naval Institute Press, 2000).

bled up onto the wall and began firing at a house overlooking the beach from where enemy fire was originating.

The remaining troops were pinned down by the machine-gun fire and were unable to follow the others onto the sea wall. Leading Seaman Jack Legrow quickly assessed the danger of his fellow soldiers and moved into action. He reduced speed to Slow Ahead and moved to a position where he was able to set up his climbing ladder against the wall. With bullets whizzing all around him, Legrow climbed onto the wall, steadied the ladder, and helped pull the troops up. As each man made it to the top, he dropped in position and returned enemy fire. During this entire action, the enemy machine-gun fire was focused on Legrow's boat.

Although completely exposed, Legrow continued his effort, showing no concern for his own safety. The attack on the beach was a success and the commanding officer of the flotilla documented Legrow's act of heroism. The coolness and gallantry displayed by Jack Legrow under enemy fire earned him the Distinguished Services Medal Cross.

GUNFIRE AT ARGENTIA AND ST. JOHN'S MADE PUBLIC JITTERY

One of the dozen or so German Raiders, armed merchant ships disguised as Allied vessels, was named the *Prairie*, which was also the name of an American naval vessel. When this information became known after the war, it fuelled suspicion that the fire which nearly destroyed the USS *Prairie* at Argentia was an act of sabotage.

The *Prairie* was operating out of Argentia in the early part of the war. While docked at the Argentia port, a fire broke out and spread rapidly. The entire base was placed on alert because the vessel carried enough explosives to be felt seventy miles away. Its cargo included 600 tons of high explosives, 300 depth charges, 103 torpedo warheads, 12,000 gallons of diesel oil, and one million gallons of fuel oil.[7]

Author Eileen Houlihan, who was teaching school at the time, was told of the fire by Father Dee, the parish priest. Fire fighters were battling the blaze, and there was no move to evacuate the area. Mrs. Houlihan recalled the incident:

> This was startling news. I couldn't dismiss my pupils without given a reason, nor could I tell them what had happened. The anxiety of those next endless hours remain vividly in my memories. But lunchtime finally arrived and I breathed a sigh of relief as they left for home. I wasn't thinking so much of myself an explosion occur but the reality of the thirty young children under my care.[8]

On March 29, 1942, President Roosevelt recommended to Prime Minister Churchill that Britain adopt the strategy of attacking the main U-boat bases and the factories that made them. Churchill agreed with the suggestion and replied:

---

[7]   Herb Wells, *Comrades in Arms: A History of Newfoundlanders in Action, Second World War* (St. John's: self-published, 1986).

[8]   Eileen Houlihan, *Uprooted! The Argentia Story* (St. John's: Creative, 1992).

> In order to cope with future U-boats hatchings,
> we are emphasising bombing attacks on U-boat
> nests, and last night went to Lubeck with 250
> bombers, including 43 heavy. Results are said to
> be the best ever. This is in accordance with your
> wishes.[9]

The Americans kept secret until after the war had ended that a German U-boat had boldly entered the harbour at Argentia and remained a threat to the base for more than three hours. The German sub entered Argentia by going beneath the protective net across the harbour. Its presence was quickly detected by the Americans. However, they choose not to attack the sub while it was in the harbour for fear of damaging its own shipping.

Meanwhile the German Captain, after observing the military presence in Argentia, chooses not to attack. He felt that if he attacked he could not successfully escape the harbour. The Americans allowed him to leave, but once the sub was clear of the harbour, USN cutters opened fire and sent the sub to the bottom of the Atlantic. There were no survivors.

SOUTHSIDE HILL OIL TANKS HIT BY GUNFIRE

On Thursday, August 3, 1944, just minutes after the gun on Signal Hill fired to announce that the St. John's Regatta was going ahead on schedule; gunfire erupted on St. John's Harbour.

---

[9] Winston Churchill, *The Hinge of Fate: The Second World War Volume IV* (London: Cassell & Co, 1951).

Bullets struck the oil tanks on Southside Hills and sent a work crew scrambling. The incident, which could have caused a catastrophe had the bullets penetrated the tanks, was covered-up and remained a secret until several years after the end of World War II.

The gunfire originated on board the HMS *Dianthus*, a Canadian corvette moored near the Southside of St. John's Harbour. The vessel was scheduled to move out to sea that morning where a drill was to take place to train crewmen on the handling of guns. Despite concern expressed by crewmen, the captain ordered them to load the pom-poms, the ship's QF 2-pounder guns. In addition to fuel tanks on the southside, there were many military vessels in port. Some of the crew were worried over the possibility of an accident occurring during the loading process.

After the flag went up at Cabot Tower and the Signal Hill gun went off to announce the Regatta, rapid gunfire was heard from the harbour area. While loading the pom-poms, a gun accidentally went off, and several of the bullets struck the oil tanks on Southside Hill. Realizing the danger, a crewman from St. John's lowered the gun so it pointed away from the tanks and then shut it down. However, before the gunfire stopped it sprayed bullets over the heads of men working on repairs to Southside Road. The men scrambled for shelter.

There were no injuries. The *Dianthus* went to sea and completed its practice on schedule.

The thousands of city folk at the Regatta that day had no idea how close St. John's had come to a major disaster.

CHAPTER EIGHT

WWII Bombs Dumped Outside St. John's Harbour

~~~

During March 1946, the RCAF in Newfoundland sent 60 tons of bombs left over from the war to be dumped in waters off the coast of St. John's. The handling of the bombs, while being loaded on the RCAF motor vessel *Beaver*, caused some concern in the city. The job of moving 500-pound bombs was assigned to longshoremen on the waterfront. In describing the scene at the coastal wharf, *The Evening Telegram* noted, "Longshoremen were pushing around 500 pound bombs like sacks of oats or any other supposedly safe commodity as they loaded them aboard the boat from railway freight cars."

The plan to dispose of the bombs was drawn up by the Canadian Navy and involved taking the shipment out to sea and dumping it into the ocean at a spot designated by the Navy. Authorities assured the public the bombs were no longer dangerous. A Navy spokesman said, "The detonators were removed at Gander, placed in a pile and exploded."

Once the bombs were loaded, an experienced bomb-disposal group from the Navy took over the cargo and the job of getting rid of it.

This was not the only shipment of unused war bombs sent out to sea from St. John's Harbour. Some months before the SS *Meigle* destroyed a similar cargo.

THREAT TO ST. JOHN'S FROM UNEXPECTED SOURCE

While authorities were concerned over the German attacks on Bell Island and the sinking of the *Caribou*, a threat to the city of St. John's, which was constant throughout the war and which came close to wiping out a portion of the city on several occasions, went unnoticed. This threat was not from the enemy, but from American bombs arriving at the Army Dock in the east of end of the harbour, and transported to be stored in Quantum Huts at the White Hills, then part of the US base, Fort Pepperrell.

On several known occasions, only good fortune avoided major explosions in the east end of St. John's. During the first such occasion, in 1943, it took six trailer loads of bombs to unload the American munitions ship in port. A driver for one of the trailers, Mike Cahill, recalled that the bombs were loaded during a heavy rain storm. After the loading was completed, and just before the drivers were to get into the trailer cabs to drive off in convoy, the rainstorm escalated into a thunder and lightning storm.

A flash of lightning, which Cahill said, "Came out of nowhere," struck one of the bombs. Immediately, the bomb heated and everyone scattered for cover. "There were a lot of silent prayers that night," said Cahill.

One of the other drivers figured that if he could get a wet tarpaulin over the bombs it would cool them down and avoid an explosion. If only one of the bombs had exploded, it would have detonated the hundreds of bombs close by.

The tarpaulin caught fire from the heat generated by the bombs. Then it seemed that prayers were answered. The fire burned out as quickly as it started, and the pelting rain cooled the bombs. The workers were able to move out with their cargoes and deliver them without incident to the White Hills.

On another occasion, flares and bombs were loaded together onto one trailer. The friction caused in loading the cargo set off the flares. Cahill said, "Boy oh boy! What a sight." The flares fired off in all directions. People ran for cover, some ran up the Monkey's Puzzle (a tenement of houses that ran up from near the dock to the Battery Road).The Americans wasted no time in sending in an emergency team to take control of the situation. They succeeded, and another wartime catastrophe was prevented. Either one of the above mentioned incidents described could have caused untold destruction of property and loss of life in St. John's. But these were not the only near-miss situations.

Joe O'Toole was driving a load of bombs up Prescott Street from Water Street when the back hatch broke open and the bombs began falling out and rolling down Prescott Street.

Joe quickly turned the vehicle toward the sidewalk, which brought the truck to a parallel position with Duckworth, and stopped the bulk of his cargo from emptying onto the street. There was nothing anyone could do about the few that had fallen out except pray. Once again, however, fortune smiled on St. John's and the matter ended without any of the bombs exploding.

RUNAWAY SPOOLS

On March 18, 1945 a similar accident occurred on Prescott Street, but bombs were not involved. Regardless, there was damage, but fortunately loss of life was avoided.

At about 11 a.m. on Saturday, March 18, an RCAF truck was heading up Prescott Street with a cargo of spools of cable weighing about 1.5 tons each. Just past the Water Street intersection, the spools broke loose from the truck and began rolling down the hill. Three of the rolls turned at about halfway on Prescott Street, between Duckworth and Water Street, and crashed into the front of the Marguerite Beauty Shop, breaking a large window, and damaging the building somewhat.

The remaining spool continued onto Water Street, where it struck and considerably damaged a car owned by William McArthur, then continued its course into the front of the building occupied by Charles R. Bell Limited. A large window was also broken in this building, and some heating fixtures were damaged. The driver and helper on the truck shouted warnings to people walking on the street, and they all managed to get out of the way of the rolling spools.

CHAPTER NINE

German Secrets
in Labrador

~~~

The only place in North America where the Germans were able to land and establish an on-land installation during WWII was on the northern Labrador coast. It remained a secret until the 1980s. This mission was accomplished in 1943 by U-537 commanded by Captain Peter Schrewe. The U-537 was the only U-boat in Newfoundland and Canadian waters in that year with a specific mission. That mission was to establish an automatic weather station near the northern tip of Labrador. Since weather conditions generally flow from west to east across the Atlantic, the weather station was expected to be vital to the enemy submarines and raider operations. Discretion as to just where in Labrador to set up the station was left to Captain Schrewe.

The weather station for Labrador was one of twenty-one land-based, automatic weather stations expected to supply the German military with weather information at regulated

U-537 at anchor in Martin Bay, Labrador, on October 22, 1943.
(Bundesarchiv CC-BY-SA 3.0 de)

predetermined times. Five of the stations were established around the Barents Sea above Norway, fourteen were established in the Arctic, and two were sent to North America. Of the two destined for North America, only the Labrador Station was ever in operation.[1] The second mission, which was being carried out by U-867, failed when on September 19, 1944, an RAF Liberator from Squadron 221 sunk the submarine off the Norwegian coast.[2]

The Labrador station was comprised of meteorological instruments, a 150-watt short-wave transmitter and antenna mast, and an array of nickel-cadmium and dry-cell batteries. The responsibility of setting up the equipment and assuring

---

[1]   Michael Hadley, *U-boats Against Canada* (Montreal: McGill-Queens,1989).
[2]   Ibid.

its operation was left to the two scientists who were part of the mission. All the equipment was packaged in ten cylinders, each weighing about 220 pounds. Each cylinder was marked with the name "Canadian Weather Service" to mislead anyone who might stumble upon it. The station was programmed to broadcast a coded weather report every three hours. Each broadcast was restricted to a maximum of two minutes.

The mission was not without its problems. Its departure from Kiel, Germany, was delayed from mid-July to mid-September due to heavy Allied bombing in the area. While crossing the Atlantic on October 13, 1943, to carry out its mission, a raging wind storm tore its anti-aircraft cannon from the deck and washed it over the side. Poor weather prevented the captain from getting an accurate astronomical fix of his position. The boat was leaking because of a broken diesel intake.

Regardless, the captain pushed on with his mission, and after five days sailing through snowstorms, U-537 arrived off Cape Chidley, the northwest tip of Labrador, on October 22. Moving southward he headed for what is known today as Martin's Bay, thirty-two kilometres south of the Cape. Captain Schrewe chose to establish the station as far north as possible to avoid contact with the local inhabitants.

A reconnoitring party, using an inflatable craft, went ashore to seek an appropriate site to set up the weather station. Once a site was determined, another team had to scale a sixty-metre cliff with the equipment for the project. A few hours later, two more inflatable rafts pulled up on shore with the equipment and armed guards to stand lookout so there would not be any surprises from the sea.

The scientists proceeded to install the weather equipment while the boat's engineering staff made repairs to the U-boat. To mislead any Allied forces or locals who might happen upon the site, they spread American cigarette packages and emergency ration tins from captured crashed aircraft.[3]

The next day, October 23, the weather station was ready for operation. Its first transmission was made three minutes later. The mission took twenty-eight hours to complete and U-537 then set out for Newfoundland's east coast, not before being warned by U-boat Command in Germany to be careful because U-220 had recently laid a minefield off St. John's.[4]

Military intelligence in Newfoundland learned of the presence of U-537 in its coastal area after intercepting a message ordering it to patrol off St. John's. Captain Schrewe became aware that his presence near the capitol city had been detected because Allied radar was constantly triggering his U-boat's radar warning devices. He remained submerged to avoid being attacked.

Intelligence tracked U-537 to an area seventy-five miles east of Argentia. The Navy sent a force of thirteen ships and several aircraft to search and destroy it. Weather conditions were poor and winds were high by the time the RCN escorts arrived. U-537 managed to slip away, and it continued its patrolling on the Grand Banks.

---

[3] Jak P. Mallmann Showell, *U-boats at War: Landings on Hostile Shores* (Annapolis: Naval Institute Press, 2000).

[4] Ibid.

The crew of U-537 established Weather Station Kurt on October 23, 1943. (Bundesarchiv CC-BY-SA 3.0 de)

On November 10, 1943, at a location 130 miles southeast of Cape Race, another opportunity arose to capture the vessel and perhaps learn of its mission in Labrador. Despite a concerted effort by the Navy and Air Force, on December 8, U-537 escaped and returned to Germany.[5]

A year later, on November 9, 1944, U-537 was torpedoed and sunk by the USS *Flounder* in the Java Sea north of Bali. There were no survivors.

The German weather station in Labrador escaped detection for thirty-seven years. Its discovery was made by Canadian historian M. Alex Douglas, of the Department of National

[5] Marc Milner, *The U-boat Hunters* (Toronto: University of Toronto Press, 1994), 78-80.

Defence, and a German industrialist and expert on German Arctic weather stations named Franz Selinger. Selinger became interested in the project after receiving pictures related to the mission, including the weather station, which he received from author Jak Mallman Showell.

Evidence gathered at the site showed that, at some point, the station had been discovered and smashed by unknown agents. When the research team arrived at the site in 1980, they found it strewn with barrel-like weather canisters. After examining the equipment, they concluded it had not been systematically disassembled, but the wires had been cut and one of the canisters was missing.

The recovered station became the property of the New-foundland Government but was sent to Museum Canada in Ottawa for restoration and display.[6]

---

[6] T. Alex Douglas, "The Nazi Weather Station in Labrador," Canadian Geographic, December 1981, 42.

CHAPTER TEN

Last U-Boat Surrendered in Bay Bulls

~~~

On May 11, 1945, U-190 had been submerged for fifty days, and its crew was not aware the war had ended on May 8. After sinking the *Esquimalt*, on which forty-four died out of a total of seventy men, Captain Reith realized he would be the target of a concerted effort by the Canadian Navy to find and destroy him. His response was to remain submerged and sail to Newfoundland coastal waters. Occasionally, U-190 moved close to the surface in an effort to pick up radio broadcasts with updates on the war.

Werner Hirschman, Chief Engineer on U-190, recorded in his diary that the broadcasts painted a bleak picture for Germany, but he noted that these reports came from American radio stations and were not trusted by the German crew.[1]

---

[1] Werner Hirschman, *Another Place, Another Time: A U-boat Officer's Wartime Album* (Montreal: Robin Brass Studio, 2011).

Captain Reith decided to leave Newfoundland coastal waters and head for Norway. On May 11, he was about five hundred miles southeast of Cape Race when he received a message from the commander of U-boats in Germany confirming the war was over. They were told to ignore the standing plan for the situation, which was to scuttle the ship and get rid of all secret documents. A few hours later, another message was received from Cape Race supplying the coordinates for them in arranging surrender. The message also ordered Reith to raise the black flag and to throw all ammunition overboard.[2]

Admiral Karl Donitz, who had taken over Germany after Hitler's death, advised U-boat commanders to ignore the plan to destroy all U-boats and to surrender. He made this concession to the Allies in exchange for some concessions for his people. An agreement was made, whether it was the concession or not, that U-boat captains would, before surrendering, discharge all crew members from the navy so that they would become private citizens. As private citizens, they were to be returned to their homes in Germany within four weeks after the surrender. Reith released his crew prior to surrendering. The Allies failed to live up to this agreement.[3] It is possible that U-190 crewmen were not treated as private citizens because they had destroyed records despite the new conditions ordered by Donitz.

The turn in events was shocking to the captain and crew of U-190. They held a short meeting at midnight to discuss what action they would take. Many U-boats ignored the Donitz order and scuttled ships. The men on U-190 did discuss

[2] Ibid.

[3] Michael Hadley, *U-boats Against Canada* (Montreal: McGill-Queens,1989).

scuttling, but they also talked about escaping to Spain, South America, or going to Germany. In the end, they decided to follow orders, as they had always done, and to surrender.

With the time approaching for the arrival of the Royal Canadian Navy (RCN) ships assigned to accept their surrender and escort them to Bay Bulls, the Captain gathered together all secret papers and stored them in special bags, which would weigh them down. He then tossed the bags overboard. While he was busy carrying out that task, the crew was getting rid of the ship's ammunition supply and firing the remaining torpedoes.

In the rush to complete things before the Canadians arrived, the torpedoes were fired too quickly and exploded too close to the U-boat, almost blowing it up. The explosion also likely tore open the bags of secrets, which began floating in the waters all around them. A second call from Cape Race informed them they would be escorted to Bay Bulls. The men of U-190 were already complaining of the cold Atlantic and were not happy about going to Newfoundland.[4]

DIARY OF THE ENGINEER

Around midnight on May 12, the shadow of an approaching Canadian destroyer was seen by the watch on U-190, who alerted the others. It was the corvette HMCS *Thorlock*. At this stage there was tension on both sides. The corvette pulled up alongside the sub and a Lt. R.B. Blackford led a heavily armed party of Canadian officers aboard to take control. They were greeted by Captain Reith and Chief

[4] Three ports were designated for surrendering U-boats: Bay Bulls, Halifax, and Sydney.

Engineer Werner Hirschman. The two officers escorted the boarding party down into the submarine. The Canadian officers spread out to search the boat while one of their members positioned a long chain from the bridge, a routine practice, to prevent any attempt to submerge by obstructing the entry hatch.

A couple of hours later, the HMCS *Victoriaville* arrived, and Lt. F.S. Burbridge led more naval officers aboard the U-boat. Captain Reith was told they would be taken to Bay Bulls, which was three days travel from their current position. Hirschman was to remain on board to assist the Canadian navigator and selected deck hands. To assist in operating the U-boat, the Germans supplied two chief petty-officers, six technicians for the engine room, and three sailors, one each at the engine, telegraph, and rudder.

Hirschman, who kept a diary of the events, noted that Captain Reith was fumbling around trying to package things he wanted to take with him. When the Canadians objected, he claimed it was all his personal property.

Once everything was in order, the two Canadian vessels departed, leaving behind Hirschman, eleven German sailors, five Canadian officers, and about twenty-five Canadian sailors. In the confusion of the situation, U-190 was left to follow with the flags of the RN and RCN flying beneath the German brass eagle clasping a swastika, which had been overlooked. Hirschman had noticed but took a little delight in the error and decided to say nothing.[5]

During the long hours aboard the submarine, the Germans

---

[5] Werner Hirschman, *Another Place, Another Time: A U-boat Officer's Wartime Album* (Montreal: Robin Brass Studio, 2011).

were surprised to learn how Canadians felt about them. Describing his conversation with a Canadian petty officer, Hirschman noted:

> A Canadian petty officer replies to my question as to the general opinion in Canada about Germany with, "Oh— the German people are very clever, but the Nazis..." and illustrates his meaning with a throat-cutting gesture. I tell him that we are all Nazis, since National Socialism did a lot of good for our country in the years before the war. He doesn't believe me and insists that all Nazis are criminals whereas we here are really easy to get along with.

Hirschman spent the time until dawn chatting with Lt. A. Stirling and Lt. S. Burbage and playing chess. By the time dawn arrived, U-190 had caught up with the two RCN cutters. During the night, some of the RCN sailors gathered the water canteens left by the German sailors, which contained alcohol. Lt. Stirling discovered this after finding several of his men sleeping in the bow torpedo compartment. The canteens, along with all personal property belonging to the German crew, were recovered and apologies made to the Germans by the Canadians.

According to Hirschman, the weather got very bad, and it became extremely cold. Everyone on board added extra clothing. A relaxed, trusting atmosphere developed, and the Canadians left their automatic guns and bayonets hanging around and lessened their watch on the POWs.

Hirschman went to the bridge and described in his diary the view as they entered Bay Bulls:

I note that we are entering a large bay surrounded by mountains. In the distance, for the first time, I see some huge icebergs. The two escorts are circling around us. Ahead there are some patrol boats, like our R-boote [Raider Boats]. We have arrived in Bay Bulls, Newfoundland.

More and more small craft are circling our sub. A motorboat with a group of photographers aboard come quite close. There is a girl on board and I must have stared a bit too intensely as Burbidge feels inclined to smile and drop a teasing remark. I explain, "The first girl in three months." He nods understandingly. A boat comes alongside and a group of sailors dressed in immaculate blue uniforms come aboard. The surroundings leave a God-forsaken impression.

A few wooden shack-like houses are perched on the rocks and the harbour area looks just as primitive. Our escorts have already tied up at a wooden pier.

NEWSMEN COVER U-190 ARRIVAL

Lt. Scott Young, the Canadian Navy Public Relations Officer, arranged for a launch to take a party of reporters out into the harbour to get a closer look at the German U-boat. On May 14, *The Evening Telegram* described the condition of U-190:

> She had nothing of the trim and graceful appearance of the Canadian war vessels by which she was surrounded. In fact, with her rusted hull encrusted with salt, she might well have been mistaken for some monstrous pre-historic creature which had come to land from the

depths of the ocean. But there she was with her whiskered crew who looked the part of wolves of the sea, but as they were herded ashore by men who had been hunting them down for years in the Atlantic, they were cowed wolves despite their attempts which met with not the slightest response to barter jokes with those lining the gangways and the rails of the ships.

Interrogation and search of the prisoners took place on board the *Victoriaville* after which, under the eyes of several hundred Canadian ratings and facing a battery of cameras, they were transferred to another naval raft on the opposite side of the jetty to await transportation to Halifax.[6]

A Canadian naval officer, acting as interpreter, told Hirschman where to moor the U-boat. As Hirschman prepared to leave U-190 for the last time, he entered one final observation in his diary. It reads, "No more—'Ready for Action! Assemble on deck—Ever. The last patrol of the U-190 finished."

NEWFOUNDLAND ACCEPTS U-190 SURRENDER

The official surrender of U-190 had taken place at sea after Captain Reith was taken on board the HMS *Victoriaville* under the command of Newfoundland-born Lt. Commander Lester Hickey of St. Jacques. Hickey received his early education in St. John's where he lived with his grandmother on Fleming Street.

At the beginning of the war, he was at sea serving on an

[6] *The Evening Telegram*, May 14, 1945.

Imperial Oil Steamships tanker running between Halifax and Peru. He volunteered for service with the RCN and was mentioned in despatches on June 2, 1943, for his outstanding performance during the Battle of the North Atlantic. Information that surfaced after the war, which claimed U-190 surrendered at Halifax, was proven to be incorrect. It is likely, though, that due to the fact that feelings were running high against U-190, because the *Esquimalt* was out of Halifax, it was decided to bring the German sub to Bay Bulls.

FROM BAY BULLS TO POW CAMP 20

The war in Europe was over, and the defeat of Japan was three months in the future. The submariners of U-190 were prisoners of war and confined in POW Camp 20 about twenty miles outside Gravenhurst, Ontario. POW Camp 20 was a far cry from the type of POW camps used by the Axis powers to intern prisoners. It was more like a resort, spa, or country club when compared to the internment camps of Germany and Japan.

Prior to being used as a POW camp, Camp 20 served as a sanatorium. It was built on a site overlooking Lake Muskoka. Werner Hirschman described it as "a very pleasant place. We prisoners were treated like guests of the country."[7]

The treatment referred to by Hirschman included a variety of entertainment, a twenty-dollar monthly allowance, and a beer ration. Inmates had access to a multi-language library and six American movies were shown weekly. Prisoners had

---

[7] Werner Hirschman, *Another Place, Another Time: A U-boat Officer's Wartime Album* (Montreal: Robin Brass Studio, 2011).

their own symphony orchestra and a swing band, a tennis court, hockey rink, and a fenced swimming area at Lake Muskoka. If any prisoner was still bored, he could work on the prison farm, which kept pigs, chickens, horses, maple trees, and potatoes.

The prisoners were disappointed after being moved to a POW camp in England. The English still held strong resentment against the Germans, and U-190 prisoners were not given the same respect and treatment they received at Camp 20. Within a year, they were all returned to Germany.

There were five German U-boats in Newfoundland waters in the last weeks of war: U-190, U-889, U-879, U-866, and U-1233.

The U-190 was commissioned into the Royal Canadian Navy in June 1945. This was followed by a summer tour of the St. Lawrence River and the Gulf as well as ports which had participated in the war against the U-boats.

From September 7, 1945, U-190 was used on anti-submarine training duties until July 24, 1947, when her service ended.

On Trafalgar Day, October 21, 1947, U-190 was towed out to sea, and many say not coincidentally, to the spot where she had sunk the HMCS *Esquimalt*. She was cut free to drift while being subjected to various forms of anti-submarine weaponry by RCN naval and air forces in Operation Scuttled. It took nineteen minutes to send U-190 to the bottom.[8]

---

[8] Kenneth Wynn, *U-boat Operations of the Second World War* (Annapolis: Naval Institute Press, 1998).

CHAPTER ELEVEN

Joe Kearney and the Desert Fox

Corporal Joseph Kearney was one of the British commandos sent behind German lines as part of World War II's most intriguing and top-secret operations. In one of the commando unit's most daring missions, they attempted to capture the notorious German general known as *The Desert Fox*, Field Marshal Erwin Rommel. Joe Kearney fought side by side with the unit's leader, Lieutenant-Colonel Geoffrey Keyes, who was killed during the raid. Kearney is portrayed in the movie *The Desert Fox* making a futile attempt to rescue the wounded Captain Campbell lying near the body of Keyes. The captain urges Kearney to save himself as two German officers, with guns drawn, approach the scene.

BORN IN ST. JOHN'S

Joseph Francis Kearney was born in St. John's on September 8, 1921, the eldest of seven children born to William

Kearney and Bridget Beer. He grew up at 11 Livingstone Street and attended St. Bonaventure's College, but dropped out of school to help support his family during the Depression of the 1930s.

When the call went out in Newfoundland for volunteers to serve in WWII, Kearney was the fiftieth Newfoundlander to enlist. Because the required age for enlistment was twenty, and Joe was still eighteen, he used a false birth certificate to join. On April 14, 1940, Kearney was among the recruits sent to Sussex, England, for training, and he became part of the 57th Newfoundland Heavy Regiment, Royal Artillery when it was formed.

In August 1940, Joe Kearney volunteered for service in an elite commando unit which was set up to conduct small-scale raids behind enemy lines. The commando training took place at Galashiels, Scotland. Twenty Newfoundlanders volunteered, but only five made the final cut. Kearney was one of the five.[1]

All five were assigned to the 11th Scottish Commando Unit sent to Egypt to join the commando brigade called Lay Force. Their first assignment was to reclaim the Kafr Badda Bridge on the Syrian coast. The commandos fought fiercely and, although sustaining heavy losses, succeeded in their mission. The Brigade was disbanded, but the 11th Scottish Commando Unit remained partially intact. Kearney was the only Newfoundlander to remain with the group.

Lt. Colonel Geoffrey Keyes, commander of the unit, origi-

---

[1] G.W.L Nicholson, *More Fighting Newfoundlanders* (St. John's: Govt. of Newfoundland and Labrador, 1969).

nated a plan for the daring raid behind enemy lines in North Africa to capture Rommel, thereby disrupting the German offensive in Africa. The German headquarters were at Beda Littoria, Libya, about two hundred and fifty miles behind German lines.

On November 10, 1941, fifty-three commandos set out for the African coast in the submarines the *Torbay* and the *Talisman*. Corporal Kearney was assigned to the *Torbay*. When interviewed on the popular CBC trivia show *Front Page Challenge* in 1961, Kearney recalled:

> At the time we were bedded down in a place called Amiya in Egypt. At two o'clock in the afternoon some fifty of us piled into lorries and were driven twenty miles to Alexandria. Here, we boarded the HMS *Medway*—a submarine shop depot. After receiving the once over by its commander, we climbed into two submarines. They were the *Torbay* and the *Talisman*. At dusk, we moved out the harbour.

A severe rainstorm was raging when the force landed on the Libyan coast. The operation, hindered by the rainstorm, got off to a bad start. Several men drowned and others were unable to land. Kearney said:

> Only twenty-eight men had managed to make it to shore. The wind by this time had increased considerably and with dawn approaching, the subs were forced to withdraw. Our casualties were one injured, six believed drowned.

> We were now two hundred and fifty miles

behind enemy lines, and fifteen miles inland over rough hilly country lay the main German headquarters. We headed off, heavily laden, and the darkness made it tough going. An hour and a quarter later we reached the top of the first encampment. This lay about a half mile inland. After a short rest, we continued on.

Despite the loss of men and equipment, the mission went ahead. However, the storm continued to rage without interruption while the commandos took refuge in a cave. After several days, Keyes decided they had waited long enough. They had a rendezvous time to get back to the submarines and escape.

Airfields were flooded and telephone lines were destroyed. Kearney described the time leading up to the attack: We blackened our faces and at six o'clock moved out. Visibility was not good. It was now dark and still pouring rain. The night turned into an inky blackness and in order to stay in touch we were forced to hold onto one another's bayonet scabbards. At 10:30, we took a short rest and started our climb of about five hundred feet. After much slipping and, crawling, we finally made the top. By 11:30, we reached a point near the headquarters building and held up. Keyes and Terry then went ahead to scout the grounds.[2]

The mission came close to being detected at this point.

[2] Herb Wells, *Comrades in Arms: A History of Newfoundlanders in Action*, Second World War (St. John's: self-published, 1986).

Fortunately, the commandoes were prepared for this type of eventuality. Kearney told how they avoided being exposed. He said:

> While we were waiting on word from Keyes and Terry, a barking dog aroused two Italian officers in a hut nearby and they asked what we were doing there. One of our party, a Palestinian, was an expert linguist. He immediately translated what they said to Captain Campbell in German who replied in the same tongue that we were German troops on patrol and for them to go away and keep their dog quiet. This was passed along by the interpreter and they returned to their hut apparently satisfied. We then moved on.

They met up with Keyes, their senior officer, near the German target. He had scouted the compound and outlined his plan of attack to his men. General details of the headquarters had been supplied by a British officer disguised as an Arab living in the adjacent town. Keyes had carried out an on-the-spot surveillance, which determined that all the doors and windows of the compound were barred. He gave his last-minute instructions, and the commandoes took up attack positions at three minutes to midnight. Their objective now was to enter the headquarters through the front door.

The daring attack failed, and Keyes lost his life. But Kearney escaped. Cut off from reaching their planned evacuation site, the remaining commandos set out overland to reach Allied lines. On November 26, near Tobruk, Kearney and six comrades were captured by Italian soldiers.

ROMMEL GIVES MILITARY HONORS

A few days after the commando attack, Field Marshal Rommel gave Lt. Colonel Geoffrey Keyes a burial with full military honors, side by side with the four German officers killed in the attack. Keyes was posthumously awarded the Victoria Cross. Biographers of Rommel suggest the joint military funeral symbolized the sense of honour and respect Rommel encouraged in his men.

Prime Minister Winston Churchill held Rommel in high regard. While the British were in the midst of coping with Rommel's strategic genius, Churchill upset some people, both inside and outside the military, with the statement, "We have a very daring and skillful opponent against us, and may I say across the havoc of war, a great general."

In his memoirs, Churchill recalled the incident:

> My reference to Rommel passed off quite well at the moment. Later on I heard that some people had been offended. They could not feel that any virtue should be recognized in an enemy leader. This churlishness is a well-known streak in human nature, but contrary to the spirit in which a war is won or lasting peace is settled.[3]

Field Marshal Rommel committed suicide shortly after being incriminated in a plot to assassinate Hitler.

Joe Kearney returned home and on November 5, 1947, married Dorothy Mahoney. They had three children: Donna, Joanne, and Francis. Kearney died on September 1, 1987.

---

[3] Winston Churchill, *The Hinge of Fate: The Second World War Volume IV* (Boston: Houghton Mifflin, 1950) 67.

CHAPTER TWELVE

Spring Rice Document Surfaced After 100 Years

～～～

During 2016, Newfoundland marked the 100th anniversary of WWI, and a remarkable collection of WWI history was made widely known to the Newfoundland people. Missing from that history was a piece of military intelligence now known as the Spring Rice Document, which had a profound effect on Newfoundland's wartime policies. That intelligence, when shared with the Newfoundland government in 1915, caused an instant change in wartime policy and resulted in severe consequences for the people of the island.

The lack of knowledge of this top-secret record has resulted in a misinterpretation of Newfoundland's wartime policies. In simplified terms, we cannot know the truth of WWI in Newfoundland without considering the Spring Rice Document.

CAPTURED GERMAN INTELLIGENCE THREAT TO NEWFOUNDLAND

In May 1915, British intelligence informed the Newfoundland governor of "reliable reports" that Germany was about to bring the war to the northwest Atlantic, and this caused heightened alarm in St. John's when, in July, the British obtained proof from an unexpected source. Details in a German document, captured in the United States, set off a chain of events in Newfoundland with widespread repercussions.

The British ambassador to Washington, Sir Cecil Spring Rice, had gained access to German documents that fell into the hands of American officials after a major intelligence break occurred in New York on July 15, 1915. Among the captured papers were references to bays and coves in Newfoundland, along with codes and the dates when U-boats would be in the areas. Because British intelligence had already gathered information on Germany's intentions to launch an all-out submarine attack on British shipping in the northwest Atlantic, Spring Rice sent this particular item to the British admiralty in London with a copy telegraphed to Captain G. Abraham, the British intelligence officer in St. John's. Abraham appears to have been Britain's top intelligence agent in North America. The British ambassador in Washington shared the secret documents with Abraham before informing Canadian intelligence officials. In fact, he assigned the responsibility to advise Canada to Abraham, who lived on York Street in downtown St. John's.

At 6:40 p.m. on July 25, just ten days after the intelligence break in the United States, Abraham received the alarming telegraph from the ambassador. However, there was little detail on where or how the information was obtained, except to state that it was taken from the briefcase of a German naval attaché. The information received by Intelligence Officer Abraham was a very small part of widespread revelations that would have repercussions on the deteriorating relationship between the then neutral United States and Germany. The captured documents were the property of Dr. Heinrich Albert, Naval Attaché at the German embassy in Washington and head of German propaganda in the United States.

The ambassador's message to St. John's did not mention the shock waves the July 15th find was already sending through the top echelons of the American government and military and, in particular, those who were strongly fighting to maintain America's neutrality. The sensational telegraph message revealed that the accompanying specific locations of several bays and coves in Newfoundland were found among the papers of the German attaché. Abraham, referring to the Spring Rice Document, explained that it seemed to refer to routes, signals, etc. of submarines from July 29 to August 11. In the course of conversation, the German attaché is said to have stated there are three men among the fishermen at Miquelon preparing to render assistance to the plan.[1] On August 15, 1915, the *New York World* began publishing details of the unravelling espionage story which were provided by the US Secretary of the Treasury, William G. McAdoo.

[1] PANL, GN 1/3/A, Box 93.

SPY DOCUMENT CONTAINED SPECIFIC NEWFOUNDLAND TARGETS

The communication was a copy of a page from the German records, which mentioned the following locations in Newfoundland, each noted with a series of numbers indicating the geographic location: Belle Isle, Groais Island, Pigeonnier Arm, Robineau Cove, and Duggan's Cove. The Ambassador's message included this statement:

> Informant is a German Spy. Addressed to Foreign Office; sent to St. John's. Canada not informed." The Intelligence Officer in St. John's was given approval from London to share the secret with the Canadian Ambassador to Washington. Less than one month later an assassination attempt was made on Sir Cecil Spring Rice when six men attacked his motor car as he was driving on a Washington Street. The attempt failed.[2]

PANIC AMONG POPULATION

The documents received by Governor Davidson appeared to confirm the contents of the Spring Rice Document. What followed was an example of the widespread fears over a possible German attack. The now long-forgotten paramilitary force in Newfoundland, known as the Legion of Frontiersmen, met with an unexpected reception from a local population when they responded to the report.

On August 1, Governor Davidson received a message from Conche noting that a submarine periscope had been sighted

---

[2] *The Evening Telegram*, September 3, page 7.

near Groais Island. Residents there tried to alert a passing steamer of their sighting, but failed to get its attention. Groais Island, and the planned presence of enemy submarines in the area in late July and early August, were mentioned in the Spring Rice Document, a fact of primary interest to the governor.

Governor Davidson was extremely concerned over the possibility of panic among the residents. He had already dispatched the SS *Fogota*, which was manned by police and members of the Newfoundland Regiment. The vessel was armed with a twelve-pounder field gun and a three-pounder from HMS *Calypso*. However, before they arrived on the scene, a near tragic situation involving the Legion of Frontiersmen developed.

The Legion of Frontiersmen, who wore unusual uniforms, including an Australian type hat, had become aware of the sighting and, rapidly responding, arrived on scene before the *Fogota*. Coastal residents had been advised to keep a sharp lookout from La Scie to Flower's Cove, and orders were given to arrest and detain all suspicious-looking strangers.

Unfortunately, not all communities were aware of the existence of the Frontiersmen or their rather unusual uniform. Neither had they seen a German in uniform. When the Frontiersmen were sighted approaching one small community, the villagers thought the enemy had landed and they prepared to do battle. Armed to the teeth with old rifles and shotguns, these patriots were ready to repel the invaders from Newfoundland soil.

The residents had mistaken the Frontiersmen for Germans.

The commanding officer of the Frontiersmen quickly convinced the resistance force that they were not German soldiers. This was followed with apologies and the extension of true Newfoundland hospitality to the Frontiersmen.

SPY SUBMARINES HEAD FOR PORTS IN NEWFOUNDLAND

Abraham also informed the governor of an unconfirmed report that British intelligence had received prior to the Spring Rice Telegram, which claimed that four submarines had left Cuxhaven in the first week of June for the United States coast. In addition, there were intelligence reports that two suspected enemy vessels sailing under a neutral flag had left American ports at the same time. The British suspected that these ships were actually supply vessels for the submarines moving to the North Atlantic coastline.[3]

The source of this information may have been from an electronic advantage gained by the British on August 5, 1914. On that date, the British cable ship *Teconia* raised the submarine cables off the German coast and cut them. This action forced the Germans to reroute all their international communications by radio or another country's cables. These passed through Allied territory and were easily monitored by the British for the rest of the war.[4]

Newfoundland was already preparing for a rumoured German offensive on North America. Just days before Governor Davidson received the spy document, he had been

---

[3] Ibid.

[4] David Miller, *U-boats: History, Development and Equipment 1914-1945* (London: Bloomsbury, 2000).

advised by British intelligence on how the enemy could mount such an offensive. Now, armed with the Spring Rice Document, that advice from the British took on an immediate priority. Captain G. Abraham explained the situation to Davidson:

> If it is the enemy's intention to send submarines across the Atlantic to attack British ships, arrangements have doubtless been made to secure means of communicating with many agents both here and on the coast of the Dominion and the United States. Their plans would understandably be completed, not only for the arrangement of bases of supply, but also for information as to the movement of British ships of war and merchant vessels.
>
> It may pay the Germans to send one or two large and modern submarines to intercept the summer traffic through the Bell Isle Straits, but I am convinced they will only be sent in company with supply ships fitted out in Europe and disguised as foreign trawlers. Assuming that a harbour has been selected suitable for the purpose, it will not, I think, be on the New-foundland coast. The submarine must come by a very northerly route, via the Norwegian and Iceland coasts, and would therefore seek a northerly base for receiving supplies.
>
> Their plan therefore would be to wait until the Belle Isle Straits are open to traffic and base

their plans for attacking the line of traffic debouching from the Straits at some point out of sight of shore but no more than one hundred or two hundred miles from their base on Labrador.[5]

BRITISH INTELLIGENCE WARNED NEWFOUNDLAND TO PROTECT LABRADOR

The Labrador area of the colony was of special importance to British intelligence. Abraham explained:

> We are concerned that if the Germans set up a Labrador base they could take control of a telegraph office for their own purposes and we might not know. The telegraph stations will remain open as usual. Each operator would be required to send on a daily basis a code word that would be changed weekly.[6]

After presenting his view on what German strategy would be, Abraham advised Davidson that Newfoundland's first move should be to seek Canada's cooperation in closing the Strait of Belle Isle to ships from Europe for the summer of 1915. He said this could easily be done in conjunction with the guarding of the route through the Cabot Strait. The intelligence officer felt that the German submarines may never receive the information that traffic was diverted from the Strait of Belle Isle, especially if they missed the usual notice in telegraphs to Lloyds of London and an

---

[5] PANL 1/3/A

[6] Ibid.

announcement in the American newspapers that the Strait of Belle Isle was, as usual, open for traffic. When this suggestion was discussed with Canada, the Canadians disagreed with closing the strait but agreed to accept the responsibility to patrol them.

Captain Abraham, just days before, had discussed other steps the enemy would have to take to follow through on its intention to send submarines to the northwest Atlantic. He pointed out that bases of supply would be needed to service the enemy fleet, and these would likely be established "in out of the way bays of Newfoundland, Labrador or off St. Pierre."

The intelligence officer suggested that part of Newfoundland's response effort needed to include a country-wide monitoring of supplies, particularly those needed to support submarines (i.e., oils, lubricating oils, hardware supplies, unusually high orders of food, water, medicines, etc.).

Upon the advice of Captain Abraham, Newfoundland customs officers were ordered to gather information from all British and neutral ships coming into Newfoundland regarding any sightings and locations of vessels acting suspiciously. They were told to report immediately any such information gathered to government authorities. All British vessels were supplied with listings of local authorities to whom such information had to be reported. Newfoundland also agreed to create a system of land patrols and patrols by small vessels to watch the coast for suspicious activity.

CHAPTER THIRTEEN

Germany: A Major Threat to Newfoundland

~~~

The captured Spring Rice Document indicated that the areas of concentration for the German plan in Newfoundland were the Strait of Belle Isle and the Great Harbour Deep area of the Great Northern Peninsula. A week after learning of the plan, the government's response strategy went into action. Two armed patrol boats, each carrying armed members of the Newfoundland Regiment, were on their way to set up military stations in coves identified in the document.[1]

A Lieutenant Norris and Lieutenant O'Grady, each in command of forty non-commissioned officers of the New-foundland Regiment, left St. John's by train for Lewisporte where they boarded the SS *Home* to begin their secret mission. Their assignment was to guard the places in the

---

[1] Plans to outfit several patrol boats for northern Newfoundland were in progress at the time the Spring Rice Document was sent to Newfoundland. Now, armed with specific information, the government stepped up its plans.

Great Harbour Deep, White Bay, area referenced in the spy document: Pigeonnier Arm, Duggan's Cove, Fourchette Bay, and Robinson Cove. The soldiers were armed with rifles only and were ordered to capture any supply ships which reached these rendezvous points and to keep the governor informed daily by telegraph. Governor Davidson felt Lieutenant Norris was ideal for the assignment because his father was the leading merchant in Green Bay and White Bay, and his brother was manager of an agency at Conche.

Around the same time, a second patrol vessel rushed to the area of Groais Island. This was the SS *Petrel* with the Hon. A.W. Piccott, Minister of Marine, in charge, and Lieutenant Commander A. MacDermott, RN, in military command. A third vessel, the SS *Fogota*, transported another forty-member detachment of the Newfoundland Regiment to join MacDermott's party and to occupy Groais Island. The SS *Petrel* also carried an experienced Royal Navy Reserve gun crew, who were trained to handle the two eight-pounder guns on board. The Marconi Telegraph Company sent an engineer to install a wireless telegraph system on the patrol boat.

Newfoundland entered into an agreement with the Canadian government for the Canadian Navy to patrol the Straight of Belle Isle. The SS *Hump*, from Newfoundland, was already on patrol and operating from a station in northern Labrador with headquarters at Nain, which had a wireless connection with the Canadian system at Belle Isle and Point Riche.

NEWFOUNDLAND CHANGES ITS ALIEN ARREST POLICY

Captain Abraham, in a confidential document sent to Governor Davidson, urged that he act immediately to arrest all enemy subjects in Newfoundland and Labrador who were still at large, as well as deporting all those "who actively sympathise with the enemy."

Abraham told Davidson:

> Should enemy submarines come to this part of the world, it is to be expected that they will have arranged for several bases or places in which to meet their supply ships on various points of the coast, partly for safety and partly to increase their range of action. It would be of value to them to have their agents in various places, especially if the latter could supply them with information concerning our precautionary measures. These duties could be performed by enemy subjects in this country or those who sympathise with the enemy. They could communicate their information to the United States in some "en clair code"[2] without arousing suspicion, whence it could reach the enemy.[3]

Davidson, armed with the specific locations and dates on which submarines were expected to be in Newfoundland waters, became more resolved in his response actions.

---

[2] The Oxford Dictionary defines *en clair code* as a code in ordinary language.

[3] PANL, G1/100, reel #2, document #295. Letter from G.E.F. Abraham.

LABRADOR MISSIONARIES ARRESTED

In view of the Spring Rice Document, the Newfoundland Governor was forced to have a further look at the presence of the Moravian German missionaries in Labrador. There were fifteen members of the Labrador mission, nine of whom were German subjects, and six were British. He communicated his views to the colonial secretary in London, Bonar Law:

> The Newfoundland Government recommends that authority be given to the Justice of the Peace officers now on duty in Labrador to arrest eight of these enemy aliens and to bring them to St. John's for the purpose of internment for the period of the war. I would advise that Bishop Martine at Nain should be permitted to stay, in view of his age and of his long residence on the coast, and remain in executive charge of the mission work. He would still have help of six persons, either the missionary or storekeepers and the only doctor to look after the affairs of the mission.
>
> I express this opinion after much deliberation, not so much because I suspect their hostile intent nor believe in their power to do mischief, but because the coast in their charge is likely to be made use of as a submarine base and because they cannot be expected to denounce their compatriots.[4]

The Newfoundland governor's resolve to deal with the pending crisis is reflected in the following message he sent to the governor general of Canada:

[4] PANL, GN 1/3, Box 93.

We should undoubtedly and justifiably be open to censure if, despite the official warning we have received, we should still permit to be at large enemy subjects and others who have openly shown their sympathy with the enemy. Moreover, apart from the anxiety and the responsibility, the Government is also put to considerable expense to guard the shores and to watch the actions of possible enemy agents. For instance, the cost of putting in commission the *Hump* as a patrol vessel is a strict outcome of our knowledge that a number of enemy subjects are at large in settlements on the coast of Labrador and then from evidence before us, not I admit of the best quality, that certain of these enemy subjects have expressed views which are not in sympathy with our cause.[5]

Although the government initiated a policy dealing with enemy aliens and censorship when the war broke out, a new, more intensified policy emerged as a consequence of the Spring Rice Document.

The governor sought and received approval from Britain for the imposing of the following policy regarding aliens. In respect to this condition, Governor Davidson, in a message to Hon. A. Bonar Law, a member of the British War Cabinet, made the following recommendations:

All enemy subjects not already in custody should 'now' be picked up and interred. I should advise that an exception be made in favour of enemy aliens of German nationality by birth, who can prove continual residence

---

[5] PANL, GN 1/3/A.

on the American continent for the last twenty years. Enemy aliens already interred be prevented from transmitting messages through third parties or other enemy subjects. As regards to persons who not being of enemy nationality can be shown to be actively in sympathy with the enemy. I know of only one person who fails in this category, namely, Mr. Rockwell Kent, a subject of the United States at present residing in Brigus. In the case of this man there is ample evidence, officially on record, to show that he is hostile in intention and I should advise that he be required to leave the colony on the first opportunity.[6]

Two days after he received the Spring Rice Document, Governor Davidson requested that the POWs in the outport jails be transferred to the Donovan's "concentration camp," which was guarded by thirty armed soldiers from the Newfoundland Regiment. The POW camp housed twenty prisoners.

Sometimes allegations of German spying led police to a dead end, as was the following case, which made the newspapers.

A foreign speaking man arriving in St. John's from Bell Island on Saturday, July 8, 1916, caused excitement among city people over rumours that he was a German spy. The incident attracted the attention of the Newfoundland Constabulary.

The Evening Telegram reported:

He registered at a certain boarding house as a Russian.

---

[6] Ibid.

By a curious coincidence, it happened that two other men of that nationality were staying there. However, all three became very friendly and started to converse. At the outset, one of the genuine Russians, having a fair knowledge of the German language, discovered that the newcomer knew nothing about the Russian tongue, as professed, but on the contrary, was found to be a versatile German, judging by his talk.

The Russians were in St. John's to purchase two Newfoundland ships for Russia. After the Russian notified the Constabulary, the mystery guest disappeared. The newspaper suggested he had been "aided and abetted by a foreign businessman whose proclivities are known not to be at all in sympathy with the flag under which he lives."

FIRST WWI POW CAMPS IN NEWFOUNDLAND

The legal basis for proceeding against enemy aliens in Newfoundland became the War Measures Act passed by the Newfoundland Legislature on September 7, 1914, and made retroactive to August 1. This legislation was modelled on similar legislation passed by the Canadian and British Parliaments. The act provided Government with "wide discretionary powers to arrest, detain, and to deport undesirables in the interest of 'the security, defence, peace order and welfare of Newfoundland.'"[7]

On August 19, 1914, His Majesty's Penitentiary on Forest Road in St. John's became the first designated POW camp

[7] Ibid.

in Newfoundland. Those POWs held at HMP complained about being treated as criminals, the lack of recreation, and poor quality of food. The governor of the penitentiary responded to this criticism:

> It is the best scale of dietary known here. Namely: tea, porridge, molasses and biscuit every morning. Fish and potatoes, biscuit, and tea for dinner on Mondays, Wednesdays and Friday. Pea Soup and biscuit on Saturdays. Fresh meat, rice, soup and biscuit on Tuesday, Thursdays and Saturdays.[8]

Soon after this episode, the POWs were moved to other facilities at Harbour Grace, Placentia, and the Bay of Islands. As a consequence of the Spring Rice Document, the government leased premises on Topsail Road, known as Donovan's and located about seven miles west of St. John's, which they converted into a detention camp for POWs. The prisoners were eventually transferred to the Donovan's "concentration camp."

Prior to this, the camp was being used for military convalescents and had an observatory in which the patients enjoyed an excellent view of the country area. The Newfoundland Regiment considered it too far out of town for them to use.[9]

During WWII the Royal Canadian Navy used the facility as a rest and relaxation camp for sailors who had spent longer than normal periods at sea. It had a large cookhouse, three quantum huts, a large outdoor swimming pool constructed

---

[8] PANL, GN/1/100 reel #2.

[9] Ibid.

on a stream, and a large cabin for officers. Today, the site is occupied by Sears of Canada.

In 1946, the Kinsmen Club of St. John's took over the property and used it as a boys' summer camp. In 1952 four wooden bunk houses were added to the three quantum huts. The wartime officer's cabin housed the camp counsellors and included a canteen. I attended summer camp and stayed in these same huts in the mid-1950s.

The famous Newfoundland singer Biddy O'Tool lived in a small white house next to the property. O'Tool was a member of the popular Uncle Tim's Barn Dance Troupe and is best remembered for the song "I Met Her in the Garden Where the 'Praties Grow," which she sang on stage at the Knights of Columbus in St. John's on December 12, 1942, when it was consumed by fire. Ninety-nine people lost their lives in that fire. The Barn Dance show was strictly a stage show broadcast weekly on radio with the auditorium filled to capacity with iron collapsible chairs. For decades after this disaster, people not there that night mistakenly claimed there was a dance taking place.

LONDON ORDERED INTERNMENT OF ALIENS

The fears that Germany would bring the war to the shores of Newfoundland were widespread from the start of the conflict and intensified as the war progressed. In December 1914, the *Montreal Star* published a news item that caught Newfoundlanders' attention. The article, raising the issue of German spies operating in Newfoundland, asked, "How far is St. John's used as a spy centre?"

The story was based on reported claims by the manager of the Nova Scotia Steel Company, owners of the Bell Island Mines, that the German arms dealer Krupp was in possession of the most detailed information about the Bell Island Mining Operation. Germany was one of the mine's biggest customers before the war. The article suggested that the information could be used by the enemy in any plans to attack or invade Canada.

During this period when anti-German sentiments in Newfoundland were growing, a rather startling incident occurred when a man who had been dead for two months, and who was a long-time active and respected member of the community, Robert von Stein, was accused of carrying out undercover work for Germany.

CHAPTER FOURTEEN

Rockwell Kent Deported from Newfoundland

~~~

The Spring Rice Document had a direct effect on the firm position taken by the Newfoundland governor regarding Rockwell Kent. A world famous artist, Kent was deported from his home at Brigus, Conception Bay, days after British intelligence passed the captured papers to the governor. In a letter to the colonial secretary, the governor stated he was concerned that public suspicions that Kent was a German spy might lead to mob violence.

Kent, a winner of the Lenin Peace Prize, chose Brigus to settle for its natural beauty and the much easier pace of living compared to the rest of North America. In February 1914, he rented a Victorian-style house there, which required some upgrading. Kent carried out the repairs himself and then sent for his wife and three daughters in the United States. Most people in Brigus welcomed Kent and his family as neighbours but were indifferent to his work as an

Renowned American artist Rockwell Kent (1882-1971) lived in Brigus for a short time before being deported. (Unidentified photographer, circa 1920, Smithsonian Institution Archives)

artist. Others viewed him with suspicion, which intensified once war broke out.

The daily news of the events taking place in Europe and North America inspired a general suspicion of all foreigners, and especially naturalized aliens. When police began rounding up German aliens for questioning, it did not take long before the people of Brigus were pointing a finger at Kent. The artist did little to help his situation. He displayed an attitude of contempt towards the people of Brigus by trivializing their wartime fears of Germans and not only mocked them but also mocked the police sent to Brigus to enforce the actions undertaken by the Justice Department in accordance with the Wartime Measures Act.

The first rumour spread about the artist was that he was a German spy and kept his art studio under lock and key because he was using it to draw geographic maps of Newfoundland for the enemy.

In reality, there was no need for concern because the artist's studio had nothing to do with German espionage but contained artwork being sent to an agent in New York to sell. In April 1915, his New York agent, George S. Chappell, found a buyer for a collection of Rockwell's drawings. When he requested directions from Kent, the artist sent the following telegraph: "Sell drawings on condition that you appropriate six for self. This is a magnificent stroke of business. I am delighted and grateful to you."[1]

It appears, because of the growing suspicions, that when he found it necessary to go to Boston in May 1915 on undisclosed legal business, Kent arranged for his family to stay at 6 King's Road in St. John's. Communicating from Boston on May 17, he sent the following telegraph to his wife:

Preliminary hearing Friday. Everything proceeding satisfactorily. There will be plenty of excitement though. I am confident of the outcome. Good lawyers are acting for me. Very lonely. Tried to hire flute but couldn't. Write to me right away and wire if anything occurs eager to hear from you.[2]

All telegraphs and letters to and from Rockwell Kent were being stopped and screened by censors before delivery. The above telegraph was referred to the deputy chief censor and then released.

[1] PANL, GN 2-14, Box 3.
[2] Ibid.

The next aspect of Kent's life that attracted the attention of neighbours was the large tool chest he kept on his property. They suggested he was using it to store bombs or the tools to make one.

When Kent stored seven tons of coal for the coming winter, another suspicion of spying was added to those already circulating. "He must be storing the coal as fuel for German U-boats operating on the Atlantic," they said. Then an incident occurred at a school concert that convinced some people that Rockwell Kent was indeed a German spy. Kent participated in the concert by singing German songs. Kent, who was not at all German, had remembered some favourite German songs from his youth, which he performed at several Brigus concerts.[3]

Meanwhile, Kent had heard all the rumours and was amused by them. He did have his supporters in the community. A dozen or so Brigus residents were genuine and loyal friends and gave no heed to the stories. Kent, however, found it amusing to joke about the situation. He painted a yellow sign on his front door that read, "Bomb Shelter, Chart Room, and Wireless Station." Beneath the sign he drew a German Eagle.

The rumours spread outside the community and reached police offices in St. John's. The inspector general of police, Charles Hutchings, was already coping with daily allegations from all over the colony about German aliens and other foreigners, and each one got police attention. As in each such allegation, a police officer was sent to inform a suspect of

---

[3] Gerhard Bassler, *Vikings to U-boats: The German Experience in Newfoundland and Labrador* (Montreal: McGill-Queen's, 2006).

the allegations, and in this case, Kent was invited to go to St. John's for a meeting with the inspector general of police.

Kent's actions continued to draw the attention of his opponents at Brigus and the Newfoundland authorities. He wrote his friends in German, knowing it would be viewed by the censors, and he even expressed in the writings a wish for German victory in the war.

Then a statement made by Kent on May 22, 1915, in the *New Republic* sealed his fate in Newfoundland. In the article he denounced Britain and cursed Newfoundland. This came at a time when Newfoundlanders were dealing with news of family members dying on the battlefronts of Europe.

Sir Richard Squires, who investigated Kent's background and gathered information from American authorities, concluded that Kent was no spy and no threat to Newfoundland. This was a view shared by Governor Davidson. Their main concern was that the hysteria developing over the issue could lead to more serious problems and a threat to the Kent family's safety.

BRIGUS LEADERS SUPPORT KENT

Some of the leading citizens of Brigus came to Rockwell Kent's defence. There were nine of them: S.W. Bartlett, William Bartlett, J.W. Hiscock, Dr. J.N. McDonald, S.E. Chafe, J.C. Cozens, R.E. Maddock, John Smith, and T.C. Makinson. They submitted a letter to the inspector general of police, who sent a copy to the governor.

The group recognized that Kent created problems for himself, but they explained that he was an intelligent and accomplished individual whose ordinary demeanour was to speak frankly without fear. They noted that Kent had a "strong liking" for the German people. This, they said, was not unusual for an American college-bred man who spent some time as a student in Germany.

The letter stated,

> It is highly improbable that Mr. Kent as a socialist has any particular regard for the Kaiser or the military aristocracy of Germany. The spread of socialism is Mr. Kent's desire, not the aggrandizement of the bitterest opponents of socialism in the world.
>
> We shall be sorry to be deprived of all opportunity to hold further conversations with Mr. Kent, and can assure him that there are Newfoundlanders who do not regard him with suspicion and dislike.

The petition of his supporters and the intervention of the American consul in St. John's were to no avail, and in July 1915, the order for Kent's deportation was issued. Governor Davidson himself did not believe that Kent was an enemy agent and felt the decision to expel him from the country would have been deferred had it not been for the German threats revealed in the Spring Rice Document. Davidson wrote,

> It had become necessary, out of consideration of public safety to intern enemy subjects of military age and to exercise surveillance over others who openly expressed their sympathy with the King's enemies. Mr. Kent

concurs in the reasonableness of this decision and has undertaken in response to this invitation to leave the country.[4]

A week later, Kent asked the governor to grant him a one month extension to his deadline to leave due to sickness in his family and the time needed to prepare for the move. The governor approved the request because he believed Rockwell Kent was neither in the employ of the enemy nor in direct correspondence with known enemy agents.

KENT'S PRIVATE TELEGRAPHS

Among the colonial secretary's files at The Rooms are several of the intercepted telegraphs to or from Rockwell Kent during WWI. Kent sent the following telegraph to Mrs. Kent in Tarrytown, New York, July 19:

> Letter arrived today. We expected you. Children in tears all upset. You must come. Will make any sacrifices and will return most remittance immediately. Daniel will assist. Visit worth any amount to K [Kathleen]. We have prepared for weeks. Come Red Cross. Best way start now.[5]

Somehow, this message escaped censors and was sent directly, which caused John R. Bennett, Deputy Chief Censor, to write to American Telegraph:

> I must express my surprise that you have passed this message, for it should certainly have been held up. You

[4] PANL, GN 1/100, reel #2.
[5] PANL, GN2-14, Box 3, Colonial Secretary's Files.

have in the past referred all these messages to this office, and this practice should have been adhered to in the present case.[6]

He asked that "all" letters and telegraphs to Rockwell Kent be first sent to the censor's office.

On July 20, Kent, who had been expecting his wife to return from the United States, sent the following telegraph to her in Tarrytown, New York:

> Don't come. We have decided, all come see you and stay. Don't know just how dispose ourselves on arrival but will find way. Kathleen delighted at decision. Best way to spend the money which I hope you have sent. Have written particulars all well and eager to return to civilization.[7]

Kent was escorted to St. John's Harbour where police made sure he left the country. On August 7, 1915, he sent the following message from New London, Connecticut, to Bessie Noseworthy at Brigus:

> We are settled in New London, Connecticut, and want you with us, as soon as you can get here. Come to the next *Florizel* and bring Marcy if you want to. I have written sending money. Don't fail us. I will meet you in New York from Halifax. - Rockwell Kent.[8]

That appears to be the last of the unfortunate Rockwell Kent episode in Newfoundland, but not the last of Kent. His

[6] Ibid.
[7] Ibid.
[8] Ibid.

reputation and stature in the arts spread worldwide. In 1968, Premier Joseph R. Smallwood acknowledged that a wrong had been done to Rockwell Kent and his family, and extended an invitation to Kent and his wife to visit Newfoundland. Kent agreed and a banquet was held in his honour at Memorial University in July 1968.

Kent was impressed with how Newfoundland had progressed since he left it and told Smallwood, "Why not let us have you on lend-lease for a while? My God, how we and all mankind need men like you today."

CHAPTER FIFTEEN

Suspected German Spies Deported

~~~

Mike Critch, an icon of Newfoundland radio history, has an interesting family connection with one of the intriguing spy stories of World War I. An uncle of Critch's, Peter Kercher, was arrested as a "German spy suspect" in St. John's soon after the breakout of WWI and allowed to leave Newfoundland in the aftermath of the Spring Rice Document under certain restrictions.

In the fall of 1914, Kercher, then thirty-five years old and a steward on the SS *Florizel*, was dismissed from his job as the result of the Government's enemy alien policy. It was a time when German aliens in Newfoundland were being rounded up, and the public was alarmed by daily news reports and speculation of German activities off the Newfoundland coast and a fear that the colony itself might come under attack. Many respectable Newfoundland citizens with German origins, who before the war were highly esteemed and treated as fellow countrymen, were being shunned by friends.[1]

Peter and Alice Kercher.
(Photo courtesy of Mike Critch)

Kercher had been a resident of Newfoundland for ten years before being accused, and had spent his childhood in the United States. While searching for the maiden name of Mrs. Peter Kercher, I learned of Mike Critch's connection to the Kerchers. In discussing the story with Critch, he commented, "Finding Peter's wife's name is not too difficult; it was Alice Critch, my Aunt Alice. As a matter of fact, I still have a picture of Peter and Alice taken at a photo studio in Brooklyn, New York."

---

[1] PANL, GN 2-14, Box 13, File 152.

Kercher was kept at the Donovan's POW camp on Topsail Road. Authorities who got to know him were most impressed by his exemplary character and his outstanding performance of work assignments. Kercher was a major influence in helping to maintain discipline and order in the camp.

His performance at Donovan's played a role in his not being sent to the Canadian POW camps when others were moved there. Instead, he was set free under the conditions that he move to the United States, pay a four thousand dollar bond to stay there, and report twice monthly to the British consular agent at New York. Although his British naturalization papers were forfeited, these were returned to him after the war.[2]

Peter Kercher became an American citizen in 1907, and in August 1914 became a British subject. He was arrested and interned in July 1915, but he was excluded from other arrested German aliens when they were deported for imprisonment in Canadian POW camps. His arrest, and the arrest of others, was part of Newfoundland's policy towards aliens during WWI.

Mike Critch never met his uncle, but he did know his Aunt Alice, who lived to be a hundred. When the epidemic of Spanish Flu swept the world in 1918 and there was an urgent need for hospital space in St. John's for sick and injured veterans returning from Europe, the government looked to the fifty-acre property on Portugal Cove Road called Escasoni.[3] Once authorities moved to rent or purchase it, they discovered it was owned by Peter Kercher, the German

---

[2] Ibid.

[3] The prominent Emerson family later obtained the property, which continued to be called Escasoni.

they had declared as an enemy alien. The governor pointed out that because of wartime legislation relating to trading with the enemy, he could not deal with Kercher. However, they did take control of the Escasoni property, and turned it into a sanatorium for the troops.[4] It was an ideal spot for a hospital and in 1918 was well outside St. John's and was surrounded by farms, grassy fields, and nearby rivers.

Mike Critch recalled that Escasoni housed a very large residence, and there was a second building on the property. He recalled having outings there many years later when the buildings had been vacated and were deteriorating. Mike said that one of the most impressive features of Escasoni was the outside balcony that surrounded the house. He recalled family photos, long disappeared, showing patients sitting outside on the balcony when it was being used as a soldiers' hospital. Critch said that when Peter was not using it himself, his uncle rented it out.

Some years later, when Kercher passed away, he left, in his will, property and money in St. John's to a Newfoundland family he had befriended while living in the colony. Mike recalled that his aunt and uncle settled down in New Jersey and his aunt kept in touch with relatives in St. John's by letters, but as time passed, they heard less and less from her. Mike Critch was awarded the Radio–Television News Directors Association of Canada's Lifetime Achievement Award in 2008.

---

[4] PANL, GN-214, Box13, File 141.

SUSPECTED SPY DEPORTED

L. Huesbsch was a naturalized American subject but, by birth, an enemy alien. At a time when British intelligence expected that German submarines were seeking out-of-the-way coves and bays along the Labrador coast as bases to attack Allied interests on the Atlantic, Huesbsch was seeking to do business in Labrador.

He was planning to travel throughout Labrador, purchasing furs for a firm to be marketed in enemy territory believed to be German owned. Newfoundland authorities had already been warned about the likelihood of suspicious visitors in Labrador scouting out the coast while operating under the guise of doing legitimate business.

When the matter was referred to Newfoundland's Justice Department, Huesbsch was advised to return to the United States. The Deputy Minister of Justice pointed out, "The export of furs of which the ultimate destination may be enemy territory has been prohibited by Order in Council, furs being conditional contraband." The governor was concerned over the possibility of foreigners on business communicating intelligence to the enemy through their business contacts.

James S. Hansen, another visiting businessman who was already travelling in Labrador buying furs, was deported at the same time and for similar reasons.

Richard Warschauer, a German businessman, moved to St. John's early in 1914 and was manager of the Newfoundland Trading Company of New York. Soon after, he married a

Newfoundland girl. His main business was the buying of tinned lobster for the firm of Rosenstein & Company, New York. This work required him to travel to the outports of the colony regularly, and he became familiar with most places. Warschauer fit the profile of an enemy operator in Newfoundland as described by Captain Abraham.

The British had supplied Newfoundland censors with lengthy lists of firms and people outside Newfoundland which were suspected of having German connections. This reference source was a major tool of the chief censor's office. It was this listing that led to the two arrests of Warschauer.

Warschauer, like Kercher, was considered an enemy alien and, as such, automatically brought under the scrutiny of the chief censor. When they noted that he was sending frequent mail to a company in Philadelphia on their index listings, he was arrested and imprisoned, but not for long. Several prominent citizens vouched for him, and he was released on four thousand dollars bail. While in prison, Warschauer was suspected of smuggling mail to the outside. His explanation for the actual mail, which was of concern to the censors, was that he was trying to collect bad debts from the Philadelphia Company. His lawyer was A. B. Morine, K.C. and M.H.A., and a prominent member of the Newfoundland Patriotic Association.

The suspected spy was not free for long. Once he was released from HMP, he was placed under police surveillance. The amount of mail he had been sending to the United States dropped significantly, which led censors to suspect he

[5] PANL, GN-2-14, Box 3.

was circumventing the censorship laws by using a third party to get mail outside the country.[5] At this time Davidson advised the Justice Department, "It is especially important at this juncture to have the strictest guard on him and his communications." Specifically referring to the Spring Rice Document, Davidson said, "In view of renewed enemy threats of hostility, it is necessary to make Warschauer absolutely secure, and I advise his being again remanded to the Penitentiary."

His bail bonds were forfeited, and he was again arrested and held as a prisoner of war. The prisoner was told that prosecution was possible under the Defence of the Realm Legislation. The fact that he was an officer in the German Reserve was an added factor in his becoming a POW. The accused was a German subject and of military age. In an interview with Governor Davidson, Warschauer admitted he had qualified to be enrolled as a German reserve officer, and if he was in Germany he would serve in the German Army. When on bail, he stayed at O'Rorke's Hotel in Holyrood, not far from St. John's. The prisoner did not face prosecution, and after a short while at Donovan's POW Camp, he was sent to an internment camp in Canada.

ST. JOHN'S REGATTA COMMITTEE MEMBER ACCUSED OF SPYING

Robert von Stein, an engineer whose professional work was evident in St. John's and as far from the city as Salmonier Line where he constructed bridges, was also famous for his work with the St. John's Regatta Committee. He served on the executive of that committee for years and introduced many novelty attractions to lakeside for the enjoyment of the general public.

The basis for the accusation was a report in the *St. John's Mail and Advocate* on September 12, 1914, which claimed that the *North Sydney Herald* had conclusive proof from private, reliable sources of Stein's systematic gathering of intelligence for the Kaiser. One of Stein's sons, Conrad, enlisted in the Newfoundland Regiment and served in the 3rd Battalion.

Stein's sister-in-law publicly defended him and denied that there was any basis to the article, which she said was nothing but "slander."

CHAPTER SIXTEEN

Newfoundland Sea Captain was German Kaiser's Hero

During 1895, Kaiser Wilhelm of Germany, perhaps the world's most powerful man at the time, had sent messages to St. John's and England in an attempt to locate Captain William Fitzgerald.

The Kaiser was indebted to Fitzgerald, a native of Carbonear, Newfoundland. The Kaiser, of whom historian H.F. Shortis wrote, "had only to stamp his foot and the whole world would stop to listen," was anxious to reward the Newfoundland sea captain for the heroic rescue of twenty-six of the Emperor's subjects from a sinking ship during a raging storm in the North Atlantic.

The sea adventure of Captain Fitzgerald had its beginning on December 21, 1893, when he set sail from St. John's in the topsail schooner *Rose of Torridge* bound for Gibraltar.

On January 24, 1894, he was nearing latitude thirty-six degrees north and twenty degrees west in a raging wind storm. While Captain Fitzgerald and crew struggled to keep their vessel on course, they were suddenly thrust into an even more treacherous dilemma. Straight ahead was the German vessel *Cassandra* flying a distress signal that read, "Ship is sinking. Wish to abandon."

Captain Fitzgerald was baffled over how to get close enough to the *Cassandra* to rescue the crew without losing his own ship and endangering his own men. Captain Fitzgerald skillfully manoeuvred his ship in circling the *Cassandra* six times, and when it became apparent time was about to run out, he moved into action. He brought the *Rose of Torridge* as close to the distressed vessel as possible and began removing the crew.

During the rescue, a block from the loft of the *Cassandra* fell and struck Fitzgerald. If it had not been for his strong physical condition, he may not have survived the mishap. He got to his feet and continued the rescue effort. Fitzgerald later recalled one of the biggest problems at that time was getting the German captain up and over the side of the *Rose of Torridge*. The Captain weighed over two hundred pounds. All twenty-six members of the Cassandra's crew made it safely to Captain Fitzgerald's ship. It was just in time. The stern of the sinking vessel raised high in the water, and it nosedived, completely disappearing beneath the crashing waves.

When the *Rose of Torridge* arrived in Gibraltar, the German survivors were taken to the German consul, and a statement was taken from Captain Fitzgerald. The consul, after confirming the amazing sea rescue, sent a dispatch to the German Emperor. Meanwhile, Captain Fitzgerald continued his trip, and after discharging his cargo took on a load of salt at Trapani before returning to St. John's, Newfoundland.

Upon his arrival at St. John's, he was approached by R.H. Prowse, German Consul to Newfoundland, with a surprising offer from the German Emperor. Kaiser Wilhelm wished to honour Captain Fitzgerald with a special gift in recognition of his heroic rescue. Prowse asked Fitzgerald to choose from among a list that included a watch, a sextant, binoculars, and a medal. The captain said he would prefer a watch, and Prowse advised the Kaiser by mail of the Captain's preference.

CHAPTER SEVENTEEN

Espionage on the Avalon

~~~~~~~

MOUNT PEARL WIRELESS STATION UNDER GUNFIRE

A September 9, 1918, memo from United States Consul to Inspector General of Police, St. John's, read:

> On August 27, 1918, an attempt was made by some persons unknown to damage the Marconi Wireless Station at Mount Pearl and to shoot Leading Telegrapher Mooney who turned out to search for the party.[1]

At the start of the war, Imperial Authorities in London viewed the Avalon Peninsula in Newfoundland as a strategic place to set up a wireless telegraph station. The site they chose was Mount Pearl, which after completion was capable of working with Bermuda, Canada, and at times England in handling important war communications. The only debate over the station was what to call it. The

---

[1] PANL, GN 2-14, Box 2.

suggested names were too long. Newfoundland had too many letters, and the name Mount Pearl had no significance to strangers. The name Avalon might direct the thoughts of the sender elsewhere, and the name St. John's would cause confusion. The one chosen was the Marconi Wireless Station, which had obvious identification potential.

Among the most serious security incidents to occur in Newfoundland during WWI was the incident on August 27, 1918, when two men attacked the Marconi Wireless Station at Mount Pearl, and also attempted to shoot a telegraph operator employed there.

The attackers were detected before they could cause real damage, and a response party from the station gave chase. One of the men in that group was Leading Telegrapher Mooney, whom the attackers attempted to kill. During the escape pursuit, one of the escapees turned his gun on Mooney, attempting to shoot him. Fortunately for Mooney, the bullet missed.

There was an immediate restriction placed on the publication of all information surrounding the attack, and Inspector General of Police Charles Hutchings,[2] acting upon instructions from the colonial secretary, initiated an investigation into the attack. Part of his instructions were to deport any person or persons considered to be "undesirables."

Around the same time that the telegraph station was under attack, Hutchings had received a report from a woman he

[2] Inspector General Charles Hutchings was married to the daughter of Captain Billy Boig, who was a partner with Captain John Keating when the two found the Cocos Island Treasure, better known internationally as The Lost Treasure of Lima.

described as "a prominent person" who had heard a stranger speaking German. The information given by the lady, which was not detailed in the archival report, led police to a Joseph R. Schnitzer. Police felt they were on the right track when Schnitzer met the description of one of the perpetrators given by the guards at the telegraph station. Yet police were not anxious to make an arrest. They simply advised him that he was an "undesirable" and told him to leave the country.

The suspect was not happy with this advice and next day sought and was given a meeting with the inspector general of police. Hutchings listened to the man's story but felt it lacked credibility. Schnitzer had told the inspector general of his business connections and related, in detail, how he spent his time after working hours.

Hutchings investigated the suspect's story and confirmed his own suspicions. He learned from Schnitzer's nephew that references to his uncle's business connections were untrue. As to Schnitzer's account of his "after work activities," Hutchings concluded, "I considered this ridiculous, and I again invited him to leave the Dominion." Still there was no mention of an arrest, and again the suspect expressed reluctance.

To impress Schnitzer with the seriousness of his situation, Hutchings set up another meeting at which time he brought in two guards from the Mount Pearl telegraph station to confront him. After meeting the suspect face to face, the two identified him as "not only one of the attackers, but he was also the man who fired the shot at Mooney." Despite this identification, the man was not arrested, but on the recommendation of Charles Hunt, his lawyer, he was allowed to return to his residence on condition he would report daily to police headquarters. Hunt's request was supported by the American consul in St. John's, a man named Benedict. The investigation of Schnitzer had extended to Washington, and Benedict felt the man should be permitted to stay in Newfoundland until the report from Washington arrived.

While still awaiting the Washington report, Schnitzer made an unscheduled visit to the inspector general and caught him by complete surprise when he said that, despite the American consul's recommendation, he was ready to leave the country. Hutchings advised him not to act hastily but to talk the matter over with Benedict. "I don't want any more trouble," Schnitzer replied and said he was leaving Newfoundland of his own accord.[3] Hutchings offered no further explanation as to why, with two confirmed eye-witness identifications and the statement from the suspect's nephew, that the man was not prosecuted. Whether he was acting as a German agent, or else had a private dispute with someone at the Marconi Wireless Station was not mentioned in archival records reviewed.

As to Schnitzer's nationality, Hutchings reported, "He was born in Jerusalem and probably of German descent as his name indicates. He went to the United States in 1901 and became a naturalized American citizen." Twelve years after, in 1913, he claimed he was a British subject. During the war, Schnitzer's family in Jerusalem were given British protection when "some notable British official visited there."

---

[3] PANL, GN 2-14, Box 2. Colonial Secretary's Letters, A letter from the Inspector General of Police. September 9, 1918.

Although the incident was kept from the press, rumours of the arrest of German spies and their attempt on the Marconi Wireless Station, although inaccurate, spread and became part of the oral history of WWI.

SPIES SEEMED TO BE POPPING UP EVERYWHERE!

On August 30, 1918, *The Evening Telegram* published the following poem by James Murphy, which lampooned the paranoia of the day:

The Isle of Fish

When folks are drinking two in one,
Today the finest savoured dish
Is cod which sticks to every tongue.
Where if a man be looking shy,
Some folks will say, he's a German spy.

A man sat on the rocky brow
Which overlooks the Battery side.
He watched the boat which sailed below
Upon the silent harbour tide.
Not thinking that some had an eye
Upon him as a German spy.

They saw him, and they took his work,
Two leaves of rhyming it did show.
He gave the German name of Burke
And then they told the spy to go.
Satisfied no bombs would fall from high
And that Burke could be no German spy.

Again we find on Monday night,
Our energetic peelers tramp.
T'was said by some, a German light
But t'was in 'Tom Seymour's' camp.
I am afraid some folks will say—bye n' bye
The man in the moon is a German Spy.

NO SUBMARINE DEFENCE AT ST. JOHN'S

Even a year after the Spring Rice Document, St. John's Harbour was still defenceless against a possible attack by a German submarine. In fact, according to Vice Admiral of the British Navy, George Patey, St. John's was without any defence whatsoever. Patey pointed out that this weakness in the colony's defence policy was reflected in the government's belief that, because it was unable to provide a defence against enemy cruisers, it would be better to do nothing at all.

Patey warned,

> This would be, to a certain extent justified in former times, but with the development of the submarine, the situation is altered. At present, it would be quite easy for one or two submarines armed with one or more guns to hold up the harbour and town of St. John's, take what they wanted and set fire and destroy the rest.[4]

The vice-admiral recommended that St. John's adopt a defence similar to that put in place by Halifax a year before. In June 1915, Halifax installed several anti-submarine nets at the entrance to its harbour. He said an added

---

[4] PANL, GN 1/3/A.

advantage would be to mount two twelve-pounder guns in appropriate places and to include the two three-pounder guns discarded by the *Calypso*, which were good for another five hundred rounds of ammunition.

Commenting on the possibility of a German U-boat attack in Newfoundland waters, Patey stated, "I understand that the latest German submarines are easily capable of covering three to four thousand miles."[5]

AN AIR BASE AT CAPE RACE

In mid-June 1918, when there was concern that Germany might attack St. John's and concentrate on shipping along the Newfoundland coast, planning was in progress to establish a land and sea air base at Cape Race. The strategists, struggling with the problem of how to best deal economically with the German threat to St. John's and the surrounding coastal area, proposed two choices. The first was the suggestion to install heavy guns at St. John's Harbour and have armed patrol boats operating from there and ready to respond. The second proposal was to provide air surveillance using aeroplanes and or sea planes.

The Newfoundland government followed up both ideas by obtaining the advice of an expert on coastal defence who, after studying the problem, recommended that government proceed with the plan to use an air defence. It was pointed out that an air patrol was faster and cheaper than the alternative. The British government wanted both heavy guns and

---

[5] Letter from Vice Admiral George Patey, June 3, 1915, to the Secretary of the Admiralty, Whitehall, London.

air patrols, but it was too late in the summer to do anything about it.

The move to set up an air base did get underway with Canada taking the initial steps. Its plan was to construct a base at Cape Race which would handle land planes, sea planes, airship balloons, and kite balloons, all to be equipped with the latest suitable instruments.

Canada, Britain, and the United States favoured the building of an air station at St. John's as an "outpost to the bigger station at Cape Race." Britain agreed to consult with its air-force experts. The American Aviation Construction Department said it could supply aeroplane model J.N.4.H., which would be fitted with a Hispano/Suiza engine with bomb dropping ability, wireless, and all the latest technology. Two planes were immediately ready for the new air base and two more shortly after. The cost of each aircraft was eight thousand five hundred dollars. The idea for motor patrol boats was dropped because it would have been too costly.[6]

The project ended with the ending of the war on November 11, 1918.

[6] PANL, GN2-14.

PART TWO

~~~

EPIC
SEA
ADVENTURES

CHAPTER EIGHTEEN

A World-Famous Epic

~~~

Charles H. Hutchings, King's Council, and later the Inspector General of Police and Minister of Justice for Newfoundland, published a story in *The Newfoundland Quarterly* about the famous Cocos Island Treasure and its connection with Newfoundland.

In this article, he revealed he was the grandson of Captain William Boig, who died during the 1841 expedition of the *Edgecombe* to Cocos Island in search of the Lost Treasure of Lima. He added that he had some of the gems his uncle brought back from the voyage.

Hutchings's knowledge of the Cocos Island events came from three sources, which he listed:

1. Letters from his uncle William Boig Jr. written to his sister, who was Hutchings's mother.

2. The extracts taken from the logbook of the *Edgecombe* by his uncle, William Boig Jr.

3. The traditions within the Boig family.

The story of Long John Silver and *Treasure Island* is one of the most famous sagas of the sea, and Robert Louis Stevenson's novel has sold tens of millions of copies around the world.

In recent years, writers and researchers on several continents claim Stevenson based his story on Captain John Keating and that the real Treasure Island was Cocos Island, a UNESCO World Heritage Site today owned by Costa Rica.

Tourist brochures in Costa Rica boast of the Stevenson connection, and international film makers, scientists, authors, historians, and academics agree it is most likely very true. Film maker and scientist Dr. Ina Knobloch brought her production crew to St. John's in 2004 to film the local haunts of Captain John Keating. Other writers and filmmakers followed. There is also the fact that, over the past hundred years, dozens of books have been published referring to the role of Captains John Keating and Billy Boig in finding the hidden treasures on Cocos Island.

THE *EDGECOMBE* EXPEDITION SAILS OUT OF ST. JOHN'S HARBOUR

With the cargo of a half-load of dried fish stored on board and adequate supplies for the adventure that lay ahead, the *Edgecombe*, Stevenson's *Hispaniola*, set sail on January 25, 1841, from the wharf in front of the Customs House, site of today's War Memorial in St. John's. Fortunately, it was a clear winter's day, and the harbour had not yet become blocked with ice. Among those waving a farewell from the wharf was Keating's first wife, Elizabeth, and his only child, ten-year-old Margaret.

Keating and Boig had done their best to keep the expedition secret. Not even the crew had been told of the real purpose and destination of the *Edgecombe*. Adding to the secrecy of the adventure was the fact that the brig was to wait at Rio de Janeiro for the arrival of a stranger. Had the weather been favourable, this meeting would have taken place on schedule. The same gale-force winds along the coast of South America that slowed the progress of the *Edgecombe* delayed the arrival of the mysterious stranger from Liverpool, England. Finally, after a lapse of six weeks, the weather improved, and the vessel from Liverpool arrived.

The long delay in the arrival of the man from Smith & Irwin, the financial backers of the expedition, likely aroused some suspicion among the crew. Why was another person needed? After all, they had a full crew and three captains on board. Boig and Keating, however, remembering their agreement with Smith & Irwin, knew only too well the purpose of the stranger about to join their expedition. The man, identified in records only as Captain Gault, arrived after the storm had ended and presented his papers to Boig and Keating when he boarded the *Edgecombe*. With the addition of Captain Gault, the vessel now had four captains. The fourth captain, identified in *Lloyds Shipping Records* simply as Captain Briz, took charge of the ship from Rio de Janeiro to the Falklands, and there transferred to another ship. It wasn't unusual for two or more captains to be on the same ship in those days. Ships' voyages would often be for long periods and would have a series of captains in charge before the ship returned to its home port. Sometimes, captains would simply change ships in a foreign port.

Meanwhile, as far as the citizens of St. John's were concerned, the *Edgecombe* was on a routine trip to deliver a cargo of fish to Rio de Janeiro. We now know Boig and Keating had actually agreed to take only half a load of fish from Job Brothers, in St. John's, to Brazil. This enabled them to conceal the true nature of the adventure, and it also provided them with some extra money towards financing the hunt for treasure. While the St. John's newspapers noted the *Edgecombe*'s voyage to Brazil with a cargo of fish, it took a page-by-page review of *Lloyds Shipping Records* to confirm the real purpose of the mission.

When the Edgecombe sailed from Rio, instead of turning north to return to Newfoundland, it turned south and headed around the Horn. Following the Lloyds records, combined with information from descendants of Captain William Boig, I was able to confirm that the *Edgecombe* stopped over at the Falkland Islands and then went on to its final destination, Cocos Island on June 18, 1841. When the *Edgecombe* sailed within view of Cocos Island, the first thing the men would have noticed would be the highest peak, Mount Iglesias, sometimes called Observation Point, which usually at that time of year had a grey cloud surrounding its peak. Stevenson's *Treasure Island* had its own Mount Iglesias. It was called Spy Glass Hill. June was not an ideal time to recover treasure from the island due to the commencement of the rainy season; it rains on Cocos Island every day from May until November.

Captains Boig and Keating chose to go ashore to scout the area first, while Captain Gault remained on board to control the crew. The two treasure seekers had studied the map, procured from a man named Thompson in return for a life-saving favour, and knew well the instructions that accompanied it. Having viewed the jungle-covered island, and experiencing the heavy rainfall, they felt it would be a major challenge to locate the treasure and remove it, particularly since it reportedly took ten long boats just to bring the Lima part of the treasure trove ashore.

The two men made their way through the jungle growth and followed Thompson's instructions closely. They were amazed that it had led them so quickly to the treasure cave. Captain Keating estimated the measurements of the cave to be from twelve- to fifteen-feet square. Boig was overcome with the sudden glitter from the treasure and believed the cave was gleaming with a strange and terrifying light. Once inside, the two men took account of the mass of wealth. It contained bars of gold and silver, and sacks of coins. The sacks were stamped with the official mark of the Bank of Lima, and bound up at the mouth with strips of hide. Some had burst, or had worn through, and a stream of gold coins poured from the canvas.

The treasure contained many beautiful church ornaments, a number of golden crucifixes and chalices; among the trove was a statue of the Madonna in solid gold. This item weighed 750 pounds and was so heavy that Keating and Boig together could not lift it, but could only push it along the floor of the cave. Once they regained their composure, Keating suggested they not tell Gault of their discovery. The two feared for their lives if the crew were to witness the sheer size of the treasure. Boig agreed, and they decided to come back later with a crew of men they could trust, and with whom they would share their newfound wealth.

Boig and Keating filled their pockets with gold coins and concealed two small sacks of jewels on their persons, which they brought back and hid on the *Edgecombe*. Once back on ship, they informed Captain Gault that it would be very difficult to find the treasure. Gault, seeing the excitement in their expressions, which they could not conceal, became convinced that they had indeed found the Lost Treasure of Lima and were not about to share it.

Captain Gault called the crew together and informed them of the treasure on the island and shouted, "Lads, we are going to share this stuff with these fellows!"

The crew threatened mutiny if the captains refused to give each man an equal share. Keating reminded them that the people who financed the expedition had the right to reap the chief part of the golden harvest, and suggested that all the crew members would receive a substantial reward.

This further angered the sailors who shouted, "The stuff is ours, and we are going to have it!" Consumed with greed, the crew then went ashore in hopes of finding the treasure.

Keating feared they had a mutiny brewing and reproached Gault for causing the problem. Captain Gault claimed it was better the sailors should mutiny before they knew the location of the treasure, rather than after the treasure had been brought on board. This was obviously true. The three captains tried to formulate a plan to avoid mutiny. When the men returned and demanded to know where the treasure had been buried, Boig convinced them he and the other captains were willing to share, but in order to do it correctly and guarantee each a fair amount, they would need to go to the British consul in nearby Panama and draw up an agreement. By this time the men were drunk, and after agreeing to the proposal, soon fell into a deep sleep.

KEATING VAMOOSES HOME

Meanwhile, Keating took his belongings and the loot he and Boig had recovered from the treasure cave, and quietly slipped into Panama. From there he made it overland to the Atlantic coast where he signed on a ship, and worked his passage back to Newfoundland. In an account of his adventure, which he wrote in 1878, Keating said:

> In Panama, I hired two mules and a guide to go across the Isthmus. The *Edgecombe* then, in charge of Captain Gault, sailed for the Pearl Islands for a load of shells. I drew a rough sketch of the island [Cocos Island] while there, as there was no chart in my time. I stated where we anchored, and where on Cocos Island, treasure was buried. I sold the gold from the treasure in St. John's for 1300 pounds sterling.

Keating's hiring of two mules suggests that perhaps the treasure he brought back was more considerable than he later claimed. Some believed Keating brought back more of the treasure than indicated in the several statements made over his lifetime. He likely did not reveal his real take from the Lima Treasure to any person because Keating was a man who mistrusted others. Rupert Furneaux, in his book *The Great Treasure Hunts*, speculated that the full value of the treasure recovered in 1841 by Keating was between $7,000 and $110,000. Charles Driscoll, in *Doubloons*, estimated that Keating brought back $15,000 in gold. At the time, even a few thousand dollars would have been a considerable amount. In those days, a seaman earned eleven dollars per month, and a judge about seven hundred dollars a year.

Two people who may have helped Keating convert the gold to money, in 1841 and 1845, were a Newfoundland industrialist and politician, Charles Fox Bennett, and a Harbour Grace merchant, Robert Trapnell, whose family later entered the jeweler business in Newfoundland. Trapnell was a close friend of Captain Keating, and served as best man at Keating's second marriage in 1871. The Trapnells of Harbour Grace operated a business importing lumber and exporting fish. Keating had worked for Bennett both as a captain and as a ship's carpenter. Bennett operated a shipbuilding yard on Water Street where the post office is located today, and a brewery on Sudbury Street. Both properties were leased by Bennett from one Johanna Keating.[1]

ENTER CAPTAIN NICK FITZGERALD

Captain Nick Fitzgerald's death notice was carried in *The Evening Telegram* on May 31, 1906, the same day he had

[1] The 1884 Last Will and Testament of Johanna Keating.

died. The message was telegraphed to the city, and because of Fitzgerald's prominence in Newfoundland, it was published on the front page that same day:

> Nicholas Fitzgerald died this morning at 6:00 a.m. after ten days illness. He was 68 years old, and carried on the fishery business the greater part of his life. His death was due to bronchitis. He left a wife, a son and three daughters. Captain Fitzgerald was better-known inside Newfoundland as a successful fishing Captain whose views on the resource were often sought and welcomed by authorities. In the death of Nicholas Fitzgerald, Harbour Grace loses one of its most prominent citizens, and the country a man of wide knowledge and extensive experience in the staple industry of our country. At an early age he took up a seafaring life, and for many years followed deep sea voyages sailing out of this port (St. John's) and Harbour Grace. Having tired of seafaring life, he settled down in the prosecution of the fishery. He devoted special attention to the herring industry in which he was the most successful of any who followed this industry on the Labrador. Here for years he advanced a better cure, and publicly expressed his opinion that more attention to the curing and packaging of our herring would make it a profitable industry.

When the story broke internationally of Captain Fitzgerald's involvement in Cocos Island, and its role in Robert Louis Stevenson's *Treasure Island*, the Captain's papers and documents were sought by writers and treasure hunters from many countries.

The former Admiral Palliser of the British Navy and Count Herve de Montmorency launched their own expedition to Cocos Island in 1896 using Fitzgerald's knowledge of where to locate the allegedly massive treasure. How Captain Nicholas Fitzgerald obtained that secret was revealed in the book Montmorency wrote about his expedition, entitled *On the Track of Treasure*. Fitzgerald had shared with the Count his own intriguing tale of entering the world of Cocos Island treasure hunters.

According to Montmorency:

> Captain Fitzgerald recalled that during late February 1868, the George T. Fog, a fishing-schooner, sailing off the coast of western Newfoundland was broken by heavy ice, and became waterlogged. Captain Nicholas Fitzgerald, of Harbour Grace, owner of the schooner, was aware of the conditions in the villages along the coast and decided to stay with his vessel as long as he could. Several other ships were wrecked at the same time, and some of the crews made their way across the ice to the community of Codroy near Port aux Basque. Despite the fact that residents of that community were short on provisions, they welcomed the shipwrecked sailors. Ice-floes, coming down from Labrador, had blocked western communities and made it impossible for supply vessels to bring them much needed provisions.
>
> Fitzgerald was about twenty miles off the coast and managed to man his vessel for almost two weeks. Fortunately, a barque came by just as Captain Fitzgerald was about to give orders to abandon ship, and success-fully rescued the Captain and crew and all their

provisions. The barque found an opening in the ice-floes which enabled it to sail straight into Codroy. Fitzgerald and his crew unloaded their provisions and shared them with the inhabitants and other shipwrecked sailors.

Captain Fitzgerald's generosity in sharing his food and whatever clothing and blankets he was able to gather went a long way in easing the burden the others stranded there were suffering through.

He came across a dilapidated old shack where several wrecked sailors were perishing before his eyes. The floor was caked with ice and the openings in the roof allowed the wind and snow in. He noticed one man far more distressed than the others. Captain Fitzgerald took pity on him, and had him carried to a room which he had engaged for himself in the village.

After putting the stranger in his bed, Fitzgerald attended and watched over him with such success that he brought him through his illness.

Then the stranger revealed to Fitzgerald a secret he had not shared with any other living person:

I've lived long, and I've never met real kindness before. In return for what you've done for me, I'll put you in the way of becoming a rich man, if you'll accept my offer. I am Keating; the men folks call me Keating of the Cocos Island Treasure. It's true that I've been to the island twice and brought treasure away with me. I can go again, and I can take you with me, if I recover. In case I do not, I will give you my secret now. Only you must promise me first that if I live, you will not reveal to anyone what I'm going to tell you, and that you'll go with me to Cocos Island and help me to remove the treasure you shall share.

The name Keating, and the enchantment and mystery attached to it, were known to Captain Fitzgerald. The two men drew up a rough agreement, which both signed. He didn't tell his story all at once, but in parts, as his strength permitted. By the time he finished he had revealed more, perhaps, than he had intended, including the details of the suspicious death of Keating's partner, William Boig.

When Keating recovered, he reminded Fitzgerald of their contract and expressed a wish to begin planning for their expedition to Cocos Island. By this time Fitzgerald had second thoughts.

Montmorency described Fitzgerald's fearful reaction and wrote:

> The closer his acquaintance with Keating, the less inclined was the old sailor to venture on any undertaking in which he might share the fate of Captain Boig. He was, however, an honest man, and he respected his part of the bargain with Keating, which compelled him to preserve the latter's secret during his lifetime.

FIRST WOMAN TO LEAD EXPEDITION TO COCOS ISLAND

During August 1896, a Newfoundland woman was making

news from California to New York for her plans to carry out an expedition to retrieve a massive hidden treasure buried on Cocos Island. She confidently told reporters, "I will have no problems finding it because my late husband, Captain John Keating, gave me the map and the directions to follow to go straight to the treasure cave."

The *New York Times* reprinted the article published in a California newspaper *The Journal*. A few days later, the story appeared in the *Daily News* at St. John's. The following is a copy of that feature.

CAPE BRETON WOMAN'S SEARCH FOR TREASURE[2]

Brave Mrs. James Brennan of North Sydney, formerly wife of Captain John Keating of Newfoundland, is organizing an expedition to a little shell of a volcanic rock, five hundred miles south west of Panama, to recover gold and silver buried there half a century ago. New York, July 29– *The Journal* says, "Mrs. James Brennan of North Sydney, Nova Scotia, has been for the past ten days in Oakland, Cal., where she is super-intending the fitting out of thee schooner *Meridian*, which had been chartered for her by a San Francisco ship agent before she left her home in the province. When the schooner is ready for sea Mrs. Brennan will occupy the cabin, and the *Meridian* will be at her disposal for a period of three months, with an option of a further period of six months. The *Meridian* is not a yacht. Mrs. Brennan is not a yachtswoman. She has never been at sea in her life, and although she has been

[2] Catherine (Woods) Brennan was from St. John's, where she met and married Keating of the Cocos. After his death, she married a James Brennan, another Newfoundlander, at Cape Breton.

married to two different seafaring men, and outlived them both, she is a demure little old lady, who looks as if she had lived an old maid's life in a quiet country village, and never seen any one more adventurous than the country parson.

And yet Mrs. Brennan is going to try to effect a landing on Cocos Island, a little shell of volcanic rock about five hundred miles south-west of Panama, an island inhabited only by herds of goats and known only as having been at one time a watering place for south sea whalers. Mrs. Brennan is going there to find some treasure, which she knows was there fifty years ago, and which she has every reason to believe has not since been removed.

The old lady has no reason for making any mystery about her plans, except of course as to the precise spot on the island in which the treasure lies, as it is a matter of common knowledge that there is a great deal of gold hidden somewhere on the island, and extensive excavations have from time to time been made by searchers, who hoped that chance would guide them to the cache, of which Mrs. Brennan knows the exact location.

Most expeditions in search of treasure are organized by mere dreamers and enthusiasts, and not a few of them by skillful swindlers. But Mrs. Brennan, who is investing no money but her own in the venture, certainly seems to be a woman of strong common sense and the story of the treasure as she herself tells it, is very much more simple and direct than are the narratives which form the stock in trade of the common run of adventurers.

Mrs. Brennan was married for the first time in 1848 to John Keating of St. John's, Newfoundland, who died in 1882. Before he died he gave her a marked map of the island and told her the story of his own connection with the treasure. In June 1835, Keating was ship's carpenter of the *Rose Blanche* of St. John's then loading in Rio Janeiro for home. [No Nfld. Ship by that name and shipping records show 1841 the date of 1st expedition.] A man who looked like a tramp came out from behind a pile of boards on the wharf one morning and asked Keating if the *Rose Blanche* would like to ship another hand.

He was, he said, an able seaman, and had been trying to do some trading on his own account in the Yguassu country, but had been robbed and made his way to the coast with great difficulty. Keating at once assumed that the man was a deserter from some other ship, if nothing worse, but as two of the crew of the *Rose Blanche* had run away at Porto Seguro, he told the man to wait until Captain Humphries came on board. He gave Thompson, as the stranger called himself, something to eat, and later in the day found the captain very glad to add one to his depleted complement.

The *Rose Blanche* sailed the next day, and as she made her northing trip Thompson, who had contracted a fever, while tramping down to the coast, was compelled to take to his berth. He was a good-natured young fellow, did what he could for the sick man, who made loud protestations of his gratitude and talked vaguely about a great reward which Keating might hope to reap for his kindness. When the *Rose Blanche* reached St. John's, Thompson said he would like to find board in some quiet place where he could regain his strength before going to sea again, and Keating said his mother would be glad to take in any well-conducted man. Upon this Thompson said he was not as poor as he looked and he showed Keating some old gold pieces, which he carried in a belt concealed beneath his tattered clothing.

At Mrs. Keating's, Thompson grew suddenly worse, and it was when he was about to die that he told John Keating the story and gave to John Keating the map, which Keating in turn, when it came his time to die communicated to his wife. The story as Thompson told it began with the voyage of the schooner, *Mary Dear*, commanded by Captain William Thompson, which sailed from Lima on the 23rd of November 1820, bound for the Galapagos Islands, under charter to the Spanish government which was then at war with the revolted colony of Peru. The *Mary Dear*, although Captain Thompson was acting as sailing master, was under the control of a young Spanish naval officer, who was accompanied by a guard of twelve marines disappeared from the narrative Mrs. Brennan says she does not know why.

Apparently, Thompson slurred over this part of what he told Keating. At any rate, when the lawfully constituted authorities vanished from the narrative, there appear six chests of inestimable treasure, which it had no doubt intended to conceal on one of the Galapagos Islands, and these Thompson and his crew buried on Cocos Island. In the course of the long continued struggle between the Spanish and the Peruvian colonists any records or documents bearing on the case would undoubtedly have been lost, and it is impossible to say now whether the gold belonged to the Spanish Government or to some private citizens who had procured a naval guard to superintend its transportation to the Galapagos Islands and its concealment there. In either case it would now be impossible for the original owners to prove their property and the present government, will not, Mrs. Brennan thinks, give her any trouble. It is a strange undertaking for a respectable little old lady, with side combs and gray curls, and gold-bowed spectacles, this search for buried gold.

But if there are blood stains on the bags which hold the coins or skulls of murdered men lying hidden with the brass-bound chests, Mrs. Brennan has nothing to do with the lawless past of which no witnesses remain. She wants the money if she can get it as earnestly and as simply as she wants the money for the crop of potatoes on her little farm three miles from North Sydney, Nova Scotia. And if it is to be gotten she will get it.

Though some of the information provided in the brief article is inaccurate (ship names, dates), Mrs. Brennan's interview with the California press, which was also published in New York, provided fodder for treasure enthusiasts and writers and was the cause of many expeditions in search of the treasure sailing into the wrong bay.

Mrs. James Brennan was originally Catherine Woods, a member of the Woods family of merchants who lived in a large house on Temperance Street at the corner of Water Street. When Captain John Keating returned with treasure from Cocos Island in 1841 and openly boasted about it, she became fascinated by him and his sudden wealth which he made no effort to hide.

A laneway ran behind the houses at Keating's Corner from Prescott Street to the site of today's War Memorial. In the darkness of night, young Catherine would slip into the laneway to peek into Keating's bedroom window to witness him examining his loot.

Captain Keating, along with his first wife and a daughter, lived at the corner of Prescott Street and Water Street, which became known as Keating's Corner. This was about a five minute walk from the Woods home. The captain's fame spread rapidly when townsfolk began referring to him as "Keating of the Cocos." He loved the title and was instrumental in its spread to other parts of Newfoundland.

Keating paid his bills with coins from the treasure. His landlord, James Barter, who lived at 9 Queen's Road, gleefully showed friends gold coins Keating used to pay his rent. A clerk at Ayre & Sons Department Store, on Water Street, a Mr. McKenzie, also kept a coin or two used by Keating of the Cocos to purchase items at the store. At the time of the old pirate's death in 1882, McKenzie still had a silver coin in his possession which he had gotten from him in the 1840s.

Keating's first wife and daughter passed away within a short period of each other due to contagious diseases, not uncommon at the time. They were buried in the family plot at Belvedere Cemetery in St. John's. By that time, Keating of the Cocos had made another visit to Cocos Island and returned with more of his pirate booty. Catherine flirted openly with the widower and wasted no time in accepting his proposal of marriage when offered. The two moved to the Codroy Valley where they opened a general store and purchased a boat to deliver mail along the west coast.

The real reason Mrs. Brennan's efforts to find the treasure failed stemmed from the fact that Captain Keating gave her, deliberately, false information. When stranded at Cod Roy Valley with Captain Nicholas Fitzgerald, he told him that he firmly believed that his wife and her brothers were going to kill him once they got the treasure map. He passed away at Keating's Corner in St. John's and left her the map he wanted her to have. Fitzgerald was given the real treasure map. Keating was buried in the Keating family plot at Belvedere Cemetery in 1882. His widow moved to Cape Breton, content that she now had the treasure map and without as much as having Keating's name placed on the grave's tombstone, which the captain had erected in memory of his first wife and child.

One of the greatest problems any serious researcher of the Lost Treasure of Lima and its connection to buried treasures on Cocos Island has in attempting to sort out fact from fiction. In my book *Treasure Island Revisited*, I faced that obstacle. However, when I found inconsistencies among books published on the subject over the past hundred years I questioned and pointed them out.

My biggest surprise was in discovering that the treasure of Lima was never stolen. In fact, Spanish troops had taken the Lima treasure and hid it in nearby hills. On the third day of the uprising in Peru, the troops brought the treasure back and stored it in the Fort at Callao, the port city of Lima.

The treasure that was stolen and buried on Cocos Island belonged to the Catholic Church. It had been stored for safety inside the Cathedral of Lima. The treasure was being shipped out of port for safety purposes when pirates, who were actually crewmen on the vessel, killed the guards and the priests. They changed course and brought the vessel to Cocos Island. They then buried it at three different locations on the island. What for more than a hundred years was referred to as The Lost Treasure of Lima was actually The Ecclesiastical Treasure.

At that stage in my research, I referred to it as it had become known in Newfoundland history as *The Cocos Island Treasure.*

THE ROBERT LOUIS STEVENSON CONNECTION

Robert Louis Stevenson's father was an engineer who built lighthouses along the Pacific Coast of South America. He was shipwrecked and managed to get ashore on Cocos Island where he lived for two years as a hermit. Stevenson's father was also a lighthouse builder on the Pacific Coast. Academic researchers tracing this man are close to proving that the real hermit of Cocos Island was actually the father of Robert Louis Stevenson. At the time Stevenson was lost there, the story of Captains John Keating and Billy Boig were already famous along the Pacific Coast and especially in San Francisco, where young Robert Louis Stevenson lived for a period and spent time in taverns listening to sailors tell of the great treasure Keating found. There is also the fact that, in that era, writers took real live characters and brought their stories to life in fictional accounts based on true stories. Robinson Crusoe and Horatio Hornblower are two examples of such a practice.

Treasure Island was initially called *The Sea Cook or Treasure Island*, and was first published in a magazine called *Young Folks* as a series of feature columns in which Stevenson used the pseudonym Captain Richard North. James Henderson, *Young Folks* editor, dropped *Sea Cook* and went with the title *Treasure Island*. It was later revised and published in book form in Europe and the United States.

The Stevenson connection to the Keating story was something that intrigued me. Although to describe Keating, Stevenson drew from the physical features of his friend and agent, William Henley, a burly one-legged man, the character that emerged as Long John Silver has multiple similarities to Newfoundland's Captain John Keating.

Both Silver and Keating had found the treasure on two occasions, and each took a small part of it home. Like Silver, Keating did not trust his wife and others. For example, it is believed by some that Keating murdered Captain William Boig, his friend and partner in the adventure.

Long John Silver was shrewd enough to outsmart his pirate friends and his wife, while Keating managed to outsmart his fellow captains, a partner, two crews, relatives, friends, and his wife.

In Stevenson's *Treasure Island*, Long John is associated with Captain Billy Bones, a name similar to Keating's friend Captain Billy Boig. No doubt the name of one of Washington Irving's characters, Billy Bones, came to mind when Stevenson was bringing Billy Boig into his tale of treasure and pirates.

Stevenson's story had young John Hawkins while Keating had young Billy Boig, who was in his late teens, and the son of Captain Billy Boig. Hawkins was haunted throughout his adult life by terrorizing memories of Long John Silver. Young Billy Boig had a lifetime of similar memories of Keating throwing Billy's father to sharks.

In Keating's story, Captain Thompson in the *Mary Dear* steals the Treasure of Lima and buries it at Cocos Island. In *Treasure Island* there is Captain Flint of the *Walrus* who steals the treasure and buries it on Treasure Island. Stevenson's map of Treasure Island bears much similarity to Cocos Island.

Stephenson's map has two small islands off the coast of the main island, while Cocos Island also has two small islands off its coast, which are called the Dos Amigos Islands. The map that Stevenson drew of Treasure Island for his son showed the island had only two "fine land-locked harbours, and a hill in the centre part marked, 'The Spy-glass.'"[3] Cocos Island has only two accessible harbours: Chatham Bay and Wafer Bay. Also, there is on Cocos Island a hill called Observation Hill.

[3] Robert Louis Stevenson, Treasure Island, edited by Wendy R. Katz (Edinburgh: Edinburgh UP, 1998) 43.

In Stevenson's work there is mention of Corso Castle. In the Lost Treasure of Lima story there is the Callao Castle.

Stevenson mentions the pirate Captain Davis, who we know had buried gold on Cocos Island.

The followers of Long John Silver turn on him and he seeks help from the doctor on the *Hispaniola*. When the *Edgecombe*'s crew mutinies at Cocos Island, Keating and Boig enlist the support of Captain Gault in quieting the mutiny.

Treasure Island had a hermit living on the island named Ben Gun. Cocos Island had its true-life Ben Gun in Augustus Gissler, who lived twenty years on the island searching for the hidden treasure.

In the end, both Long John Silver and John Keating escaped justice.

While Stevenson's papers do not include any specific mention of the Lima Treasure, or of Captain John Keating and his partner, Captain Billy Boig, it does contain what might be a clue to his real inspiration. Boig was not at all a common name, especially for a dog. Yet Stevenson had changed his pet Skye Terrier's name from Wattie to Boig. B-o-g-u-e[4] was the spelling used in early writings on Keating and Boig, and it was the spelling that Charles Driscoll used in his book *Doubloons*. The dog was known to be ill-tempered, and perhaps this trait reminded Stevenson of Keating's partner and victim Billy Boig.

[4] Hunter Davies, *The Teller of Tales: In Search of Robert Louis Stevenson* (London: Sinclair-Stevenson, 1994).

With so many similarities between the Lima Treasure story and *Treasure Island*, it is not surprising that writers, authors, and television documentaries have zeroed in on Cocos Island as the real Treasure Island, and the true story of The Lost Treasure of Lima as Stevenson's inspiration for *Treasure Island*.

Author Jack Fitzgerald (foreground) with Steward Fraser, a descendant of Captain William Boig. Some of the jewels recovered by Boig from The Lost Treasure of Lima are still in Fraser's possession. (Maurice Fitzgerald Photography)

CHAPTER NINETEEN

Shipwrecks, Adventures, and Disasters

～～～

SHIP OF DYNAMITE THREATENED ST. JOHN'S

A burning ship in St. John's Harbour on November 14, 1895, carried enough explosives to wipe out the hundreds of men, women, and children nearby and to cause major destruction of property along the St. John's Waterfront. The firemen willingly boarded the burning vessel thereby putting their lives in danger to prevent an even greater disaster.

The burning vessel was the *Aurora*, a famous whaler of the time. She was tied up at the Bowing Co. wharf on the south side of St. John's Harbour. Dozens of ships with hundreds of workers were either tied up nearby or anchored in the harbour. Not far from the wharves was the Southside Road residential area with dozens of families. Most of them were out watching the fire. The city had several fire stations. There was one at Southside Road, one in the west end, one in the centre, one in the east end.

Fire-alarm boxes were placed on poles strategically throughout the city. Each was connected to the fire-hall system. In case of fire, the public used these to call in the alarm.

The steamship *Aurora* was a 356-ton vessel and carried a crew of sixty men. She participated in the whale hunt in the summer of 1895 and had battled hurricane-force winds on her return to St. John's.

It was in November that the *Aurora*, while docked in St. John's Harbour, had the potential of being at the focal point of a major disaster. About six hundred pounds of dynamite and ten thousand rounds of ammunition were stored below deck. The families, workers in the area, and spectators who came over from the north side of the harbour had no knowledge of the treacherous cargo on the *Aurora*.

This drama on the harbour began when Second Officer Tom Walsh, standing on deck, noticed a trickling of smoke coming up the companion way. At first, he was not bothered by this, but in minutes the smoke began to bellow up the companion way. When he went to investigate, he found the cabin directly below full of smoke and the captain's room on the starboard side was engulfed in flames. Stored, not far from these flames, were the dynamite and ammunition.

Walsh alerted captain and crew, and a man was sent to call the alarm at fire-box 43 on Southside Road. While the crew tried to control the fire with what little resources they had, firemen at the West-End Station responded to the alarm. They hitched up their horses to the fire wagons, put on their suits, and in just six minutes were at White's Wharf, a couple of hundred feet west of Bowring's, and ready to do battle. This was as close as the firemen could get to Bowring's Wharf that day.

Although the central firemen were expected at any minute, Captain Dunn chose not to take a chance. He sent a man back to the West-End Fire Hall near Job Street. In a short time, he was back with a sufficient length of hosing. When Captain Dunn moved onto the deck of the *Aurora* to take full control of the fire-fighting effort, he was joined by firemen from central, the west end, and the south side.

The bellowing smoke and flames from the burning vessel were attracting spectators from all around St. John's. Some came by foot while others rowed across the harbour. The firemen knew the *Aurora* was carrying explosives and were aware of the potential for disaster. Regardless, Captain Dunn, accompanied by Sgt. Daniel Mulrooney and Fire-Constable Reardon, risked their lives to go below deck and into the cabin where but a single wall separated the fire from the explosives. They remained steadfast in position until the fire was out and the threat to the public ended.

The next day, the *Daily News* commented on the heroic deed, "They were perfectly aware that at any moment a terrible explosion might occur; that the cabin, in fact might prove their grave, but duty called and a true fireman knows no fear in such a case."

An eye-witness in a letter to the *Daily News* asked, "What

would have been the result had that quantity of powder exploded. Can anyone measure the possible destruction of life and property likely to have accrued therefrom?" The writer suggested the men be recognized for their outstanding display of courage in risking their lives to bring the fire under control and to avoid certain disaster in St. John's Harbour.

The men were honoured within days by Sir Edgar Bowring, and two years later awarded medals. Sir Edgar Bowring sent a cheque for one hundred dollars to Inspector-General J.R. McCowan for the men "as a slight recognition of the valuable services rendered by the Fire Brigade in so promptly suppressing the fire which broke out on the *Aurora*." In response to this gift, Inspector-General McCowan replied, "I feel proud of being in command of such men who, notwithstanding the knowledge of the extreme danger of the position in which they worked, yet performed their duty fearlessly because it was their duty." The danger was even greater than first thought because there were other vessels in the harbour carrying explosives.

Governor Murray was instrumental in having the men awarded medals in recognition for their heroism in fighting that fire. In 1897, in honour of Queen Victoria's Diamond Jubilee, the awards were presented to the following men: Inspector-General McGowan, District Chief Dunn, and Fire Constable John Reardon received the Silver-Star; Sergeant Daniel Mulrooney and Fire Constable James Howard, received the Silver Medal for conspicuous gallantry and bravery.

NEWFOUNDLAND'S *MARIE CELESTE*

The strange fate of the brig *Resolven* in Newfoundland coastal waters in 1884 remains a mystery to this day and was described in the 1920s by journalist Arthur Ainsworth of London as being in the same class as the *Marie Celeste*. A dark cloud seemed to hang over the *Resolven*, and there was speculation it was a cursed ship. From the day in August 1884, when news of the ship's strange experience first broke, to the day it was lost in a shipwreck four years later, bad luck seemed to follow it.

The 143-ton *Resolven* was built in Nova Scotia of softwood, and carried a crew of six men. Her captain was E. James, and it hailed from Aberystwyth. The *Resolven* arrived at Harbour Grace on July 14, 1884, with a cargo for John Munn & Co. Ltd. and was under charter to proceed to Labrador to take a cargo of fish to the Mediterranean. She departed Harbour Grace on August 27 and carried four passengers, who were going to Labrador to work at trimming herring for John Munn & Co. Ltd. The passengers were Doug Taylor and Bernard Coldford of Carbonear; Edward Keefe of Harbour Grace; and Bill Bennett of Bell Island.

Soon after starting the voyage to Labrador, the *Resolven* experienced a tragedy the cause of which has remained a mystery since that time. By August 29, just two days after departing, word was received in Harbour Grace that the ship had run into trouble on the Atlantic and was in tow to Catalina by the HMS *Mallard*. Shipwreck and tragedy were not unknown to Newfoundlanders, but when people heard the story of the *Resolven*, it sent chills up the spine of many

Newfoundlanders and attracted international attention.

The vessel had been found deserted at the mouth of Trinity Bay. A rescue party could find no sign of life on board, and a search of the area failed to turn up any trace of the crew, passengers, or anything that would give even the slightest hint of what the *Resolven* had encountered.

The mystery was heightened by the discovery that the sails were set, a fire was alight in the galley, and no wreckage or disorder was to be seen. The only thing out of place was the yardarm, which was broken and some ropes left dangling.

One discovery that gave them hope was that the lifeboat was missing. From all appearances, the crew and passengers had left in a hurry to escape some kind of imminent danger. Not a trace of the men or the missing lifeboat was ever found.

AMAZING ATLANTIC SEALERS RACE

The Newfoundland-built *Fanny Bloomer* was one of the most successful sealing ships of the nineteenth century. During that era, she was closely identified with the famous Southern-Shore sea-faring family, the Jackmans of Renews. When Captain Thomas Jackman was injured on the *Fanny Bloomer* by a swinging tiller, his son, William, took command. It was his first command, and he was a natural. When Bowring Brother's made him a lucrative offer to take command of the *Sally Ann*, he accepted, and his brother, Captain Arthur Jackman, took command of the *Fanny Bloomer*. Captain Arthur became one of the most successful sealing captains of Newfoundland history.

The *Fanny Bloomer* and another Newfoundland vessel, the *Mary Belle*, earned notoriety not only as great sealing ships, but for an impromptu race across the North Atlantic during the winter of 1856-1857. This remarkable story began mid-December 1856. The *Fanny Bloomer* was under the command of Captain John Flynn, and the *Mary Belle* was under the command of Captain James Day, a former member of the Newfoundland Legislature for St. John's West.

The two ships were being towed down the Mersey in England by the same tug boat when Captain Day shouted to Captain Flynn, "I'll bet you twenty-five pounds I'll be in St. John's before you."

"I can't bet you that much, because I have no money to pay you only out of my wages, but I'll bet ten pounds," answered Captain Flynn.

The race was on. Both crews felt it would add excitement to the long and often treacherous return trip across the Atlantic. Side by side, the *Fanny Bloomer* and *Mary Belle* sailed down Saint George's Channel, in England, keeping each other in sight for several days. It wasn't smooth sailing and wind and rain storms quickly separated the two rivals. Yet, although out of sight of each other, each captain never forgot he was in a race. By mid-way, they were again in sight of each other, and signals were sent back and forth between the ships. Once again, the oceans tossed and they lost sight of each other until they neared land at which time they were about three-quarters of a mile apart.

At this point, the ships were between Bay Bulls and Petty Harbour. When they caught sight of each other, the competitiveness of the crews showed. On went studding sails and every inch of canvas was hoisted and respective house flags (Bowring's and Tessier's) were posted to the foremast head, as signal to Cape Spear. The ships passed the cape as they had started in England, with less than a hundred yards separating them. Finally, after a thirty-eight day crossing, they passed through the Narrows of St. John's Harbour. The harbour-pilot boarded Captain Day's vessel first because she was to the windward of the *Fanny Bloomer*. He then boarded the *Fanny Bloomer*. The ships had entered the Narrows at the same time, and the race was declared a draw. The two ships ended the race as they started, side by side. This was hailed as a remarkable feat, and the story became one of Newfoundland's many colourful tales of the sea.

In 1870, Captain Arthur Jackman took a cargo of seal-oil and skins to Liverpool in the *Fanny Bloomer*. It was sold there and spent the remainder of its years carrying coal between Wales and Waterford, Ireland.

STRANGE FORCE AT WORK

Was a supernatural phenomenon involved in the rescue of the *Orion* near Bell Island in 1867, or were the strange circumstances leading up to that rescue purely coincidental? Whatever took place, it was responsible for saving five men from freezing or starving to death on a shipwrecked vessel.

Captain James Keefe and Captain Nicholas Fitzgerald were best friends. During October 1867, one of them was fighting for survival on the Atlantic and the other was mysteriously drawn towards him by a compelling but unexplained force.

This remarkable tale of the sea started on October 9, 1867, during a heavy wind storm that struck Corbett's Harbour, Labrador. Captain James Keefe of the brigantine *Orion*, his brother, and four crew members struggled to put out line when the near hurricane-force winds drove the vessel from her moorings.

Before reaching the open sea, the *Orion* struck Coveyduck Island at the harbour's mouth and hung there for a short while. One of the crew managed to jump from the jib boom and succeeded in reaching dry land. When the others attempted to follow, the badly broken vessel had filled with so much water that only the forward part remained above water. The *Orion* drifted south for four days and, to survive, the men had to tie themselves to the rigging. To obtain food and liquids, one man at a time would unleash himself to get supplies to feed the others. The only food on the vessel was a supply of dry flour and some fat pork that had been stored in the forecastle, the only dry place left on the *Orion*.

On October 13, with Captain Keefe wondering how much longer he and his crew could survive, his friend, Captain Nicholas Fitzgerald,[1] was departing Snug Harbour, Labrador, on a return trip to Harbour Grace. His schooner, the *George H. Fogg*, was considered the fastest vessel in the country. From the start of the trip, Captain Fitzgerald was tormented by something, but had no idea what was bothering him. He felt compelled to change his course and had no explanation to offer his men when he suddenly altered the ship's course by two points. The crew members were puzzled by the change and Fitzgerald had no reason

---

[1] This was the same Captain Nicholas Fitzgerald who was given the map to the Lost Treasure of Lima by Captain John Keating.

other than he felt compelled to take this action.

Then, about twenty miles east of Bell Island, Captain Fitzgerald spied a wreck and as he approached it, he recognized it as the *Orion* carrying his friend, Captain Keefe. Fitzgerald and his men quickly rescued Keefe and his crew and provided warm blankets, food, and refreshments. A day later, they were all back at Harbour Grace and celebrated their rescue at Captain Fitzgerald's home.

ICEBERG NINE MILES LONG

During April 1892, the *Miranda*, an ore boat, was on a trip from New York to Pilley's Island in Notre Dame Bay to take on a load of copper. By the time the ship arrived at her destination, the captain and crew had an amazing story to tell. They had passed by an iceberg, but not just any iceberg! This iceberg was nine miles long and all in one piece. It reared itself 200 feet above the surface of the water and was 1000 yards wide. The 200-feet height of the iceberg gives an idea of just how big this mountain of ice measured because icebergs are known to be nine-tenths under the water. In this case, the berg would have been 1800 feet, or 300 fathoms below the surface.

The *Miranda* took exactly forty-eight minutes, travelling her normal speed, to steam past the island-mountain of ice. According to newspaper reports, the giant berg later drifted south to the Grand Banks where it broke off into a dozen pieces, each of which made very large icebergs.

THE RAISIN SHIP

The Raisin Ship was known throughout Newfoundland for decades and nostalgically recalled because of its connection to Newfoundlanders' penchant for figgy-duff pudding. The *Caroline Brown*, which became famous in Newfoundland as the Raisin Ship, was a United States-based vessel carrying a cargo of raisins in bulk from Greece to the United States. In Atlantic waters near Newfoundland, it became encircled by a raging winter storm and was abandoned by its captain and crew. Fortunately, they were rescued the next day after drifting a long distance south of their abandoned ship.

The *Caroline Brown* survived the storm and was found by Captain John Kennedy of Carbonear, who took the prize in tow to St. John's. Word rapidly spread throughout the capital city of the enormous cargo of raisins on the rescued ship tied up in the harbour. Small kids went away with pockets full of raisins and much more found its way into kitchen ovens as part of a figgy-duff.

The abundance of raisins in the city prompted the public to refer to the *Caroline Brown* as the Raisin Ship, and the name stuck. Stories of the Raisin Ship and the figgy-duffs spread to Conception Bay. The vessel was purchased by John Munn & Co. Ltd. and taken to Carbonear with a half-cargo of raisins still aboard. It didn't take long for the women and children of the community to seek out a share of the raisins. Munn's sold them for three cents a pound, but no child was refused a handful of the fruit. Never in Newfoundland's history had so much figgy-duff been eaten by so many people in one season.

AFTER WORST STORM AT SEA, THE ENGLISH REFUSED TO HELP NEWFOUNDLANDERS

Not all shipwrecks bring out the best in people. For example, when the *Blanche*, owned by Job & Co. of St. John's, was abandoned and sunk in the Atlantic, the survivors were not well treated by at least some residents of Dover, England. The adventure of the *Blanche* began on December 7, 1904, when it set sail from St. John's with a cargo of salt cod for Brazil. Captain William Sinclair was in command of the crew of seven men: J. Newhook, the mate; J. Caldwell, the boatswain; and G. Shave, T. Smith, T. Walsh, J. Glynn, and T. Williams as crewmen.

Rarely has a ship encountered as many winter storms on the North Atlantic as the *Blanche* experienced in its terrorizing voyage that year. From the day the *Blanche* sailed out the Narrows of St. John's Harbour, it fought high winds. As the days went by, these winds were replaced by blinding snow storms, blizzards, and hurricanes. Captain Sinclair and his crew were experienced seamen who were forced to use all their skills and endurance not only to keep the ship afloat, but to keep themselves alive.

During a blizzard, the foresail bust, and the vessel was put under small reaching canvas. When a hurricane hit, the jibs and headgear were blown away. The hurricane worsened and throughout the night, mountainous waves washed over the *Blanche*. These took with them the mizzen, and the fore gaff topsails were torn to ribbons. While the ship was being dismantled around them, the crew fought against the elements: the winds, gigantic waves, and freezing sprays;

snow pellets like sand cut their skin. A deep hard frost threatened their survival.

Several lulls in the storm allowed the captain and crew some time to attempt repairs. When the big hurricane they expected hit, quicker than anticipated, they were not prepared. None of the crew, including the captain, had ever experienced a storm like it. In the midst of the hurricane, the *Blanche* turned over on its side and the men felt the end was near. Nevertheless, they were determined to fight to the best of their ability to the end, and they worked throughout the night to cut away the foremast in hopes of righting the ship. By next morning, with the men near exhaustion, their efforts and prayers were answered. The ship righted itself.

But their struggle was not yet over. Sometimes they fought the elements waist-deep in water. They cut away the spars and the jib-boom until the *Blanche* resembled a floating log. Meanwhile, the lifeboat had washed away in the storm. To keep the vessel afloat, they now had to jettison 300 barrels of cargo. Another 300 barrels had been lost into the sea when the hold broke open after being smashed by a mountainous wave.

Captain Sinclair told the men their only hope of survival was to make it to the major shipping lane and hope for rescue. On December 22, at 10:00 a.m., the *Blanche* was spotted by Captain J. Christianson in the SS *Seveland* which was sailing from Sweden to Bremen, Virginia. The Swede sent a lifeboat to rescue the Newfoundlanders.

The courageous Newfoundland crew had survived a three-week battle with the worst of Atlantic storms. The captain knew there was one last duty to perform before abandoning ship. He realized that if he left the ship afloat it would remain as a danger to shipping in the area. He decided to sink the *Blanche* by removing its hatches so it would fill with water and sink. After performing this last duty, Captain Sinclair boarded the lifeboat and was taken with his crew to the safety of the *Seveland*.

Nine days later, the rescue vessel came across a Scottish pilot off Dungeness, but he flatly refused to take the survivors to port. Off the coast of Dover, another pilot vessel was encountered, and this time the pilot demanded payment of one pound sterling, per man, to take the Newfoundlanders to port. This angered the Swedish captain, and an angry exchange of words erupted that could have resulted in violence if the English had been closer. Finally, the captain chose to deliver the survivors himself. Despite the captain's efforts, the board of trade at Dover refused to take charge of the men as their contracts read that they were to be paid off in Liverpool.

Finally, the Liverpool Shipwrecked Marines Society took charge of the survivors, and on New Year's Day sent them to Liverpool. By mid-January, the captain and crew of the *Blanche* were at home in Newfoundland. They had all experienced a life-threatening challenge they had never before dreamed of nor would they want to again.

MYSTERY DISAPPEARANCE OF THE *SOUTHERN CROSS*

The tragic story of the *Newfoundland* disaster of 1914, with its loss of seventy-eight sealers, was making headlines across Newfoundland. And with public attention focused on that disaster, an even greater tragedy had occurred, but remained unknown for days. The *Southern Cross*, with a crew of 173 men and a bumper cargo of seal pelts, had disappeared, leaving no trace as to what tragic circumstances had overtaken it. Almost one hundred years have passed since its disappearance, and still no evidence has surfaced to shed light on this, the greatest mystery of all Newfoundland marine disasters.

The *Southern Cross*, under the command of Captain John Clarke, sailed from St. John's on March 12, 1914, heading for the annual Gulf-seal hunt. Other vessels at the Gulf at the time were the *Terra Nova*, *Neptune*, *Eric*, *Viking*, and *Seal*. It was a practice at the time for ships to telegraph regular progress reports to St. John's where they were posted outside the general post office on Water Street. After 'tea' each day, crowds would gather outside the GPO to read the latest news on the sealing fleet.

For some unexplained reason, the *Southern Cross* failed to supply any direct progress messages. Instead, other ships relayed progress reports from the *Southern Cross* to St. John's. This suggested that either the vessel had no telegraph machine, or else, if it had one, it had broken down.

On March 30, those with loved ones on the *Southern Cross* were elated by a message which they believed referred to the ship. The message read, "Steamer passing out of the gulf, distant; supposed to be the *Southern Cross* or the *Terra Nova*; flags flying, looked well fished."

Many in the crowd argued that the vessel mentioned in the dispatch was actually the *Terra Nova*. Their optimism was based on previous reports that the *Terra Nova*, just five days before, had 24,000 pelts on board. No reports had been received that mentioned the number of seals taken by the *Southern Cross*.

The attention of the crowd turned to speculating on what date the ship referred to would arrive. By most calculations, it was predicted that, if the vessel was the *Terra Nova*, it would arrive in St. John's by Wednesday, April 1, and if it was the *Southern Cross*, she would make Harbour Grace by the same day. The land-based experts added that their predictions were based on the assumption that favourable weather prevailed.

On Tuesday, March 31, nobody suspected that the *Southern Cross* was in trouble. *The Evening Telegram* reported the latest information on the sealer:

> The *Southern Cross* has not been reported since passing St. Pierre yesterday afternoon, and the general opinion is that she is 'hove to' in Placentia Bay. The night being fine, she evidently passed St. Lawrence and Burin, or she would have been reported from either of these places.
>
> Assessing that she reached Dodding Head about 11:00 p.m. yesterday, she would likely shape her course for Cape St. Mary's. As she is heavily laden, and can only steam a little over five knots, she would not be due at Cape St. Mary's until about 8 or 9 o'clock this morning. The storm came on about 7:00 a.m., and experienced mariners venture the opinion that she is about 15 or 20 miles west of Cape St. Mary's.

The *Newfoundland* disaster occurred on March 31. However, there was still no public alarm over the non-arrival of the *Southern Cross*. On April 1, *The Evening Telegram* reported:

> Messer's Bowring Brothers Ltd., received a message from Captain Connors of the S. S. *Portia* today saying that he passed the *Southern Cross* five miles W.N.W. of Cape Pine, at 11:00 a. m. yesterday. It is supposed that she ran into St. Mary's Bay, and harboured at North Harbour.

Public attention, during this period, was focused on the *Newfoundland* disaster and the loss of seventy-eight lives. Consequently, those with loved ones on the *Southern Cross* were becoming anxious. The April 1 message from Captain Connors was the last reference to any sighting of the *Southern Cross*.

On April 3, the Cape Race wireless station reported that the *Southern Cross* had not passed the Cape or Trepassey, and a message from Captain Connors confirmed she had not arrived at St. Mary's Bay. At this point, and while dealing with the tragedy of the *Newfoundland*, authorities became alarmed over the fate of the *Southern Cross*. Contact was made with the US *Seneca* which was in the vicinity of Cape Race. The Seneca was joined by the *Kyle* in a joint search effort for the missing sealing vessel.

Although there was a level of concern over the *Southern Cross*, the public remained optimistic, and there was a perception that her delay in returning to St. John's was caused by bad weather. On April 4, *The Evening Telegram* reflected this public optimism, "If she had been driven off to sea, which is the general opinion expressed by experienced seamen, it would take her some days to make land again. The ship is heavily laden, and cannot steam at a great speed."

By April 7, the *Fiona* had joined in the search. Authorities questioned many schooner captains in the area where the *Southern Cross* was last seen, but not a trace of the vessel could be found. The only possible clue to the fate of the sealing vessel came on April 11.

The *Kyle* reported seeing two white-coat pelts off Cape St. Mary's while on route to St. John's. The captain explained that due to the weather conditions, visibility was very limited. When the *Kyle* picked up supplies in St. John's, it set out for the Cape St. Mary's area to renew the search for the *Southern Cross*. Days passed into weeks, then months, then decades, and not a trace of the *Southern Cross* was ever found. The ship, its cargo, and 173 men seemed to have disappeared off the face of the earth.

NEWFOUNDLAND WAR HERO IN MIDDLE OF INTERNATIONAL INCIDENT

When the captain of the US Coast Guard cutter *Walcott* told the Newfoundland captain of a rum-running vessel to "Heave to!" he got an unexpected answer.

"See you in hell," said the Newfoundlander, who made a valiant attempt to outrun both the *Walcott* and the *Dexter*.[2]

Captain John Thomas Randell was hired by New York

---

[2] Janice Patton, *The Sinking of the I'm Alone* (Toronto: McClelland and Stewart, 1972).

mobsters to command their rum-running vessel, the *I'm Alone*. His confrontation with American authorities ended in a six-year court battle, during which time Captain Randell became a famous personality in the US and Newfoundland.

Randell was drawn into the mobster-rum-running operations by a representative of the New York mob, Big Jamie Clarke. On behalf of his mob-friends, Big Jamie had purchased a schooner called the *I'm Alone* at Lunenburg. The sole purpose of the vessel was to bring illegal whiskey from St. Pierre, Belize, and British Honduras to the United States to supply the bootlegging and speak-easy establishments operated by New York mobsters.

Big Jamie paid $18,000 for the *I'm Alone*, which was an impressive looking schooner. It weighed ninety tons, and measured 125 feet long and twenty-seven feet wide. To command and take charge of the operation to pick up whiskey and deliver it to the mobsters, Big Jamie sought out an experienced, tough, and smart sea captain who was dependable. He found such a guy in Captain John Thomas Randell.

Randell, a seasoned captain and adventurer, served with distinction during World War One in the Royal Navy. He came out of the war a Newfoundland hero. Captain Randell was awarded the Distinguished Service Cross and the Croix de Guerre for his part in a battle with a German U-boat. He was just the sort of man the New Yorkers wanted in their operation.[3]

---

[3] *The Evening Telegram*, April 1929.

After agreeing to take the job, Randell and Big Jamie worked out a plan to minimize the risks in getting the contraband liquor past the coast guard. Randell was well aware that the coast guard had no jurisdiction in international waters. He agreed to purchase the liquor cargoes from St. Pierre and Belize and to rendezvous with Big Jamie off the coast of Louisiana. The two men took a bundle of fifteen US bills each, with the middle one torn in half, and each one-half was placed in the middle of each bundle. The serial number on the half bill became the password to use by each party to identify themselves.

Between his rum-running trips, Randell was often entertained by the mobsters. He was always ready for an invitation to socialize, and always took along an impressive wardrobe. This included a tuxedo, dinner jacket, six dress shirts, twelve dress collars, eighteen pairs of silk socks, several pairs of black leather shoes, and a top hat.

The first encounter between the *I'm Alone* and the US Coast Guard occurred during a delivery of whiskey from St. Pierre to Big Jamie off the Louisiana coast. The *I'm Alone* arrived at night at the rendezvous point, and after the passwords were confirmed, Big Jamie began unloading the whiskey into his motor boat. He was successful in landing one load on shore, and had returned for a second load when, seemingly out of nowhere, the US Coast Guard moved in to make an arrest.

Big Jamie doused his cargo with gasoline, dumped it overboard, and used a flare gun to set it afire. While the coast guard was distracted by Big Jamie, Captain Randell made an escape at full speed. He sailed the schooner to Belize, British

Honduras, where he continued his illegal operations until March 20, 1929, when the *Walcott* again caught up with him.

Unarmed, the captain of the *Walcott* went on board the *I'm Alone*, and he informed Randell that he was operating illegally, and ordered the Newfoundlander to surrender. Randell claimed he was in international waters and the coast guard had no jurisdiction to challenge him. The captain returned to his ship, and after a short delay, sent several shots across the bow of the *I'm Alone*. When the coast guard gun jammed, Randell used the opportunity to escape. The *Walcott* followed close behind. Gunfire from the coast guard during the chase struck Randell in the leg. Serious injury did not result because only rubber bullets were used.

What happened next sparked an international controversy that made newspaper headlines across Canada and the United States. Captain John Thomas Randell was smack in the middle of the dispute, which dragged out in US courts for six years.

The chase continued into the next day. In the Gulf of Mexico, the *Walcott* was joined by a second coast guard cutter, the *Dexter*.

Using a megaphone, the captain of the *Dexter* ordered Randell to "Heave to."

Once again, Captain Randell repeated that he was in international waters, and beyond the jurisdiction of the coast guard. The *Dexter* fired a volley of shots across the bow of the *I'm Alone*, and when it refused to stop, launched an all-out attack on the rum runners. Real bullets ripped apart the sails of the schooner, which was damaged to the extent that Captain Randell ordered the crew to the lifeboats. Randell remained on board until the last minute. When the schooner tipped to dive down into the ocean, he jumped into the water, and was rescued by the Americans. One crewman of the schooner drowned during the confrontation.

Once on board the *Dexter*, the survivors were arrested, but treated well. They were given warm clothing, hot coffee, and food. Following this, they were taken to New Orleans and placed in jail. When arraigned in court, Randell insisted they were 200 miles off the US coast when arrested by the coast guard, and there was no legal right for the authorities to arrest them.

The case lingered on for six years in American courts. It finally ended in favour of the rum runners. Because the *I'm Alone* was a Canadian registered vessel, the American government extended an apology to Canada and paid the Canadian government $25,000. A total of $25,666.50 in compensation was paid to the crew of the *I'm Alone*. Captain Randell received $7,906, the family of the drowned man got $10,000, and the remaining crew members divided the remainder among them.

MOST UNUSUAL ENCOUNTERS AT SEA

Two ships, the *Massasoit* and the *Miranda*, sailing in Newfoundland waters ten years apart, both encountered massive icebergs, which are believed to be the largest ever witnessed by any ship in Newfoundland waters. One survived the unusual confrontation, the other was destroyed.

Newfoundland history is full of accounts of ships being lost after going ashore on reefs, running into cliffs, and sailing into rocky coves and bays in fog. The wreck of the American schooner *Massasoit* doesn't fit into any of those categories and stands out as one, if not the only, shipwreck of its kind in this province's history.

THE *MASSASOIT*

Wrecks involving icebergs usually occur when the ship hits a submerged spur of ice, or else simply runs head on into the towering icy wall. The *Massasoit* was lost after sailing into the big bight of an iceberg off the Southern Shore in a dense fog during June 1882. This vessel had left Gloucester on June 8 bound for the summer fishery on the Grand Banks of Newfoundland. Her master, a Captain Bond, had decided to go on to St. John's to pick up provisions. The vessel passed Cape Race on Friday, June 16, and sought information about ice conditions along the Southern Shore from a passing Newfoundland skiff. Captain Bond was informed by the skipper of the skiff that there was no sign of ice. Based on this information, Captain Bond made no effort to shorten sail and did not reduce speed.

About twenty or thirty miles southeast of Cape Ballard, the ship ran into a fairly thick bank of fog, but it was not thick enough to cut off all visibility. They could still see a short distance in all directions. The Captain maintained speed until after sunset and took in a little canvas after dark to reduce speed. The vessel did continue at a good speed because of the information received that there was no ice in the area.

It was not a very dark night, but the gloomy and gray fog pressed around them.

Neither captain nor crew noticed that the fog was growing lighter and that it was getting more white than grey on both sides of the ship and ahead. This whiteness was not due to a reduction in the thickness of the fog. It was far more deadly. Unknown to those on the *Massasoit*, they were running into the huge bight or cove of a gigantic iceberg. The brightness on the port and starboard bows and straight ahead was caused by the great iceberg shining through the thinning fog.

Before they realized what was happening, the ship was right up to the head of the bight, and the sides of the bay of ice closed in around them like the cliffs of some rock-bound cove. By this time, the *Massasoit* was moving too fast to be saved. She crashed headlong into the iceberg, which was an island of ice more than five miles long. It towered more than six times the height of the schooner's mainmast.

Because the iceberg was so far south, it was starting to break up, and great cakes and blocks of ice, dislodged by the impact of the vessel's collision, came tumbling down into the sea or crashing on the decks. Newspaper reports noted that the southerly wind fortunately was not strong, and it was fairly calm in the bight of the iceberg. Captain Bond and eight of his crew got into one of the dories and rowed away from the stricken *Massasoit*. The newspaper *Newfoundlander* reported:

> The remaining five men who made up the crew stayed behind to remove some of their belongings. They

believed the vessel would not sink immediately. Hardly had the first boat left her than she sunk in a swirl of ice and foam and the five men were never seen again, for the fog closed in and swallowed up everything. Captain Bond and his eight men were rescued and brought to St. John's.

CHAPTER TWENTY

Monster Squid in Newfoundland Waters

～～

On September 18, 1966, the United States Naval Oceano-graphic Research vessel *San Pablo* was operating in waters 120 miles east-northeast of Cape Bonavista, Newfoundland, when the crew noticed something unusual breaching the water within viewing distance of the vessel.

The spectacle that followed was something no man on the boat had ever witnessed, and not likely would again. A life and death battle was being played out between a sperm whale and a giant squid. Which sea creature won the battle is not known, but this was not the first battle of this nature to be witnessed by man.

In 1875, F.T. Bullen, British journalist, was a passenger on the whaling ship *Cachelot* and watched through his binocu-lars an encounter between a giant squid and a sperm whale. That incident inspired Newfoundland poet E. J. Pratt, in

1926, to write his epic poem "The Cachelot," in which he immortalized the battle between two monsters of the sea.

The giant squid, known by other names, including, kracken, devil fish, and cuttlefish, has terrorized Newfoundland fishermen over the centuries, and has been the inspiration in many tales and myths. According to the late Dr. Fred Aldrich of Memorial University, a world authority on the giant squid, the first clear historical reference to the creature was made in 1555 by Olaus Magnus, Archbishop of Upsala and Sweden, who described a monstrous fish seen off the coast of Norway. The Archbishop noted, "Their forms are horrible, their heads are square, and they have sharp and long horns round about, like a tree rooted up by the roots."

It was Olaus Magnus, according to Dr. Aldrich, who coined the word *kracken* in describing the giant squid. For more than 300 years after Magnus wrote about the kracken, there was practically no scientific work to verify the existence of this sea creature. Sailors around the world told exaggerated and often mythical tales of the monster squid. Jules Verne, in *Twenty Thousand Leagues Under the Sea*, described an encounter between Captain Nemo and the crew of the *Nautilus* with a giant kracken.

The author Osmond P. Breland observed:

> Since Homer's Odyssey, with its account of Ulysses' battle with Scylla, who was evidently a giant squid, stories of blood-thirsty, many armed monsters have been told by seafaring men.[1]

---

[1] Osmond P. Breland, "Devils of the Deep," *Science Digest*, October 1952, 31-33.

By the end of the 19th century, Newfoundland became the world's focal point for knowledge and evidence that proved the mythical devil fish or kracken really existed.

In 1873, when two fishermen and a boy were fishing in Conception Bay, a few miles north of St. John's, the existence of the sea-monster called the devil fish was only a tall-tale. By the end of the day they had the solid proof the world's scientific community was looking for. It also marked a day of terror that remained instilled in their memories for a lifetime.

It was October 26 when Theophilus Piccott, his twelve-year-old son Tom, and Daniel Squires set out for the fishing grounds in the tickle near Bell Island. Tom was proud to be at the tiller and enjoying workingwith his father, when suddenly terror struck. Dan Squires had noticed a darkened brownish object floating a short distance from the boat. After he pointed out the item to Theo, young Tom was told to steer the boat towards the object. Both men agreed that it was likely some kind of wreckage. When the boat drew near enough, Dan prodded the object with his boat hook.

> I gently lowered the grapnel down
> Towards its mighty jaws,
> And all at once some lengthy arms
> Was wrapped around the claws.
> I pulled away with all my might–
> To discover was my wish
> What had devoured my grapnel
> Such a monster looking fish![2]

---

[2] T.E. Tulk, "My Adventure with a Giant Squid," *Newfoundland Quarterly*, March 1954, Vol. 53 (1) 18.

Suddenly, the dormant floating object turned into a raging sea monster that sent waves of terror down the spine of the three fishermen. They had come face to face with the mythical devil fish. The creature swiftly emerged from the water and launched an attack upon the little fishing boat. What appeared to be a dozen snake-like tentacles, ranging between ten and thirty-five feet in length, lashed towards the boat with two of the tentacles gripping around it. The body of the creature measured ten feet long and eight feet wide. The two men were almost mesmerized by the two large black eyes, about eight inches each in diameter, which fixated on them. A bulk of tissue in the centre of the head opened, and a large parrot-like beak projected, opening and closing and viciously attacking the gunwale of the boat.

One of the tentacles fastened to the boat while the other encircled it and began to drag it down into the ocean. Water began pouring into the boat, but the two men, still in a state of terror, did not move to fight off the attack.

It was at this moment, when death seemed imminent, that young Tom regained his composure and launched a direct attack on the devil fish. He grabbed a tomahawk lying on the bottom of the boat and began chopping at the tentacle holding the vessel. After severing the tentacle that encircled the little craft, Tom succeeded in chopping off the second tentacle that had attached itself to the boat. Tom single-handedly defeated the creature which retreated down into the ocean while emitting a dark fluid to hide its trail as it disappeared from view.

Tom had the presence of mind to make sure that the two

severed tentacles were in the boat before his father and Dan Squires rowed to shore in fear that at anytime the creature may attack again. When the trio arrived home in Portugal Cove, Tom left the shorter tentacle near the front door to his home where it was dragged away and eaten by dogs. He took the long arm and preserved it as a trophy of his victory over the creature. His action on that date contributed to the scientific community's ability to move the existence of a giant squid from myth to reality.

The story of the terror on the tickle near Bell Island spread throughout Portugal Cove, and attracted the interest of the Anglican Minister in the community. He visited the Piccott family, and after hearing the first-hand account of the adventure, and seeing the tentacle cut from the creature by young Tom, the minister suggested Tom take it to Dr. Moses Harvey in St. John's. Dr. Harvey was Minister at St. Andrew's Presbyterian Church, and known internationally for his interest in science and nature.

Rev. Dr. Harvey's interest in giant squid was sparked by stories he had heard from Newfoundland fishermen about a creature they called "the big squid," which had horns, or arms that measured from twenty to thirty feet in length. The story that truly captured his attention was a fisherman's tale of a narrow escape he and two others had on the coast of Labrador.

> The little vessel of some 25 or 30 tons in which they were in, in the still water of a harbour, suddenly began to sink, until the deck was nearly on a level with the water. There was no water in her hold to account for

this. In alarm, they launched their boat to escape. This startled a big squid that had attached itself by its suckers to the bottom of the vessel, and was dragging it under the waves. The moment it relaxed its hold, the vessel rose to its former position, and the men saw the squid, some 30 or 40 feet in length, shooting rapidly through the water, and in a few minutes, was out of sight.[3]

After hearing this story, Harvey became determined to someday capture or find a giant squid. He had dreams of being able to solve the problem of centuries.

Since Tom was eager to profit from the rare item in his possession, the next day he and his dad placed the tentacle in a tub on their wagon, which they ordinarily used to bring supplies to and from the city, and set out to bring the piece of scientific evidence to the Plymouth Road residence of Dr. Harvey. When they arrived and showed Dr. Harvey the monster's tentacle, he immediately recognized that this could be the evidence the scientific world was seeking to prove the existence of a giant squid.

> How my heart pounded as I drew out of the tub in which he carried it, coil after coil, to the length of nineteen feet, the ducky red member, strong and tough as leather, about as thick as a man's wrist. I knew at a glance it was one of the tentacles or long arms of the ancient's Kraken, or modern giant cuttle fish. Eureka![4]

Young Tom was happy to receive ten dollars from Dr. Harvey

[3] Rev. Moses Harvey, "A Sea Monster Unmasked," *Science Digest*, 1899.
[4] Ibid.

for the specimen, and Theo Piccott agreed to have Dr. Harvey visit him at Portugal Cove next day to discuss the encounter with the creature.

When Dr. Harvey arrived at Portugal Cove, Theo, Dan Squires, and young Tom were present to answer his questions. When Tom finished telling his remarkable story, he casually added, "I thought I was done for by the big squid." In his notes, Dr. Harvey recorded that Tom had regarded the episode as a lark, but the two men had not recovered from the terrorizing encounter. He said that the senior Piccott and Dan Squires showed fear in their eyes as they described the creature. Dan Squires said, "It had eyes as big as saucers, gleaming with fury, and a fierce parrot-like beak that was ready to tear us apart."[5]

They estimated that the length of the creature was sixty feet, and its head was as round as a six-gallon keg. Stories had long been told among Newfoundland fishermen of monster-size squid, but Dr. Harvey had never encountered, or heard of one being sighted in Conception Bay. After examining the tentacle, and considering the information given to him by the three witnesses, he concluded the giant squid weighed about 1,000 pounds with tentacles as long as thirty-five feet. He arranged to have the tentacle photographed, then began writing his scientific paper.

Dr. Harvey later described his thoughts at the time:

I was now the possessor of one of the rarest curiosities in the whole animal kingdom—the veritable arm of the

5 Michael F. Harrington, "The Sea Monsters in Conception Bay," *Atlantic Guardian*, June 1957, Vol. 14 (6), 23-29.

hitherto mythical devil fish about whose existence, naturalists had been disputing for centuries. I knew that I held in my hand the key of the great mystery, and that a new chapter would be added to natural history. I was thus, by good fortune, the discoverer of a new, and remarkable species of fish, the very existence of which had been widely and scornfully denied, and had never been absolutely proved.

Although Harvey was thrilled over having the tentacle of a giant squid, he lamented not been able to obtain a complete creature.

Destiny, however, had something better in store for me than the acquisition of the tentacle. Only three weeks after the event described, a message reached me which threw me into a perfect fever of excitement. Another devil fish had been brought ashore in perfect condition at a place called Logy Bay, a few miles north of St. John's.[6]

Dr. Harvey wasted little time in getting to Logy Bay. The fishermen were excited about their find and were eager to talk about their experience. Harvey was delighted to see that, with the exception of the head, the remainder of the creature was intact. He knew that he had something that no museum in the world possessed.

The creature was captured by the Logy Bay fishermen after it became entangled in their net. When they began hauling in the net, they realized they had something more than fish

[6]   Rev. Moses Harvey, "A Sea Monster Unmasked," *Science Digest*, 1899.

in it. The net was much heavier than usual, and when they moved it, whatever was trapped in it began a ferocious battle to escape. The net was shaken, moved, and pulled in all directions.

When the fishermen got the net to the surface, they were astonished to see a sea monster struggling to free itself. The huge eyes and wriggling snake-like tentacles struck fear in the Logy Bay fishermen. Several tentacles extended through openings in the net and sought to grasp the boat. They were about to release the net when one man regained his composure, drew his splitting knife, and slashed the blade across the creature and severed most of its head. With the creature now dead, they managed to get it to shore. The man who had killed the monster told Harvey he would not wish to repeat the experience of the half-hour battle with the giant-squid for all the money in the world.

Harvey offered the men "a few dollars" for the creature, and after getting it on board his wagon, took it to his home in St. John's, where after storing it in brine, he placed it in a shed in his back garden. Word about the capture of a devil fish spread rapidly and crowds began visiting Dr. Harvey's shed to get a glimpse of the historic find. This creature was smaller than the one encountered by the Portugal Cove fishermen. Its body measured about six feet long, and the tentacles were up to twenty-four feet. The creature's total length with tentacles extended in opposite directions was fifty feet.

Dr. Harvey completed his study of the specimens and presented his papers, along with the giant squid specimens, to Professor A. E. Verril of Yale University, a world authority on cephalopods. Based on Harvey's papers, Professor Verril wrote a series of scientific papers on the cephalopods of North America, which gave Harvey international recognition. Dr. Harvey noted in his records, "Professor Verril did me the honor of naming the specimen *Architeuthis Harveyi* in honor of its discoverer."

Rev. Harvey also sent copies of his papers to Sir William Dawson of McGill University, who presented them to the National Historic Society of Montreal.

The noted Swedish Ichthyologit Jean Louis Agassiz wrote Harvey expressing his delight in the discovery, and asked permission to examine the creature. Unfortunately, Agassiz died weeks later, on December 12, 1873, without getting a chance to visit Dr. Harvey.

Dr. Harvey began receiving many requests from those wanting to purchase a giant squid, including offers from P.T. Barnum, owner of *The Greatest Show on Earth*.

Around the same time that Dr. Harvey was preparing his scientific paper, and getting ready to ship his specimens to Professor Verril, another giant squid turned up on the north shore of Newfoundland. Businessman Archibald Munn took possession of the parts of this creature from the fishermen who caught it. The parts saved consisted of jaws which were four inches long, and suckers which were an inch in diameter. Mr. Munn sent these specimens to the National Museum at Washington, DC. The Munn items were also studied by Professor Verril.[7]

---

[7] *Harper's New Monthly Magazine*, February 1874.

246 TREASURY OF NEWFOUNDLAND STORIES • VOLUME III

During the appearances of giant squid in Newfoundland waters in 1873, the mystery of the Sea-Devil's Rock (Bishop's Rock) in Conception Bay, Newfoundland, was solved, but not without a terrorizing confrontation with two St. John's fishermen.

The Legend of Sea Devil's Rock in Conception Bay became reality for Sam Wilney and Pat Daly during October 1873.

While most fishermen avoided the area because of a belief that something evil was connected with it, Sam Wilney and Pat Daly anchored their boat there one day at a respectable distance from the rock. Wilney was searching for his axe to repair an oar when Daly was startled to see something surface then disappear.

He shouted, "Faith! If I believed in the sea-serpent, I should say there's one over there now."

"What nonsense are you talking?" Wilney said. "You're up to some game."

"No, be Jasus!" Daly declared. "I swear I saw a great long thing rise out of the water, wriggling and twisting about like a serpent. Hanged if I don't begin to think there's something uncanny about that rock."

Wilney disregarded Daly's alert, and after fixing the oar, rowed round the rock. It was a calm day on Conception Bay with not even a ripple on the water. About twenty-five feet to the side of the little fishing boat, which was halfway to the Sea-Devil's Rock, Wilney noticed what appeared to be a big bunch of seaweed.

Wilney described the terror of the next moments:

> I could see some dark streaks like strings of
> seaweed floating out through the water, and I
> says to Pat, "It's nothing, but a lot of seaweed."
> Suddenly, out like a flash shot something from
> beneath the water, and lay across the middle of
> the boat. It came so quickly, it was simply like
> lightning. All we saw was that something had
> made a great leap, and the next thing we knew
> was that there was a thing like a long serpent
> lying across the boat, making it rock from side
> to side, and dragging it bodily towards the rock.
>
> Before you could look around, in a flash comes
> another one with a wriggle in the air, and a sort
> of flying leap. Then there were two long brown
> things like snakes lying right across the boat,
> and dragging it towards the rock. I could see
> twenty feet or more of each of them, and the
> boat was nearly tipped over.
>
> The creature pulled the boat until the gunwale
> was near the water, and then it rushed over the
> side into the boat. I sat like a stuck pig, when Pat
> cries out, "Chop it off, man! Chop now! Chop
> for your life!"

Sam grabbed the axe and began chopping furiously at the
creature. He succeeded in cutting off two of the tentacles
that had seized the boat, and they fell wriggling to the floor.
However, the attack was not yet over.

Sam Wilney described the next few moments:

> I got hold of the paddles, and got the boat's head round to row away, when up out of the water rose, not one, or two, but four or five great wriggling snakes, and a big thing as large as a tub, with two eyes as big as soup plates. Then and there, I knew what it was. It was a tremendous devil-fish, and it had been lying just under the water, hanging onto the rock with two or three of its arms.

Sam had seen many small squid, and on occasion had one jump out of the water and fasten onto his arm or hand. He could easily free himself from one by squeezing its windpipe, and it would let go immediately. Sam's experience with small squid convinced him that the monster squid in front of him was about to leap at him. He thought that if the creature made the sudden leap, it would capsize the boat, and he and Pat wouldn't have a chance.

"Thank heaven, he didn't!" exclaimed Sam. "He only gave a great plunge, and disappeared, leaving the water all round us as black as ink. Well, I thought he'd likely come up again, so you bet I rowed. Yes, sir! And I never stopped till I felt the bow touch the shore, and then I think I fainted."[8]

Four years later, another giant squid was driven ashore at Catalina during a severe windstorm that struck Newfoundland on September 22, 1877. The bewildered creature of the deep tried to escape by swimming backward, and stuck its

---

[8] Frank Aubrey, "A Newfoundland Terror," *Fore's Sporting & Sketches*, 1896, Vol. 13, 10-15.

tail on a rock which rendered it powerless. An unidentified fisherman, watching it from shore, described its actions:

> In its desperate effort to escape, the ten arms darted out in all directions, lashing the water into a foam. The thirty feet long tentacles, in particular, made lively play as it shot them out, and endeavored to grasp onto something with their powerful suckers so that it could drag itself into deep water. When it was exhausted and with the tide receding, a group of fishermen, who had gathered on shore, approached it.

The fishermen kept a respectable distance from the creature as they tried to determine if it was dead or alive. Once satisfied it was dead, and not able to harm them, two fishermen from the group took possession of it. On September 26, they took it by boat to St. John's. News of the presence of the dead monster fish in St. John's drew widespread interest, and crowds began showing up at the harbour wharf to see it. In response to the public show of curiosity, the government allowed the fishermen to display it in a drill shed near the harbour.[9]

When removed from the water, the creature's color was a dusky red, but soon after, it turned white. It was similar in dimensions and features to the two which were studied by Dr. Moses Harvey in 1873. Many groups expressed interest in purchasing this giant squid, and it was sold to the New York Aquarium for $500. The Aquarium housed the creature in an specially built glass tank that measured

---

[9] Don Morris, *Evening Telegram*, St. John's, Newfoundland, September 13, 1963.

twenty-five feet long, five feet wide, and three and a half feet deep.

On October 27, 1877, the *Canadian Illustrated News* reported:

> The latest addition to the remarkable collection of the New York Aquarium is by far the most curious of specimens. It is a monster cuttle-fish (squid) made familiar to the public by Victor Hugo as the devil fish. It is a most horrible looking creature.

In 1882, a giant squid taken from Newfoundland waters was on display at Worth's Museum in the Bowery, New York, which was one of the most popular museums in America in the 19th century.

The museum distributed posters around New York to promote the attraction which it described as a "devil fish" from Newfoundland. According to the St. John's *Evening Mercury*, January 5, 1882, "A huge Woodcut on the head of the advertising placard showed ten arms flung out, two of them grasping and curling round two human beings who are writhing in agony."

Newspaper competition in St. John's was strong in those days, and often the animosity between competing editors spilled over into the daily news items. In this instance, the editor at the *Evening Mercury* took a swipe at the editor of the *Evening Telegram*:

> Some people here, who have examined this woodcut, say that one of the sufferers grappled by the Devil Fish has a striking resemblance to the head editor of the *Evening Telegram*, his photograph having been forwarded along with the fish, but we are unable to

concur in this opinion. The figure in the woodcut is not nearly as handsome.

Giant squid were more plentiful in Newfoundland waters than many thought. Osmond P. Breland, science journalist, noted in his writings, "A flash of 25 to 30 of the giants were found at one time. All of them were cut up for bait by members of a fishing fleet." Breland did not elaborate on this incident in his article.

In 1912, two brothers, Josiah and Henry Sheppard, set out from Lark Harbor to go fishing. The older brother, Henry, used his motor boat to tow Josiah's dory to the fishing grounds. Upon arriving there, Josiah transferred to the dory, and Henry slackened the tow line which allowed the dory to drift 200 yards.

While attaching bait to his line, Josiah became temporarily paralyzed with fear when he was suddenly confronted by a large creature, the likes of which he had never seen before. The creature's head came high out of the water, and its huge eyes fixated on the bait-codfish in the bottom of the boat. This action was followed by the creature's tentacles leaping from the water, and the longest one wrapping around the dory. The head then submerged and began dragging the dory beneath the water. The quick action knocked Josiah off balance, and he fell into the water. Josiah shouted to his brother for help. While he struggled to keep afloat, the dory resurfaced bottom up. The boy regained control of his thoughts, and knew he had to get out of the water while waiting for his brother to arrive. He managed to climb up on the dory, and not long after, Henry arrived and helped him get into the motor boat.

The Sheppards, fearing a return of the giant creature, abandoned their fishing efforts and returned to shore. Henry and Josiah knew they had encountered a giant squid. Josiah was convinced that had it not been for the bait in his boat, the squid would have attacked him.[10]

In 1937, Constable W. Davis, a Newfoundland ranger, recorded that two fishermen from Tack's Beach had to run their boat ashore to save it from sinking after it had been attacked by a huge fish with teeth like arrowheads.

> On Saturday last, whilst Joseph Warren and his hired man were hauling their cod net, a huge brown-backed fish seized the keel forward and almost overturned the boat. Letting go the stern, the fish seized the keel amidships, and then near the stern, lifting the boat so much out of the water that the bow went under, and a lot of water was shipped.

The men decided to head for land, and to beach the boat which was rapidly sinking. The move succeeded in breaking the boat away from the creature. When the bottom of the boat was examined, it showed that the keel had been almost torn from the timbers. Three of the monster's broken teeth were found embedded in the keel. These were sent to Dr. McPherson of the Newfoundland Fisheries Research Office, but could not be identified.

During the 1940s there were sightings of giant squid in the Placentia Bay area. Abe Brinston, a fisherman from Arch Cove, was confronted by one of the creatures. He was trying to repair his boat's motor which had broken down while he

---

[10] "Attacked by a Sea Monster," *Downhomer*, October 1999, Vol. 12 (5), 85.

was fishing when a monster suddenly surfaced very close to his boat. He described it as, "Nothing less than the devil himself. It tried to climb into my boat, and was holding the boat with a monstrous set of claws."

Brinston battled and defeated the monster with his boat hook, which he used to cut at the claws and head of the creature. On his trip to shore he thought, "Nobody will ever believe this story."

The next day, Clayton Stacey, a fisherman from Sound Island, near Arch Cove, encountered a similar creature. The description given by Stacey was similar to that given in the community by Brinston. Stacey was carrying a gun, which he used to fight off the monster. He said he hit the creature with a shot, and it disappeared beneath the water, followed by a trail of blood. Stacey did not feel he had killed the creature.

When word spread throughout Placentia Bay that there was a wounded monster in the area, fishermen began carrying weapons. Several days passed and another monster from the sea, perhaps the wounded one shot by Stacey, showed up near the beach at New Harbour. One man who witnessed it told an *Evening Telegram* reporter, "It was big around as a puncheon, and an awful length. It tried to pull itself up on the rocks close to shore. Each time, it slipped back into the water."

A Mr. Glavine, while jigging for cod off Philip Head, Notre Dame Bay, snagged a giant squid in 1957. It was about a meter below his boat. Mr. Glavine cut the line before the creature could react, and it quickly disappeared.

While swimming near the surface of the water, a giant squid is often mistaken for a monster sea serpent, and is often described by those seeing it as a very long snake-like creature. The *New York Sun* on November 30, 1879, explained why someone seeing a giant squid swimming might think they are watching a monster serpent:

> The giant squid while swimming with portions of its body visible above the water is sometimes mistaken for a monster serpent. While swimming, the giant squid brings its many arms together in a line, thus affording the least possible resistance, and propels itself by ejecting water from its syphon. Giant squids move with an up and down motion exposing parts of their bodies like a snakes going through water.[11]

Not all encounters in Newfoundland waters with the giant squid were without casualties. In 1874, Bill Darling was the only Newfoundlander serving on the *Peril*, a 150-ton schooner. While sailing in Newfoundland waters, the crew sighted an unknown creature floating near the surface of the water a short distance from the boat.

The *Peril*'s Captain, James Flood, described his action after seeing the creature, "I went into my cabin for my rifle, and as I was preparing to fire, Bill Darling came on deck and looking at the monster said, "Have a care master, that ere's a squid and will capsize us if we hurt him." Smiling at the idea, I let fly and hit the squid, and with that, he shook. There was a great ripple all around him, and he began to move."

---

[11] "Sea Serpent Accounted for in 1879," *Shortis*, 1879, Vol. 3 (469), 411.

"Out with your axes and knives," shouted Bill, "and cut away any of him that comes aboard. Look alive and Lord, help us."

Captain Flood replied, "I had never seen a giant squid before and was not aware of the danger. I did not give any orders, and it was no use touching the helm or ropes to get out of the way. By then, Bill and three other men had axes, and were looking over the side at the advancing monster. We could see a large oblong mass, moving by jerks, just under the surface of the water, and an enormous train followed."

The monster was about half the size of the vessel, according to Edward R. Snow, author of *Mysteries and Adventures Along the Atlantic Coast*. He estimated it to be about 100 feet long.

Captain Flood remarked, "Quickly, the brute struck, and the ship quivered under its thud. In another moment, monstrous arms, like trees, seized the vessel, and she keeled over. In yet another moment, the monster was aboard and squeezed in between the masts."

"Slash for your life," Bill Darling shouted.

The slashing seemed to have little effect on the creature as it slipped its large body overboard, and pulled the vessel down with him.

Bill Darling said, "We were thrown into the water, and just as I went over, I caught sight of one of the crew, squashed up between the masts and one of those awful arms. For a few seconds, our ship lay on her beam ends, then filled, and went down."

The schooner *Stratbowen* was near enough to witness the attack. It moved into the area in time to rescue Flood and the surviving members of his crew.

In 1963, Doctor Fred Aldrich initiated an effort to capture a giant squid for scientific study. Based on his research, Dr. Aldrich put forward a theory that the giant squid surfaced in Newfoundland waters in thirty-year cycles. He concentrated his efforts during autumn, and launched a publicity campaign inviting people to report any sightings of the giant squid. The appeal was successful, and he received many reports of sightings of the creature, and in a few cases, reports that a giant squid had been stranded on shore. Reports of sightings came from Portugal Cove, Harbour Maine, King's Cove, Dildo, Coomb's Cove, Fortune Bay, Chapel Arm, Deer Island, and Lance Cove.

During 1964 and 1965, Dr. Aldrich acquired five giant squid. The first and largest was taken during October 1964, at Conch, White Bay, on Newfoundland's Great Northern Peninsula. It weighed 330 pounds, was thirty feet long with tentacles twenty-one feet in length. This creature was discovered by a fisherman who was hauling wood at Cape Fox, and he towed it to Conch. The man had not heard of Dr. Aldrich's appeal. The employees at the bait depot in Conche were aware of Dr. Aldrich's interest, and they contacted him regarding the find. He arranged for Eastern Provincial Airways to fly the creature to St. John's.

Several weeks later, other giant squids, similar in size to the one taken at Conch, were found at Chapel Arm, and at Lance Cove, Trinity Bay. In November 1964, one was recovered at

Springdale, Notre Dame Bay. After examining the creatures, Dr. Aldrich reported, "One unexpected result of these dissections has been the discovery of the world's largest nerve axon or nerve fibre." He added, "None showed signs of reproductive maturity and none had food in its digestive tracts."

A live giant squid was captured by a Spanish fishing vessel. The following item appeared in the *Atlantic Advocate*, November 1970:

> A 33-foot squid, taken alive by a Spanish trawler off the coast of Newfoundland, has been brought to St. John's for examination by scientists. The huge squid was caught in late September, and according to Dr. Frederick Aldrich, director of the Memorial University Marine Sciences Research Lab, it's the largest of seven which he has examined in the past ten years.

The monstrous oddity was taken alive by the Spanish fishermen, but it was dead by the time it reached port in Newfoundland. Up to this point, the largest was a 29.5 foot squid caught off northern Newfoundland in 1964.

There are many different species of giant squid, no fewer than four of these have been found in Newfoundland waters, and 47 species in waters around Scotland. Some may be larger than others. The one that attacked Tom Piccott was over a 1000 pounds. Those caught since the 1960s have been much smaller, some weighed 350 pounds.

The eating of squid is a common practice throughout Newfoundland, and the assumption was that giant squid would taste no different than the ordinary squid. When a party of scientists in St. John's in 1974 tasted giant squid for the first time, it led to an important scientific discovery. Dr. Clyde Roper of the Smithsonian Institute and several other scientists were guests at the home of Dr. Chung-Cheng Lu in St. John's when Dr. Roper raised a question about how a cooked giant squid would taste.

Dr. Cheng Lu had some pieces of a giant-squid stored in his freezer, and offered to have it prepared and cooked for the gathering. It was cut into frying pieces, some seasoning was added and it was then pan-fried. Each persons' response after tasting the exotic dish was to show a sour-face and utter the word "Awful!"

Instead of depositing the "lot" in a garbage bin, the group of scientists wondered why the taste would be so different than that of a regular squid. To satisfy their curiosity, the cooked squid was examined in a lab and an important discovery was made. The examination discovered that instead of the salt solution found in the tissue of many squid species and other animals, the giant squid had in its flesh ammonium chloride. Ammonium chloride is lighter than saltwater and makes the giant squid more buoyant and easier to control its depth. The giant squid attracts fewer scavengers because of this chemical.

CHAPTER TWENTY-ONE

Women and Children Last

The story of the *Arctic* bursts from the pages of the history of Newfoundland shipwrecks, not only for the great loss of life, but for the disgraceful conduct of some of the crew in rushing to abandon the sinking ship and leaving women and children on board to face certain death.

A PROPHECY

During the summer of 1854, William Brown, part-owner of the Collins Shipping Line, one of the world's largest passenger-mail steamship services, stopped at the shop of a fortune teller in London, England, to have his palm read. It was a day of recreation for Mr. Brown, and the idea of having his future told amused him. Partway through the session, the fortune teller's facial expression contorted as she grasped Brown's wrist tightly and whispered, "You will die in a horrible shipwreck." Mr. Brown sought more detailed information, but the session ended abruptly with the comment, "I have nothing more to tell you." As she left the room, Brown was more amused than alarmed. After all, he was a sophisticated, wealthy businessman, who claimed to have "no superstitions."

When Brown stepped onto the deck of the *Arctic* to begin his cross-Atlantic trip to his home in New York, he suddenly froze as he recalled the fortune teller's warning. He quickly dispelled these thoughts as mere superstition and walked confidently over to greet Captain James Luce, the ship's captain and a long-time friend. On September 20, 1854, a week later, William Brown's body was floating in the Atlantic waters off Cape Race, Newfoundland, and the *Arctic* lay on the bottom of the ocean. The *Arctic* shipwreck was all but forgotten until 66 years later.

COMPARED TO *TITANIC*

It is no wonder that, for decades afterwards, many in Newfoundland wanted to forget the *Arctic* disaster. However, the circumstances surrounding its sinking and the willful abandonment of women and children to drowning earned the tragedy a chilling place in Newfoundland's shipwreck history.

Following the sinking of the *Titanic* in 1912, journalists across North America sought out stories to parallel the tragedy. They focused comparisons with the sinking of the *Arctic* fifty miles off Cape Race in 1854. The 3000-ton vessel carried a total of 383 people: 233 passengers and 150 crew members.

AMONG THE *ARCTIC* PASSENGERS

Among the *Arctic*'s passengers were the wife and two children of the general manager of the Collins Line. Like the *Titanic*, the *Arctic* failed to carry enough lifeboats to evacuate all on board. The vessel carried the minimum number of lifeboats required by law.

In 1854, the *Arctic* was the *Titanic* of its day. Reverend John Stevens Abbott, who crossed the Atlantic in 1852 aboard the *Arctic*, wrote in *Harper's Magazine*, "Never did there float upon the ocean a more magnificent palace." The vessel measured 284 feet long on deck, 277.3 feet on keel, and 45.8 feet wide across the main deck. The width expanded to 72 feet in the area where the paddle-boxes on the side of the ship were located.

At this time in history, when shipping was moving from sail to steam engine, the great American Collins Shipping Line[1] was in strong competition with the British Cunard Shipping Line in the trans-Atlantic passenger-ervice business. The Collins Liners were faster and more luxurious than the Cunard vessels. Both the Collins Line and the Cunard Line received very large subsidies from their respective governments to carry mail across the Atlantic. In the case of the Collins Line, that subsidy was $33,000 per round trip. They had succeeded in getting the US mail contracts based on their commitment to provide the fastest cross-Atlantic service.

---

[1] The legal name for the Collins Line was the New York and Liverpool U.S. Mail Steamship Company, which was incorporated on November 1, 1847.

THE *ARCTIC* DEPARTS LIVERPOOL

On September 13, 1854, the *Arctic*, under the command of forty-nine-year-old Captain James C. Luce, sailed into Liverpool Harbour. At noon, September 20, the *Arctic* departed from Liverpool for New York. All passenger tickets had been sold and some wishing to purchase tickets had to be turned away. Among the passengers were several wealthy New York residents, a French duke going to Washington to take up a diplomatic post with the French embassy, a courier named George Burns of Philadelphia carrying despatches for US President James Buchanan, and the wife of the Collins Line general manager and part owner, Mrs. Edward Collins and their two children, Mary Anne and Henry.

Among those unable to book passage was a group of nuns who were travelling to serve in a convent-school in California. The eighteen nuns were disappointed when told they had to wait for the next ship leaving Liverpool for the United States. Little did they know what a blessing that delay would be.

THE *ARCTIC* REACHES THE GRAND BANKS

The *Arctic* had reached the Grand Banks of Newfoundland on Wednesday, September 27. Checking his compass about fifty miles from Cape Race, Captain Luce was pleased with his progress in crossing the Atlantic. He was now only three days from New York. The early morning fog had improved very little. It continued with intermittent intervals, which at times of visibility enabled officers of the *Arctic* to see one or two miles ahead. Regardless of the visibility, Captain Luce gave no thought to reducing speed because the vessel was making record time. However, at least one passenger, a Scotsman, was anxious about the situation. The fact that the ship had no alarm bells or steam whistle to warn of danger added to his anxiety.

At 12:15, a lookout shouted, "There's a steamer ahead." This was followed seconds later by a deck officer's command, "Hard a-starboard," and then "Stop her!" The ship's annunciator was used to signal the order to stop and change directions.[2] The sudden change in the ship's course caused Captain Luce to drop what he was doing and rush to the deck. He arrived there just as a dark bark-rigged steamer emerged out of the fog on a line of collision with the *Arctic*.

THE *VESTA*

The dark ship emerging out of the fog was the 250-ton French steamer and sail ship the *Vesta*, which had just left St. Pierre carrying 150 fishermen home to France for the winter. It had been built at Nantes, France, in 1853 for the firm of Hernoux ET Compagnie of Dieppe, France, and carried a crew of fifteen. The *Vesta*'s sixty-horsepower engine needed the help of the vessel's sails to gain speed during its Atlantic crossing.

By the time the *Vesta* came into view of the *Arctic*, both vessels were travelling at twelve knots, which was the top speed of the era.

The crews of both vessels initiated actions to avoid a collision. But it was too late. There was not enough distance

[2] An annunciator was an in-house bell communication system used to communicate within a ship, building, or house.

between the two for manoeuvring, and the fate of almost six hundred people was sealed.

Although the impact of the collision was hardly noticed on the *Arctic*, it was significantly felt on the *Vesta*. The *Vesta*'s passengers rushed to the deck in a state of confusion and were convinced by what they saw that their ship was going to sink. Two lifeboats were launched in hopes of getting to the *Arctic* which at first appeared not to have suffered any serious damage. During the escape effort, one of the lifeboats capsized and the second was ordered by the vessel's captain to remain by the ship.

ARCTIC FELT IT HAD ESCAPED DAMAGE

The *Arctic*'s captain, at first, felt his ship would survive the collision and sent Robert J. Gourley, his first mate, along with eight of his crew, to offer assistance to the *Vesta*. Soon after these men left the ship, Captain Luce was made aware that the *Arctic* had been seriously damaged. The collision had left the *Arctic* with a wide hole in its side beneath the water line. Some crewmen, led by the ship's carpenter, made an unsuccessful attempt to cover the hole with sailing canvas.

ARCTIC DESERTED *VESTA*

The *Arctic* circled the *Vesta* twice while Captain Luce assessed the impact of the damage. Those on the *Vesta*, seeing one of the *Arctic*'s lifeboats approaching and the *Arctic* circling, were convinced they were going to be rescued. The fog quickly covered the area, and when it lifted, Captain

Alphonse Duchesne, his crew, and passengers were astounded to watch the *Arctic* sail away.

The Captain and crew of the *Vesta* turned their attention to keeping their vessel afloat, while Captain Luce had concluded that the only chance to save the *Arctic* was to move full speed towards the Newfoundland coast before water pouring into the ship from the damaged section below the water line filled and sank her. He had no time to communicate his intentions to those on the *Vesta*. This decision would later cause confusion and bad feelings towards *Arctic* survivors as they arrived at St. John's.

CREW PANICKED

During its move from the accident site, the *Arctic*'s paddle crushed a *Vesta* lifeboat carrying eight men. Only one man survived. A young German passenger on the *Arctic* tossed him a rope and succeeded in pulling him to temporary safety. About 40 miles from Cape Race, the sea had flooded the engine rooms and shut down the engines. The *Arctic* slowed to a complete stop, and despite the efforts of Captain Luce and a few loyal crewmen, some of the crew disregarded the principle of "women and children first" and took control of some lifeboats for themselves. There was a great deal of confusion and panic as others attempted to escape the sinking vessel. Due to the inadequate number of lifeboats, most on board were unable to escape and tragically went down with the ship. Those who were in lifeboats fought for survival in the rough seas along Newfoundland's south coast. Many challenges needed to be overcome in order to make it safely to shore.

SURVIVORS ORGANIZE

Two of the *Arctic* lifeboats, carrying a total of forty-five crew and passengers, met as they distanced themselves from the damaged vessel. A quick discussion took place between both groups and a joint decision was made to make Second-Mate William Baalham their captain and allow him to direct their efforts to row safely to the Newfoundland coast. A suggestion that they return to the shipwreck scene to rescue more survivors was quickly dashed by those who thought that those struggling to get out of the water might cause the lifeboats to tip over or sink. They also felt there was a great danger in being close when the *Arctic* finally tipped and submerged into the ocean, perhaps dragging those nearby with them. A few on board were willing to take the risk, but they were outnumbered.

REACHED CAPPAHAYDEN

After rowing forty-two hours and enduring cold, dampness, and hunger, Baalham's lifeboats came within view of Cappahayden (Broad Cove in the 19th century) at about 4:00 a.m. on Friday, September 29. Baalham took time to size up the coastline and then selected an area on Cappahayden Beach most suitable for an easy landing. His decision proved to be a sound one, and the two lifeboats easily landed at the site.

Once safely on land, the survivors bowed their heads and offered up a prayer of thanksgiving for their deliverance. One survivor praised Baalham's skill and leadership in bringing them to safety.

While preparing to leave the beach, they heard a dog barking, which led them to the house of a Jack Fleming near the top of a crest overlooking the beach. Fleming, a fisherman, occupied the small cabin with his son, Joseph.

He had little in the way of supplies but what he had he shared willingly. As meager as the rations of hard tack and water were, they were more than the survivors had eaten in two days.

Fleming briefed the survivors on the route to St. John's and the communities they would pass through on the journey. The first of these would be Renews. Fleming had sent news on ahead to Renews to advise them that shipwreck survivors were on the way. The good people there moved quickly to welcome them and offer assistance. Jack Fleming became known for decades after for his stories about the terrible *Arctic* disaster and the survivors who made it to Cappahayden.

Two of the survivors who had been injured during the mad rush to take control of the lifeboats while evacuating the *Arctic* were left behind in Fleming's care. Baalham then led the remainder of the group on the four-mile trek to Renews. By the time they arrived, the people there were waiting to welcome them into their homes. Food, medicines, warm clothing, and bedding were supplied to each of them.

Baalham was determined to get back to the shipwreck scene as quickly as possible. Along with the *Arctic*'s purser, John Geib, they hired two small fishing schooners, one to return to the *Arctic* to search for survivors and the other to take the remaining survivors to St. John's about fifty miles east of Renews.

When the schooner sent to St. John's was forced to take shelter in Ferryland due to a terrible wind storm, a small band of six of the survivors chose not to wait for the weather to improve, and they set out by foot towards St. John's where they arrived around on October 2. This group of *Arctic* survivors was amazed to learn that the *Vesta* had survived. It had made it safely to St. John's with all but a dozen of its crew and passengers who had died during escape efforts soon after the collision.

CONFUSION REIGNED

Before leaving Ferryland, Geib unaware of the *Vesta*'s arrival in St. John's, sent a message to the US consul at St. John's with the request that it be forwarded onto the Collins Office at New York. The *Vesta*'s damage appeared to be so serious that the *Arctic* survivors were convinced it could not have stayed afloat any more than a half hour. In his message to St. John's, Geib reported with certainty that the *Vesta* had gone down. In addition to this mistaken report, Geib also reported that the family of the general manager of the Collins Line had made it to Geib's lifeboat but were washed overboard and drowned. But this was not correct.

ARRIVED AT ST. JOHN'S

It is important to record the efforts of Captain Alphonse Duchesne to make it to St. John's, five hours away. He first calmed his passengers and crew who were visibly upset by what appeared to be the *Arctic*'s callous abandonment of them.

Duchesne felt his ship had to be further lightened to survive. He ordered that the barrels of oil and fish representing the fishermen's hard work and earnings for the fishing season be jettisoned into the Atlantic before the *Vesta* would set out for St. John's. His efforts paid off, and the ship made it to the safety of St. John's Harbour just as a heavy windstorm was striking. Had that storm hit earlier, it is doubtful whether the *Vesta* would have survived. The *Vesta*, with two hundred people on board, had lost only thirteen in the disaster. One was killed in the collision, others died after jumping into the sea, and the remainder were crushed by the *Arctic*.

Fortunately, the *Vesta* had been better built to survive at sea than the large, more expensive, luxurious *Arctic*. Her biggest advantage over the *Arctic* was a safety system that involved three water-tight bulkheads, which divided her holds and engine room into separate compartments.

Touissant's Hotel on Water Street[3] opened its doors to *Vesta* survivors and assisted those who could not be accommodated in finding shelter at other hotels and lodging houses in the city. The *Public Ledger*, a St. John's newspaper, praised the actions of Captain Alphonse Duchesne in keeping his damaged vessel afloat and making it to St. John's. It noted, "Nothing but the most indomitable energy, unwavering perseverance, and the most superior seamanship could have succeeded in bringing the *Vesta* to port."

The first word of the *Arctic* disaster was received in St. John's by American Consul William Henry Newman on Saturday afternoon from John Geib. At the time, Geib sent his

---

[3] Touissant's was located where the King George V Building is now located on the eastern end of Water Street.

message to St. John's, he was not aware that the *Vesta* had survived. His letter reflected this belief, and incorrectly reported that the Collins family (wife and children of E.K. Collins) made it off the ship in a lifeboat but the boat was swamped and they were all drowned. Testimony given at the enquiry held later showed that Mrs. Collins and her two children remained on the *Arctic* to the last.

Meanwhile, *Vesta* survivors sheltered at St. John's began telling outrageously disturbing stories of the *Arctic* abandoning them and sailing away from the crash scene without offering help. A few days later, when the *Arctic* survivors began trickling into St. John's, they were not given the same warm welcome and support that had been so generously given along the Southern Shore of the Avalon Peninsula.

While the survivors of the *Arctic* fought for life just five hours from St. John's, the response to news of the tragedy in the capital city was disgraceful. Those in a position to initiate an immediate response did nothing. Although the governor, prime minister, American consul, and steam-ship manager all lived within a one-mile radius of each other, they never came together in one unified meeting to develop a rescue strategy. Instead, there was a spectacle like something out of a Buster Keaton movie, with key players resting on Sunday, bumping into each other on St. John's streets over the next days, exchanging suggestions on what should be done, then running off in all directions, all this while precious hours were passing, and men, women, and children were struggling to survive not far from the capital city.

Instead of sparking an all-out organized search for survivors, there was little sense of urgency, and the matter was tossed back and forth among those who had it in their power to respond immediately.

The first person to react was Bishop Edward Feild, Anglican Bishop of Newfoundland. Bishop Feild, upon hearing of the tragedy, rushed to the Commercial Chambers in downtown St. John's where some of the prominent merchants of the city were relaxing and discussing the news of the day. Feild told them that his yacht, the *Hawk*, was ready to go immediately to search for survivors and asked, "How many of you are willing to join me?" "We will not send a ship without assurances that we will be paid!" responded a prominent figure among them. Disappointed and upset by this refusal, Bishop Feild sought help through the American counsel in St. John's as well as Prime Minister Little and Governor Kerr Baillie Hamilton for help. The American counsel sent a message to Washington and began the process of getting help for the victims.

Although the American consul had been informed of the tragedy on Saturday, September 30, in the afternoon, and had initiated efforts to relay his information to the United States and to initiate a search, Prime Minister P.F. Little was not moved to action until Monday, October 2. In a letter to local newspapers on October 7, 1854, he explained:

> Between 2 and 3 o'clock, p.m. a gentleman called on me, stating that no steps had been taken by anybody in St. John's to rescue such of her surviving passengers and crew as had not reached the land, and were then supposed to be at the mercy of the waves not far from

our coast. I immediately waited on Mr. Newman, the American Consul, in company with my informant, and inquired from him what measures he had taken, and if he had solicited the Governor's assistance to save the unfortunate survivors. He replied that he had sent off a letter to a vessel bound to Boston, to be delivered at some intermediate port, for the purpose of telegraphing the news of the disaster to New York, but that she had sailed; that, Dr. Feild had kindly offered his yacht, which he was about to fit out and dispatch in search of the *Arctic* and her boats; that he had been at the Commercial Room, where cold water was thrown on his efforts by some of the mercantile gentlemen present, who asked him "who was going to guarantee the expenses of sending out vessels?" and that he was going to the Governor.

Prime Minister Little's letter drew an angry response from the Editor of the *Newfoundlander*, who on October 9 wrote:

The question will inevitable suggest itself to every rational inquirer, why information which reached the hands of the American Consul at 7 o'clock on Saturday evening was not sufficiently "certain" to have impelled men in the name of a Government to immediate action for the rescue of human life. Will they inform the American or British people, what they did on Saturday evening on receipt of this "not certain" intelligence? And why sailing craft—abundant in port—were not dispatched at least by daylight next day in quest of the *Arctic's* victims? Then they conveniently ignore the intervening Sunday and tell us of a communication of the Government to Mr. Newman, "on Monday morning"—this turning out to have been on Monday between 2 and 3 o'clock when Mr. Little was in conversation with the Consul. But even if this "morning" statement were not a proven falsehood, what were they about all Sunday. Was the best of day a *dics non* in the estimation of this Christian Government, while the lives of 350 fellow-beings hung upon the thread of an immediate deliverance?

Meanwhile, while Prime Minister Little was meeting with the American consul on Monday, he encouraged the consul to go see Governor Kerr Baillie Hamilton as soon as possible. The prime minister said:

> Steam vessels should be sent to the calamity without delay, and distinctly authorized him to inform his Excellency that I should undertake on behalf of the majority of the House of Assembly, to indemnify him for any outlay that would be necessary in the adoption of every available means to rescue the lives of the survivors. While we were conversing, a letter was received by him from the Secretary's Office tendering the cooperation of the Governor in any efforts that he might deem expedient to adopt under the circumstances.[4]

Following his meeting with Newman, Prime Minister Little obtained support from a majority of members of the House of Assembly, who signed an indemnity to the governor to

[4] *The Newfoundlander*, St. John's. Monday, October 9, 1854.

cover the costs the American consul would need to incur immediately in obtaining a vessel or vessels to go to the rescue of survivors. According to the prime minister, while he was out that night, the American consul accompanied by Mr. Joseph Crowdy of the Secretary's Office had called at the prime minister's house. When the PM learned of this visit, he went to see the consul, but he was not at home. The PM did not make contact with the consul again until noon the next day. The two men, who were in a position of sending aid to the shipwreck scene, encountered each other while walking on a downtown street. Even with the fact that hundreds of passengers were drowning in Newfoundland waters, the two gentlemen showed no sense of great urgency to help.

Neither did they discuss calling immediately for a joint meeting with the governor to mount an organized rescue effort. The consul informed him that he could not come to an agreement with Chandler White, Vice-President of the New York, Newfoundland and London Telegraph Company over the hiring of the *Victoria*, which was owned by the Telegraph Company. Once again money was the stumbling block.

This time it was a dispute over the mode of payment. The *Victoria* was operating out of St. John's laying the western end of the Atlantic Cable. She was fully equipped for sea and ready to sail.

Chandler White, after listening carefully to how Newman outlined the plight of the *Arctic*, shocked the American consul by, without hesitation, demanding $500 a day for use of the *Victoria* in a rescue effort. While the dispute over money continued, men, women, and children had already drowned and others were praying for rescue.

Newman had felt this amount was "robbery" and well beyond what he could authorize. He communicated the situation to the American Secretary of State, William L. Marry, in Washington. Just weeks before the tragedy, Roman Catholic Bishop J.T. Mullock had publicly praised Chandler White for his philanthropy in giving a generous donation to the Roman Catholic Church.

Little offered to meet with White to make sure he understood the commitment the government had made to the American consul. By this time, the American consul had little faith that any more survivors could be found. He viewed all efforts at this point as "keeping up appearances." The prime minister said he did not agree and had convinced White to accept an order on the local government payable in thirty days for the use of the *Victoria* at the rate agreed to by Mr. Newman.

When informed by the prime minister of White's acceptance of a deal, Newman responded that it was too late. He said he had obtained the services of the mail ship *Merlin*. Despite this turn of events, there was still no sense of urgency.

On Tuesday evening, seventy-two hours after news of the disaster had reached St. John's, the agents of the *Merlin*, the only steamer ready to respond, posted a notice at the post office that the mails should be closed at the usual time, as it was not their intention to send the steamer off unless commanded to do so by the governor.

The failure to mount a rescue effort continued, and on Wednesday morning, E. Shea, MHA for St. Mary's and Placentia, volunteered to meet with the governor and present him with the letter of indemnity the prime minister had prepared two days earlier.

On Wednesday morning, four days after learning of the *Arctic* disaster, the politicians were still arguing over who would pay and, as a consequence, they had not initiated any rescue effort. The American consul contacted the prime minister on Wednesday morning to find out why the *Victoria* was getting up her steam. He was anxious to know where she was going and told the prime minister that he had been "humbugged" by the agents of the *Merlin* "who did not intend sending her away before the usual time." Newman resolved to have nothing further to do with the *Merlin*.

Realizing the desperate situation that had been allowed to develop, he told the prime minister that he regretted not taking advice in reference to the employment of the *Victoria*. Newman also had held discussions with a Captain Salt concerning his vessel *Cleopatra* on Tuesday night, and Captain Salt displayed no sense of urgency. The Captain said he had no doubt the *Arctic*'s boats, having the passengers on board, had outlived the storm, as he had been for days himself in an open boat in worse weather off the coast of Ireland.

Incredibly, at this late time in the tragedy, all the prime minister could tell him was that "it was possible the Government was sending off the *Victoria*," as Mr. Shea had gone to Government House to get the governor to dispatch the vessel. He told Newman he should check this out with Chandler White.

To this the American consul replied:

> If you and Mr. Shea get the *Victoria* off, to you
> alone would be the credit due of having done
> anything substantial towards the relief of the
> *Arctic*'s passengers and crew.

When Prime Minister Little later visited Chandler White, he learned that no offer had been made to him by the governor to engage the *Victoria* in a rescue effort. Mr. White told the prime minister that the *Victoria* was ready for sea and he was willing to detain her for one hour to await the result of Mr. Shea's meeting with the governor.

The Prime Minister went back to the American consul and told him of White's offer and recommended that the Consul go immediately to Government House:

> And even if he would not undertake any
> responsibility in his representative character,
> he should express his concurrence in any
> arrangement which His Excellency might make
> with Mr. White.

Just minutes after the consul left for Government House, Mr. Shea arrived and met with Prime Minister Little to inform him that the governor was not taking any action. He said that the governor offered to consent to guarantee any agreement the consul would make. The prime minister sent Mr. Shea back to Government House to again plead for action. However, when he arrived, he learned that the American consul had not gone to Government House as promised. Under the circumstances, all that Mr. Shea could get from the governor was a written guarantee from the colonial secretary for any contract the consul would make in regards to the *Arctic*.

Prime Minister Little addressed the situation in a letter to the *Newfoundlander*:

> Mr. White called on me near the end of the hour for an answer, and I told him that the Government would not undertake to engage the *Victoria*, and would only guarantee any undertaking which the Consul would give; and, that gentleman [Chandler White] declared that he would give no undertaking, or incur no such liability, consequently he had better not permit himself to be any longer misled.

The *Newfoundlander* was stinging in its criticism of the government's inaction. The newspaper pointed out that authorities misled the outside world into thinking no steamers were in St. John's Harbour to respond to the disaster while, in fact, there were. The paper concluded that it was greed, inaction, and bumbling that had thwarted a quick response that might have saved lives:

> What we want to know is why men who had authority to do all this, at the eleventh hour, to save appearances, were void of all power while the time yet remained for the saving of human life? And this, we opine is the question which will arise—to readers in America and England.

There was outrage among the people of St. John's over the handling of the response to the unfolding disaster at

Newfoundland's doorstep. Much of the criticism was directed at Governor Kerr Baillie Hamilton, with public demands for his resignation.

Meanwhile, Chandler White, after enduring criticism for demanding an exorbitant fee to participate in the rescue operation, on the evening of October 3, sent written instructions to the captain of the *Victoria*, ordering him to begin the search as soon as possible. In a letter to Peter Cooper, President of the Telegraph Company, Mr. White blamed Governor Kerr Baillie Hamilton for the long delay in starting the rescue. He claimed the governor would not guarantee payment for the rescue service and that he, Chandler White, finally took the matter into his own hands and sent the *Victoria* to carry out a search. One letter writer to the *Public Ledger* newspaper suggested that White's efforts were little more than a sham to cover his failure to react to the disaster instantly.

Another letter critical of Governor Hamilton appeared in the *Newfoundlander* on October 7, 1854. The letter, signed "Colonist," attributed the source of Newfoundland's public embarrassment over the incident directly on the shoulders of Kerr Baillie Hamilton. It stated:

> Your profession of philanthropy had induced a general belief that the cause of humanity at least would have elicited from you and your government some spark of energy, some vigorous effort to save the lives of hundreds of human beings known to have taken to the boats of the *Arctic* but a short time previous to the information reaching St. John's within fifty miles of

the land, and in soundings of the waters of Your Excellency's jurisdiction.

The writer pointed out that Governor Hamilton could have acted instantly on the basis that the *Arctic* was the National Mail Steamer in the employment of the United States of America. He added that the governor, as commander-in-chief and vice admiral, had direct control over the movements of the steamship *Cleopatra*, employed in government service:

> You permitted that vessel to remain in harbor over fifty hours, when she was quite able to be at sea, and most probably would have saved the unfortunate *Arctic* and hundreds of her ill-fated passengers and people. No effort was made by your government to expedite the steamer *Victoria*, nor has the R.M.S. *Merlin*, over which you have an absolute control by the express terms of the contract, been dispatched to the locality of the dreadful catastrophe. Some generous philanthropists have indeed sent unsuitable sailing craft; in doing so much they have done their best; but the Governor and Council of Newfoundland have emphatically declared themselves incapable. What will the British Government and the British people, who have cheerfully annually volunteered their searches for Sir John Franklin and his ill-fated crew, say to the Executive of Newfoundland? What will the generous America and her citizen people, who nobly contributed hand-in-hand to the fruitless search of the Arctic Expedition, say to your heartless treatment of her drowning sons and their ruined property in her National Mail Ship, within five hours sail of your residence.

Many *Arctic* survivors, including the two originally left behind at Cappahayden, fumed after being charged four to six pounds by the Newfoundland vessel, the *Merlin*, for their passage to Halifax, where a steamship of the Cunard Lines generously provided free transportation to their original port of destination, New York.

The full debate over Newfoundland's mishandling of the *Arctic* shipwreck did not reach the United States, and the public there were told that Newfoundland could not respond because there were no steamships in port at the time.

Not all Newfoundlanders were slow in responding to the crisis. Unable to get the support of local merchants, Bishop Feild, without charge to the Americans, gathered a crew for his yacht, the *Hawk*, and on Tuesday, October 3, sent the vessel out to search for survivors. The American consul had hired the salt-fish carrier, the 93-ton brig *Ann Eliza*, which departed for the shipwreck scene on Monday, October 2. Unlike those who sought to gain financially from any rescue effort, Warren Brothers of St. John's, owners of the *Ann Eliza*, unsuccessfully searched the area for survivors and, when offered payment by the American consul, refused to accept it.

While the *Public Ledger*, a St. John's newspaper known to favour the government in power at the time, claimed that no expense had been spared and that the government and Mr. Newman were worthy of praise, the *Newfoundlander*, minced no words in putting forward its opinion. Referring to the American consul and the government, the *Newfoundlander* editorialized, "We are to deal with the fact that between them, they have perpetrated an atrocity which is sufficient to infamous the name of the country."

Throughout the first couple of weeks after the shipwrcck of the *Arctic*, the fate of Captain Luce remained unknown. Many thought he had gone down with his ship. However, he had been rescued and taken to Quebec where he penned a letter to his employer detailing the story of the disaster. The letter, dated October 14, 1854, appeared in newspapers on both sides of the Atlantic. For the first time the outside world received a detailed account of the *Arctic* disaster:

> Mr. E. K. Collins, New York
>
> Dear Sir–
>
> It becomes my painful duty to inform you of the total loss of the noble steamship *Arctic* under my command, together with your wife, son and daughter. The *Arctic* sailed from Liverpool on Wednesday, September 20, at 11 a.m. with 233 passengers and about 150 crew. Nothing unusual occurred during the passage until Wednesday, September 27th when at noon, on the Banks of Newfoundland.
>
> At noon I left the deck for the purpose of working out the position of the ship. In about fifteen minutes afterwards a cry of "Hard to Starboard" came from the officers on the deck. I rushed on deck and just got out when I felt a crash forward, and at the same moment saw a strange steamer under the starboard bow. In another moment she struck against the guards of the *Arctic* and passed astern of us. The bows of the strange ship appeared to be cut off literally for about ten feet

and seeing that in all probability she must sink in a few minutes, after taking a hasty glance at our own ship and believing that we were comparatively uninjured, my first impulse was to try to save the lives of those on board the stranger.

The boats were ordered for launching and the First Officer and six men left in one of them. It was then found that our own ship was leaking fearfully. The engineers were now set to work being instructed to put on the steam pumps and the four deck pumps were worked by the passengers and crew.

The ship was immediately headed for the land which I judged to be 50 miles distant. I was compelled to leave the boat with the First Officer and his crew to take care of themselves. Several ineffectual attempts were made to stop the leaks by getting sails over the bows, but finding that the leak gained upon us very fast notwithstanding all our most powerful efforts to keep her free, I resolved to get the boats ready and have as many ladies and children placed in them as they could carry. But no sooner had the attempt been made than the firemen and others rushed into them in spite of all opposition.

Seeing this state of things, I ordered the boat astern to be kept in readiness until order could be restored. To my dismay, I saw the rope in the bow had been cut and they soon disappeared in the fog. Another boat was broken down by persons rushing at the davits by which many were precipitated into the sea. This occurred while I had been engaged in getting the starboard guard boat ready to launch, of which I had placed the second officer in charge. When the same fearful scene was enacted as with the first boat, men leaping from the top of the rail, a height of 20 feet, bruising and maiming those who were in the boat hanging alongside. I then gave orders to the Second Officer, Mr. Baalhan, to let go and drop astern of us, keeping under or near the stern to be ready to take on board women and children as soon as the fires were out and the engines stopped.

My attention was then drawn to the other quarter boat, which I found broken down but still hanging by one tackle. A rush was also made for her, when some fifteen passengers jumped in and cut the tackle and were soon out of sight. I now found not a seaman or carpenter was left on board. The only officer left was Mr. Dorian, Third Officer, who aided me and with the assistance of many passengers who deserve the greatest praise for their coolness and energy did all in their power up to the last moment when the ship sank.

The chief engineer, with several of his assistants had taken the smallest of our deck boats and had with fifteen persons pulled away before the ship sank. We had succeeded in getting the fore and main yards and two top gallant yards overboard, together with such other small spars and materials as we could collect, when I became fully convinced that the ship must go down in a very few minutes and that not a moment was to be lost in getting the spars lashed together to form the raft, to do which it became necessary to get out the life boat, the only boat left. This being accomplished, I placed Mr. Dorian in charge of the boat taking care to keep back the oars, so that the boat might not be taken away as I still hoped to get most of the women and children in this boat at least. We had made considerable progress in the connecting of the spars when an alarm was given that the ship was sinking and the boat was shoved off without oars or any means of helping themselves and when the ship sank the boat was probably 1/8 mile away. Instantly, at about 15 minutes to 5 p.m. the ship went down carrying every soul on board with her. I soon found myself on the surface again and after a brief struggling with my helpless child in my arms I again felt myself impelled downward to a great depth and before I reached the surface again I had nearly perished and had lost my hold on my child. As I again struggled to the surface of the water, a most awful and heart-rending scene presented itself to my view, women and children struggling together amidst pieces of wreckage of every kind, calling on each other and God to assist them. Such another appalling scene may God preserve me from ever witnessing. I was in the act of trying to save my child again when a portion of the paddle box came crashing up edgewise and just grazed my head and fell with its whole weight on the head of my darling child. In another moment, I beheld him, a lifeless corpse on the surface of the waves.

I succeeded with eleven others in getting on top of a piece of the paddle box. One who found that all could not be supported by this piece of the paddle box let go and swam to another piece nearby. The others remained in the water until one by one they were relieved by death. We stood up to our knees in water at 45 degrees and frequently the sea broke directly over us.

We were soon separated from our friends on other parts of the wreck and passed a terrible night, each one expecting every hour to be his last.

At last, the long wished for morning came accompanied by fog. Not a living soul but our own party to be seen of which only seven men were left. In the course of the morning we saw water casks and other things belonging to our ill-fated ship, but could get nothing that would afford us any relief and our raft was rapidly sinking as it absorbed water.

About noon Mr. S.M. Woodruff breathed his last and all the others except Mr. George F. Allen of NY and myself began to suffer excruciatingly for want of water. In this respect we were very much favored although we had not a drop of fresh water on the raft. The day continued foggy except just at noon, as near as we could judge, when we had a clear horizon for about half an hour.

Nothing could be seen but water and sky. Night came on thick and dreary and our minds were fully made up that neither of us would again see the day. Very soon three more, of our suffering party, were washed off and sank to rise no more, leaving only Mr. Allen and myself. Feeling myself very much exhausted, I sat down for the first time about eight o'clock on a trunk which had providentially been bound among the wreckage. In this way I slept a little through the night and became somewhat refreshed. About an hour before daylight, we saw a vessel's light near us and all three of us exerted ourselves to the utmost of our strength in hailing her until we became quite exhausted.

In about a quarter of an hour, the light disappeared in the eastward. Soon after daylight, a barque hove in sight to the northwest, the fog having lightened a little. She was apparently steering for us, but in a short time, she seemed to have changed her course and we were again doomed to disappointment, yet I felt a hope that some of our fellow sufferers might have been seen and rescued by them.

Shortly after we had given up all hope of being discovered or rescued by the barque, a ship was discovered to the eastward steering directly for us. We now watched her with intense anxiety as she approached. The wind changing caused her to alter course several points. About noon they fortunately discovered a man on a raft near them and succeeded in saving him, the second mate jumping overboard and making a rope fast to the man on the raft and he was drawn aboard.

He proved to be a Frenchman who had been a passenger on board the steamer with which we had collided. He informed the Captain that others were near on pieces of wreckage and ongoing aloft, he saw us and three others.

We were the first to which the boat was sent and were safely aboard at 3 p.m. The next picked up was James Smith, a 2nd class passenger on the *Arctic*. The others saved were five of our firemen. The ship proved to be the *Cambria* of Quebec, from Glasgow for Montreal, commanded by Captain John Russell who had commanded the British barque *Jessie Stevens*, and was rescued from the wreck of that vessel by

Captain Nye of the Collins steamship *Pacific*, as will be remembered.

Of Captain Russell it would be scarcely possible to say enough in his praise for the kind treatment we received from him during the time we were on board his ship. His own comforts he gave up in every respect for our relief. The Rev. Mr. Walker and wife and another gentleman, who were passengers on the *Cambria*, have been unending in their efforts to promote our comfort. To them and all on board we shall ever owe a debt of gratitude for their unbounded kindness to us. From the Frenchman who was picked up, we learned that the steamer with which we had been in contact was the screw steamer *Vesta*, from St. Pierre and Mc Quelon, heading for Granville, France.

As near as we could learn, the *Vesta* was steering E.S.E. and was crossing our course within two points with all sail set, the land being W by N.

Her anchor stock, about 7 by 4 inches, was drawn through the bows of the *Arctic* about 18 inches above the water line. An immense hole had been made at the same instant by the fluke of the anchor, about 2 feet below the water line, raking fore and aft the planks and finally breaking the chains and leaving the stock remaining in and through the side of the *Arctic*. It is more than likely that so much of the French steamer's bows had been crushed in that some of the heavy longitudinal pieces of iron running through the ship may have been drawn through our sides causing the loss of the *Arctic* and I fear many valuable lives.

I have safely arrived at Quebec but am without a penny in the world wherewith to help myself. With sincere gratitude to those from whom I have received such unbounded kindness since I have been providentially thrown among them, I am about to separate from them and go to New York—a home of sorrow. I learned from the doctor at quarantine, last evening, that the *Vesta* had reached St. John's with several passengers from the *Arctic* but could not learn the particulars. As soon as I can get on shore I shall make arrangements to leave for New York with the least possible delay. I shall take the steamer for Montreal this afternoon.

I am respectfully
James C. Luce.

It took seventy-two hours after the *Arctic* went down for word of the disaster to reach St. John's. In that time, the lifeboats rowing away from the scene, not knowing which direction to go, could have covered a lot of miles. The situation required a swift rescue effort with steamships that could travel at a fast speed and cover large areas in a short time. Unfortunately, such a rescue was not mounted because those with power to do so failed to act. Of the 383 passengers and crew on the *Arctic*, only 86 people survived.[5] There was not a woman or a child among the survivors.[6] This sad fact was attributed to the failure of many crewmen to put women and children first in evacuating the ship and seizing lifeboats for themselves.

The *Vesta* was forced to remain in St. John's until the spring while Newfoundland's genius shipbuilder, Michael Kearney,

---

[5] Other accounts of the disaster have reported varying figures regarding the number of persons lost in the tragedy.

[6] The total number of people reported to be on the *Arctic* has also varied.

repaired the damages to the vessel. The French Naval vessel *Camelion* took the *Vesta*'s survivors home to France, leaving the captain and a skeleton crew to look after its interests and return the vessel to France when repairs were completed. The captain found it necessary to publish advertisements in St. John's newspapers advising the public he would not be responsible for bills incurred by his crew.

For his leadership and courage throughout the ordeal, the French government made Captain Duchesne a *Chevalier of the Legion of Honor*.

In the aftermath of the disaster, American newspapers speculated on what action could have been taken by Captain Luce to avoid the tragedy or lessen the numbers of those lost in the tragedy.

The most positive result of the *Arctic* disaster was the new shipping laws that established sea lanes across the Atlantic.

In the months following the tragedy, there were several newspaper reports of people who refused to board the *Arctic* because they had premonitions of the disaster. One could only wonder about the reaction of the fortune teller, who foretold Brown's death, when she later picked up a newspaper reporting on the loss the *Arctic*.

CHAPTER TWENTY-TWO

Two Outstanding Vessels

~~~

Two ships which stand out among Newfoundland sea stories are the *Edmund B. Alexander* and the HMS *Calypso*. The *Alexander*, which brought the first American troops to Newfoundland in 1941, was at one time a German vessel. After its capture by the Americans during WWI, it played a fascinating role in American history.

The HMS *Calypso* was used in Newfoundland to train Newfoundlanders for service in the Navy during WWI and was eventually abandoned and used for decades as a coal boat in St. John's Harbour. Following this, its history took a fascinating but sad twist.

THE *EDMUND B. ALEXANDER*

The *Edmund B. Alexander* became as much a part of Newfoundland history as any Newfoundland vessel.

Throughout WWII, the sinking of the *Edmund B. Alexander*

remained a priority for German U-boat commanders, with the promise of the immediate conferring of the Iron Cross to the commander responsible for the destruction of this US troop carrier. The *Edmund B. Alexander* measured 668 feet in length and was designed to carry 4,000 passengers, which was twice the passenger capacity of the *Queen Mary*.

The *Edmund B. Alexander* arrived in St. John's in January 1941, and remained moored on the south side of the harbour where it was used as a floating barracks for several months while Camp Alexander was being prepared to house troops at Rennies Mill Road and Carpasian Road.[1]

Apart from the historical significance of landing the first American troops in Newfoundland, the *Edmund B. Alexander* had an exciting and adventurous history. The troop carrier was built at an Irish shipyard in 1905 for the German-owned Lloyd Ship Line. It was originally named the *Amerika* to attract passengers from the United States, and operated as the *Breman* to New York.

One of the first adventures of the *Amerika* involved the *Titanic* disaster. Had the officers of the *Titanic* acted upon warnings and information provided by the *Amerika*, the tragedy could have been avoided. When travelling eastbound on the Atlantic on the afternoon of August 14, 1912, the *Amerika* cautiously encountered and passed through ice fields south of Newfoundland. She alerted the *Titanic* and provided the exact locations of the icebergs.

It was revealed later at the enquiry into the sinking of the

---

[1] Troops were housed at Camp Alexander until Fort Pepperrel at Pleasantville was completed.

Titanic that the *Amerika*'s warning was received and plotted on the *Titanic* charts, but then ignored. The price paid for this mistake is now history.

The *Amerika* had another encounter in 1912 that made news around the world. Unknown to the captain of the *Amerika*, it was sailing directly in a path that crossed with that of the British submarine S-12. The captain of the submarine gave orders to surface, and as the craft rose, he took the usual sweep with his periscope. The captain was horrified to see one of the largest ships in the world bearing down on him, just yards away. News reports noted that he barely had time to shout "crash dive" before the *Amerika* sliced the submarine in half. Only one person on board the submarine survived the sinking.

In 1914, WWI broke out, and the future of the *Amerika* was changed forever. She was one of ninety German ships caught in neutral and enemy ports, and was interred in New York. The *Amerika* remained there until the United States entered the war in 1917. The K in *Amerika* was changed to C, and as the *America*, the vessel was converted into a troop-transport ship. In her short service in that war, she had carried 40,000 soldiers to France. Then, once again, the *America* was touched with tragedy. While embarking troops at Hoboken, New Jersey, in 1918, it sank with the loss of several lives. Having been refloated, it was repaired and the vessel used to carry troops home from Europe at the end of the war.

In 1920, the *America* was assigned to clear up a problem created by the Germans during WWI. In 1915 the Germans conscripted thousands of Czechs into the army, and these troops were sent to the Russian front. Large numbers of these conscripts were captured by the Russians and sent to prison camps in Siberia. The *America* sailed from New York in 1920 and travelled through the Panama Canal and across the Pacific Ocean to Vladvistock. In that port, the vessel carried the Czechs, who were released from Russian prisons, to the newly created Czech Republic.

In 1929, the *America* was involved in a remarkable rescue at sea. The rescue took place at night during a severe wind storm. The Italian steamer *Florida* was in distress and sinking in the North Atlantic. The *America*'s first officer, Harry Manning, was responsible for the miraculous rescue of the entire *Florida* crew. He is credited with the rescue through a spectacular navigation manoeuvre which brought the massive vessel close enough to get everyone off the Florida. Harry Manning later became commodore of the United States Lines, and was commanding officer of the luxury liner *United States* on her maiden voyage.

In 1932, the *America* was laid up in Maryland, and attempts to sell the vessel were unsuccessful. After the Japanese attacked Pearl Harbour, the ship was again converted into a troop-transport and renamed the *Edmund B. Alexander*, after the man who commanded the 3rd United States Infantry in the Mexican War of 1846-1848. The first assignment of the *Edmund B. Alexander* was to transport American troops to St. John's, Newfoundland. The troop carrier made two trips to the port of St. John's.

The next adventure of the *Edmund B. Alexander* occurred during WWII. In 1942, she had undergone a major overhaul, and converted from coal to oil. While on her last run with troops, she crossed the path of a German U-boat, and the captain, after identifying the ship, saw his opportunity to earn the Iron Cross. The U-boat had only one torpedo remaining when the *Edmund B. Alexander* was sighted. After shouting "Fire one!" the captain ordered the crew to dive.

An alert lookout on the troop ship saw the submarine's periscope, and the vessel made a successful evasive move, passing over the submarine within inches. The U-boat moved up to periscope depth in time for the commander to get a view of the *Edmund B. Alexander* moving off at full speed, and with it, his hopes for the Iron Cross. At the end of the war, the *Edmund B. Alexander* carried troops home from Europe.

The famous vessel had one more dangerous encounter before meeting its end. During October 1946, near the German coast, it was struck a glancing blow by a floating mine left over from the war. The explosion was strong enough to move the engines from their beds. The vessel was towed to port where repairs were made, and it returned on its own power to Baltimore, Maryland. The ship was laid up there until 1957 when finally sold for scrap to Captain George Anstey, a St. John's harbour pilot who has the distinction of being the man who brought the *Edmund B. Alexander* into St. John's Harbour on January 29, 1941.

HMS *CALYPSO* PLAYED HISTORIC ROLE IN WWI

Sir Roger Keyes, Admiral of Britain's Grand Fleet in WWI, described Newfoundland sailors as, "The finest small ship seamen in the world." The skills and training which these Newfoundlanders displayed so well were acquired through training on what is now a lost piece of Newfoundland heritage, the *Calypso*, which was renamed the *Briton*.

The story of the *Calypso* in Newfoundland is connected with the British tradition of using Newfoundland as a training ground for its navy, a tradition that began around the time of Sir Humphrey Gilbert's visit to Newfoundland in 1583.

When British troops withdrew from Newfoundland in 1870, there were those in the military who argued that the training of British seamen in Newfoundland should continue. They argued the program would also provide some military protection for the colony which had been left defenseless by the withdrawal of the British military.

In 1878, a Captain Sullivan of the HMS *Sirius* put forward a plan for a Royal Navy Reserve Unit and a training ship to be stationed in Newfoundland. The Lord Commissioners of the British Admiralty, who were alarmed at some of the problems experienced by several similar programs in England, refused to approve the proposal. The lords claimed they had no suitable ships for training boys for the reserves.

In England at the time, there was a small fleet of training ships known as "industrial training ships," which were privately operated by local groups and financed by public contributions. Several of these vessels were used to rehabilitate and train wayward boys to enable them to follow a seafaring career. These training ships served the Royal Navy well and turned out some of the best sailors in the British Navy.

In 1883, the Royal Navy launched a new warship at the navy dockyard at Kent, England, which was christened the *Calypso*. The vessel was designed by Sir Nathaniel Barnaby and was the last of the class of ships known as steam-sail corvettes. It measured 235 feet long, weighed 2770 tons, and could travel at a speed of 15 knots.

The *Calypso* was well armed with four mounted six-inch breechloaders, two on each side, fore and aft, as well as twelve five-inch breechloaders, six to a side. In addition, there were six Nordenfeldt machineguns on the upper deck and two fourteen-inch torpedo tubes on the main deck. Below main deck was a protective steel deck that could stop the heaviest of shells. In 1885 the *Calypso* went into service with the Royal Navy's training squadron. By 1898, her career with the Royal Navy had ended, and the vessel was destined for the scrap heap.

Newfoundland authorities had not forgotten Sullivan's idea of reviving the colony as a training ground for British seamen. The British finally agreed and responded to efforts to save the *Calypso* by assigning her to the Newfoundland project.

On September 3, 1902, the vessel was commissioned as a drill ship. A crew of 167 men was assembled from the HMS *Prince* and the HMS *Vivid* under Commander Frederick Walker to sail the *Calypso* to Newfoundland where the Royal Newfoundland Volunteer Naval Reserve had been organized and were waiting to start training. The RNVN was created as an imperial force rather than a colonial force in recognition of Newfoundland's imperial role in the Commonwealth's defence.

The *Calypso* had a rough trip across the Atlantic and encountered some violent storms. She arrived in St. John's on October 15, 1902. Work began almost immediately to convert the vessel to suit the needs of the trainees. The fore, main, and mizzen masts, and the funnel, were all removed. The flush deck was roofed over with a peaked roof to form a huge drill hall. The hull, from which much of her armament had been removed, became the quarters for the Newfoundland reservists.

When the fishing season ended each year, fishermen from all over Newfoundland went to St. John's to train on the *Calypso*. About 500 reservists were "messed" and slept there between 1902 and the outbreak of World War One. When war was declared, the British Admiralty sent out a call for trained seamen, and the Newfoundland reservists were first to respond.

The Crow's Nest, the magazine of the Royal Canadian Navy, in its fiftieth anniversary edition in 1960, described the Royal Newfoundland Naval Reserves as, "The first really effective naval reserve in what is now Canada." An estimated 2000 Newfoundland reservists served in WWI with about 200 of those lost in action. Another 150 were injured and sent home. Several members were awarded medals and other military honours.

In 1916, the *Calypso* was renamed the HMS *Briton* to release the name for a new fighting ship which was about to be commissioned. The Naval Reserve was abandoned in 1922, and the name "The Old *Briton*" survived for decades in Newfoundland.

A. H. Murray Ltd. purchased the *Briton* and used it as a floating salt-storage depot. It remained a familiar site in St. John's Harbour for years, frequently surrounded by a flock of small schooners taking on salt cargoes. In time, the salt fishery declined, and the *Briton* was moved to Lewisporte and used as a coal hulk. In 1966, in a state of deterioration, the *Briton* was offered for sale.

Among those who expressed an interest in preserving the *Briton* was Captain Tom Dower of Grand Falls, a sea adventurer who built his own small boats and sailed solo across the Atlantic. Dower purchased the vessel from Murray with plans of re-rigging the ship to its original state. When the government failed to assist the project financially, Dower was forced to drop the venture.

The large hulk had become an eyesore at Lewisporte, and the people there wanted it removed from their harbour. In response, Dower sold the vessel to a businessman from Notre Dame Bay who scrapped it and sold the iron and copper fittings, bronze propeller, and other parts to scrap dealers.

Dower donated one of the vessel's guns and a hand-powered steering wheel to the Royal Canadian Legion at Grand Falls as a tribute to Newfoundlanders who sacrificed their lives at sea in war time. The seafaring tradition carried on by the old *Briton* continues today through the HMCS Cabot Navy Reserves, established on September 20, 1949.

CHAPTER TWENTY-THREE

Mutiny and Mass Murder

~~~

Among the list of unusual crimes recorded in the annals of Newfoundland's criminal history is the crime of mutiny. Such a crime took place aboard the HMS *Latona* in St. John's Harbour on August 3, 1797. This incident was part of a universal spirit of mutiny, which existed throughout the British Empire at the time. A ringleader of the dissidents aboard the *Latona* refused to go aloft and demanded to be put in irons. Captain Sotherton moved decisively to crush the mutiny by arresting the instigator and ordering that he be punished.

Newfoundland's Governor William Waldegrave, after being informed of the incident, angrily reacted, ordering his troops to kill immediately any person attempting to lead a mutiny and, if necessary, sink the *Latona* with all on board if any further mutinous acts were committed. Other mutineers tried to save their leader, and strongly demanded that he not be punished. Captain Sotherton responded by ordering his marines to surround the men and draw their

bayonets. In their rush to retreat, some of the men accidentally cut themselves on the bayonets.

With the crew under control, the ringleader was stripped to
the waist and whipped. The men were angry and expressed
their discontent among themselves. One marine guarding
the men said, "The language of the seamen in their
hammocks was terrible. They promised bloody work and
threatened to throw the marines overboard as soon as the
ship was in blue water."

During the following days, the crew caused trouble when
they went ashore, and they attempted to incite the garrison.
Citizens of St. John's were outraged by the men's disorderly
conduct. On September 6, Governor Waldegrave received
word that the mutiny and rebellion had ended, and Parker,
its leader, had been executed. The governor, accompanied
by marines from the Royal Artillery and a company from
the Royal Newfoundland Regiment, went to the waterfront
to address the British seamen in port.

He told them:

> I'm happy to have this opportunity to thank you
> in person for your gallant and steady behaviour
> in support of your officers. You have shown
> yourselves to be good soldiers and true and
> faithful to your King and Country. There is not
> a person in St. John's but feels a regard and
> esteem for you while, I am sorry to say that,
> they look on the seamen of the *Latona* with
> equal horror and detestation, and indeed, it is
> impossible that they should do otherwise

considering the infamy of their conduct both on shore and afloat.

But if I am to judge from your conduct, I must think that the majority of you are either villains or cowards. If the greater number of you are against your officers and refuse to obey their lawful commands, I have a right to say that you are traitors to your King and Country. If there are only a few bad men among you which you presented to be the case, I maintain that you are a set of dastardly cowards for suffering yourselves to be bullied by a few villains who wish for nothing better than to see us become slaves of France.

You were all eager for news and newspapers to see how your great delegate Parker was doing. I thank God that I have the satisfaction to inform you that he has been hanged with many other of his atrocious companions. You looked up to him as an example whilst he was in his glory. I recommend you look to his end as an example also. You may now indeed reap the advantage from contempt of the conduct of the vile incendiary.

Waldegrave then ordered his officers to kill instantly any sailor attempting to incite a mutiny. He also ordered the officers commanding the batteries at the entrance to St. John's Harbour, "To burn them with red hot shot if there were any further signs of mutiny."

He explained, "I know in this case the officers must perish with you, but there is not one of them but is ready to sacrifice himself for the good of his country in any mode whatsoever."

The Governor then ordered the mutineers "to go into church and pray to acquire the respect and love of their countrymen and eternal happiness in the next world."

The incident created a great deal of fear and mistrust among the military. Officers of the Royal Newfoundland Regiment offered twenty guineas for the capture of any person spreading false rumors about their loyalty. The non-commissioned officers offered thirty guineas, and the officers added another twenty guineas for the same purpose. A short while later the *Latona* left St. John's and all talk of rebellion and mutiny left with them.

A CASE OF MASS MURDER

Eric Cobham, a French magistrate, after confessing his sins to a priest on his death bed, passed the priest a detailed written confession of his early life of crime and asked that it be published in full after his death. The priest carried out Cobham's wishes, but when the book was published, the magistrate's heirs travelled all over France buying up every available copy.

A single copy of that book exists today and, although badly worn, is preserved in the national archives of France. It tells of an almost unbelievable life of crime led by Cobham and his wife, Marie, involving torture, mass murder, and piracy in Newfoundland.

Although a French magistrate, Cobham was not French. He was born at Poole, England, and by his late teens was involved in rum smuggling between England and France. On one trip, after landing ten thousand gallons of French brandy at Poole, he was captured and imprisoned at the infamous Newgate Prison, where some of England's most gruesome executions took place.

After being flogged, he served two years there before being released. He was twenty years old when he was set free. Cobham went to work as a clerk in an Oxford inn, but he had learned little from his prison experience and found himself in trouble again after he robbed one of the inn's guests of a bag of gold. Theft was a more serious offence than rum smuggling. The penalty was execution by hanging. Cobham managed to cast the blame for his deed on the inn's owner, who was found guilty of the theft and hanged at Newgate Prison.

Cobham planned to increase his sudden wealth. He went to Plymouth, invested in the purchase of a ship, recruited a crew, and armed the vessel with fourteen guns. From Plymouth, Cobham launched his career as a pirate. His first act of piracy netted him forty thousand pounds sterling in gold.

It was common for pirates of the eighteenth century to be lenient towards prisoners, but Cobham was a ruthless and cruel man. After capturing and taking gold from an East Indian ship, he scuttled it, and everyone on board was drowned.

When he returned to Plymouth, he met and married a girl

named Maria Lindsay. Maria enthusiastically joined Eric in his piracy. After they captured and scuttled another ship near New York, they sailed to Newfoundland where their piracy flourished and their wealth grew.

It was 1740 when the Cobhams set up headquarters at Sandy Point, Bonne Bay. Sandy Point, at the time, had no civil authority and was sparsely inhabited by aboriginals and a few fishermen from Acadia. From the protection of the snug harbour, the Cobhams were able to attack ships travelling to and from the Maritimes, mainland Canada, and the French colony of St. Pierre. Furs were as valuable as gold in those days, and the Cobhams captured many rich cargoes which they sold on the French black market.

The Cobhams went undetected for years because they murdered every person they captured. Ship owners believed their vessels had simply gone to the bottom of the Atlantic during severe storms. Maria Cobham excelled her husband in the art of torture and killing. She often carved up prisoners with her sword or had them tied to masts. She practiced pistol shooting on them while taking care to avoid killing them until a limb had been severed.

On one occasion, she had an entire crew sewn alive into sacks and tossed overboard. At another time, she set a captured West Indian crew at ease by inviting them to join her in the galley for lunch. She fed them food laced with laudanum and poisoned all of them.

After twenty years of murder and piracy, the Cobhams had accumulated a magnificent fortune and selected France as their permanent home. They purchased a mansion and large estate from the Duc de Chartier, at Lavre. They owned a private harbour and a private yacht and quickly became the envy of the French aristocracy.

When the Cobhams became bored with their lives, they would use their yacht for brief flings of piracy. On one such escapade, they captured a West Indian brig, massacred the crew, and sold the ship at Bordeaux, France.

Impressed by the Cobham wealth, prominent French people used their influence to have Cobham appointed a judge in the French county courts. As the years passed, Maria slowly grew insane, and one day she went to the cliffs near her estate, took laudanum, and jumped off the cliff to assure her suicide.

Cobham lived for years afterwards and died a natural death. Following his death, his family was elevated to the French aristocracy.

When the deathbed confessions of Eric Cobham appeared in print, the Cobham heirs quickly got them off the market. Some British merchants got hold of the confession, compared the details given by Cobham with their own records, and were satisfied with the accuracy of the infamous Cobham Confession.

RED-FACED POLICE AT PETTY HARBOUR

During February 1868, a detachment of police went to Petty Harbour to deal with a report that the people there had invaded a visiting cargo ship and stripped it of its cargo. The

Mary Curley was on a trip from New York to St. John's with a cargo of meal and flour for Harvey & Co. when it went aground at Petty Harbour. The next day the police received reports that after the captain left Petty Harbour to go to St. John's for help, the men of the community invaded the ship, stole four hundred barrels of flour and, tossed hundreds of pounds of meal overboard.

In response to the report, a detachment of police was sent to the community to put a stop to the attack upon the vessel and to arrest the perpetrators of the offence. However, when the police arrived and investigated the charges, they learned that the men had taken the flour off the ship, but no crime had been committed.

Before leaving for St. John's, the captain of the *Mary Curley* was worried that the vessel would be smashed to pieces unless freed from the point where it was grounded. He invited the people of Petty Harbour to come on board and save as much of the cargo as possible. The men of Petty Harbour responded and, by removing the cargo, lightened the ship, which floated away from the rocks. At this point, the mate of the ship asked the men to stop discharging the cargo and they complied.

Police agreed that the rumour of a crime at Petty Harbour against the *Mary Curley* was nothing more than exaggeration and rumour that had gotten out of hand. The captain and crew of the ship were happy to receive the help of the men of Petty Harbour.

BIBLIOGRAPHY

Aubrey, Frank. "A Newfoundland Terror." *Fore's Sporting &
Sketches*, Vol. 13, 10-15, 1896.

Bassler, Gerhard. *Vikings to U-boats: The German
Experience in Newfoundland*. Montreal: McGill-Queen's,
2006.

Breland, Osmond P. "Devils of the Deep." *Science Digest*,
October 1952.

Churchill, Winston. *The Hinge of Fate: The Second World
War Volume IV*. Boston: Houghton Mifflin, 1950.

---. *The Grand Alliance: The Second World War Volume III*.
Boston: Houghton Mifflin, 1950.

---. *Triumph and Tragedy: The Second World War Volume
VI*. Boston: Houghton Mifflin, 1953.

Davies, Hunter. *The Teller of Tales: In Search of Robert Louis
Stevenson*. London: Sinclair-Stevenson, 1994.

Douglas, T. Alex. "The Nazi Weather Station in Labrador."
Canadian Geographic, December 1981.

Ferrell, Robert H. and John S. Bowman, eds. *The Twentieth
Century: An Almanac*. New York: World Almanac
Publications, 1984.

Fitzgerald, Jack. *The Jack Ford Story: The Newfoundlander in Nagasaki*. St. John's: Creative, 2008.

Hadley, Michael. *U-boats Against Canada*. Montreal: McGill-Queens,1989.

Harrington, Michael F. "The Sea Monsters in Conception Bay." *Atlantic Guardian*, Vol. 14 (6), June 1957.

Harvey, Rev. Moses. "A Sea Monster Unmasked." *Science Digest*, 1899.

Hirschman, Werner, *Another Place, Another Time: A U-boat Officer's Wartime Album*. Montreal: Robin Brass Studio, 2011.

Houlihan, Eileen. *Uprooted! The Argentia Story*. St. John's: Creative, 1992.

Hoyt, Edwin P. *U-boats Offshore: When Hitler Struck America*. New York: Stein and Day, 1978.

Keegan, John. *The Second World War*. New York: Penguin, 1989.

Lambe, James B. *The Corvette Navy: True Stories from Canada's Atlantic War*. Halifax: Nimbus, 2010.

Manchester, William. *The Last Lion: Winston Spenser Churchill Alone, 1932-1940*. New York: Little, Brown and Co, 1988.

Miller, David. *U-boats: History, Development and Equipment 1914-1945*. London: Bloomsbury, 2000.

Milner, Marc. *The U-boat Hunters*. Toronto: University of Toronto Press, 1994.

Neary, Steve. *The Enemy on our Doorstep*. St. John's: Jesperson, 1994.

Nicholson, G.W.L., *More Fighting Newfoundlanders.*
St. John's: Govt. of Newfoundland and Labrador, 1969.

Patton, Janice. *The Sinking of the I'm Alone.* Toronto:
McClelland and Stewart, 1972.

Peterson, Laurence. *The First U-boat Flotilla.* Annapolis:
Naval Institute Press, 2002.

Quigley, Gene. *Voices of World War II.* St. John's: Jesperson,
2006.

Showell, Jak P. Mallmann. *U-boat Command and the Battle
of the Atlantic.* St. Catherines: Vanwell, 2000.

Smallwood, Joseph R. *Encyclopaedia of Newfoundland and
Labrador: Volume 1.* St. John's: Newfoundland Book
Publishers, 1981.

Staff of the *New York Times. Churchill in Memoriam.*
New York: Bantam, 1965.

Stevenson, Robert Louis. *Treasure Island.* Edited by Wendy
R. Katz. Edinburgh: Edinburgh UP, 1998.

Thomas, Gordon and Max Morgan Witts. *Enola Gay.*
New York: Pocket Books, 1977.

Tulk, T.E. "My Adventure with a Giant Squid."
Newfoundland Quarterly, Vol. 53 (1), March 1954.

Wells, Herb. *Comrades In Arms: A History of
Newfoundlanders in Action, Second World War.*
St. John's: self-published, 1986.

Wynn, Kenneth. *U-boat Operations of the Second World
War: Volume I.* London: Chatham, 1997.

OTHER SOURCES

The Provincial Archives of Newfoundland and Labrador (PANL)

Archives and Special Collections, Queen Elizabeth II Library, Memorial University, Joseph R. Smallwood Collection

NEWSPAPERS AND MAGAZINES

The Canadian Legion Veteran Magazine. 1958.

The Daily News. St. John's, Newfoundland, 1939-1948.

The Express. St. John's, Newfoundland, 1940-1941.

The Evening Telegram. St. John's, Newfoundland, 1939-1947.

The Newfoundlander. St. John's, Newfoundland, 1854.

The Public Ledger. St. John's, Newfoundland, 1854.

ACKNOWLEDGEMENTS

I am grateful for the assistance and support given me during the writing and preparation of this book for publication. Special thanks go to my son, Maurice Fitzgerald, for cover design; Bob Rumsey for editing and advice; and Donna Francis for support and encouragement. I am grateful to the editorial and production staff at Breakwater Books for their patience and invaluable help.

JACK FITZGERALD was born and educated in St. John's, Newfoundland and Labrador. During his career he has been a journalist, a feature writer, a political columnist; a public affairs writer with CJON and VOCM news services; and editor of the *Newfoundland Herald* and the *Newfoundland Chronicle*.